Windows NT® Security

ISBN 0-13-083990-6

90000

9 780130 839909

PRENTICE HALL SERIES ON MICROSOFT® TECHNOLOGIES

PRENTICE HALL SERIES ON MICROSOFT® TECHNOLOGIES

MICHAEL McINERNEY

Windows NT®
Security

Prentice Hall PTR, Upper Saddle River, NJ 07458
http://www.phptr.com

Library of Congress Cataloging-in-Publication Data

McInerney, Michael
    Windows NT security / Michael McInerney.
       p. cm. — (Prentice Hall series on Microsoft technologies)
    ISBN 0-13-083990-6 (alk. paper)
    1. Microsoft Windows NT. 2. Operating systems (Computers)
3. Computer security. I. Title. II. Series.
QA76.76.O63M39875   1999
005.4'4769—dc21   99-39655
                                      CIP

Editorial/production supervision: Jane Bonnell
Cover design director: Jerry Votta
Cover design: Scott Weiss
Copyeditor: Mary Lou Nohr
Composition: Ronnie Bucci
Manufacturing manager: Alexis R. Heydt
Acquisitions editor: Mary Franz
Editorial assistant: Noreen Regina
Marketing manager: Lisa Konzelmann

Published by Prentice Hall PTR
Prentice-Hall, Inc.
Upper Saddle River, New Jersey 07458

Prentice Hall books are widely used by corporations and government agencies for training, marketing, and resale. The publisher offers discounts on this book when ordered in bulk quantities. For more information, contact Corporate Sales Department, Phone: 800-382-3419; FAX: 201-236-7141; E-mail: corpsales@prenhall.com
Or write: Prentice Hall PTR, Corporate Sales Dept., One Lake Street, Upper Saddle River, NJ 07458.

Printed in the United States of America

10   9   8   7   6   5   4   3   2   1

ISBN 0-13-083990-6

Prentice-Hall International (UK) Limited, London
Prentice-Hall of Australia Pty. Limited, Sydney
Prentice-Hall Canada Inc., Toronto
Prentice-Hall Hispanoamericana, S.A., Mexico
Prentice-Hall of India Private Limited, New Delhi
Prentice-Hall of Japan, Inc., Tokyo
Prentice-Hall (Singapore) Pte. Ltd., Singapore
Editora Prentice-Hall do Brasil, Ltda., Rio de Janeiro

This book is dedicated to the memory of Grace McInerney.

The best of mothers when she was here.

Missed now she is gone.

C O N T E N T S

SIX   Cryptography   133

SEVEN   Proxy Server   147

System security is a tricky subject to write about. The measurement of what is secure and what isn't secure is highly subjective and dependent on many factors. The individual or group view of today's requirements for your organization, assumptions, and any known facts concerning the situation in the future and views on the criticality of your systems are all factors relating to this measurement.

It would be very easy for me to preach about what I think you should do to secure your systems, but without knowledge of your individual environment and needs, it would also be very wrong.

With this book I have approached the subject of security in two ways. First, I have tried to show why you may consider implementing a particular security feature or process. This attempt has been included to prompt the discussions between you and your colleagues that are a necessary part of the design process for the security model. Second, I have included step-by-step guides for implementing the security feature itself. You will be able to use the step-by-step guides to implement the security features and thresholds that are right for your organizational needs, adapting the examples as necessary.

Audience

Windows NT Security targets Systems and Network Administrators, Security Professionals, System Audit Specialists, Compliance Officers, Developers, and anybody who needs to understand Windows NT and Windows 2000 security features.

Concern over data security today means that management focus is moving more than ever toward data and system security. Sadly, this focus and the ensuing demand for performance are not always accompanied by a large budget allowing for add-on tools and specialist consultants who can design your security model and help to implement this design. The responsibility for the design, implementation, and maintenance of the security model falls on the shoulders of the System Administrators or other in-house group of professionals who may not have needed to face this particular challenge before.

The content of this book requires a good administrative knowledge of Windows NT systems and also Windows 2000 systems if you wish to leverage the Windows 2000 content to its fullest potential. Many of the functions and features discussed in this book focus on the system registry as both a source of information and also the place to make changes to move toward the target of securing your systems. For this reason, the reader knowledge level for this book has been set between intermediate and advanced. Readers should be comfortable using the registry editing tools for browsing and amending settings before attempting any of the exercises that include this type of activity.

Organization

Windows NT Security is divided into three parts.

Part One, *System Security Overview*, is an introduction to security concepts and how these concepts can be mapped to the Windows NT security architecture. This is a good starting point for all readers and will give you grounding in this particular topic. Seasoned Security Professionals who feel comfortable with their own knowledge in this area may still want to cover this part of the book simply as a comparison tool to their own thoughts.

Part Two, *Windows NT 4.0 Security Components*, looks at the security related components of Windows NT 4.0. This part of the book looks at all of the built-in features of Windows NT and how they can be best leveraged at your own site to meet the needs for security and also give the flexibility required to run a business.

Part Three, *Looking Forward to Windows 2000*, looks at Windows 2000 and the changes in the security model between Windows NT 4.0 and Windows 2000. This part contains an introduction to the Active Directory and then moves on to look at the security-specific features contained in the new operating system. Encrypting file systems, distributed file systems and the security concerns around this technology, the security configuration tool set, and group policies are discussed in this part of the book.

Each chapter is organized as individual unit. The chapter can be looked at on its own, and because of this organization, the seasoned NT professional can use the book as a reference guide to each topic. The main focus, however, is on building a security model for your organization, and as readers work through the book, the security model can be defined around the concepts and discussions contained in each chapter. Readers will gain the most benefit from this approach to the book.

ACKNOWLEDGMENTS

Writing this book must rate among the most difficult pieces of work that I have ever undertaken. My admiration for seasoned authors of any subject matter knows no bounds after this experience. This project would not have been completed without the help of many people in different ways.

First and foremost I must thank my wife Linda. Support, encouragement (and, when needed, a push in the right direction) was never in short supply. Her many hours of editorial input during the writing and production process helped to keep me sane and on the right track. The project would not have worked without this support.

Vincent Daly and Thomas Niestroj, my colleagues and friends at IBM, must be next on the list to thank. The time and effort put into technical proof reading was much appreciated. Many thanks go to Curt Aubley, author of *Tuning and Sizing NT Server* (Prentice Hall), who provided invaluable advice on the structure and content of the book.

Jane Heffernan is next in line. Jane always has an opinion and never feels that she has to hold back in expressing it. You couldn't ask for a better friend.

To the whole team at Prentice Hall. Mary Franz, who gave me the opportunity of writing this book and provided all the support you could ask for, and everybody else who worked on this book. Working with professionals always makes a job less stressful and more fun.

Finally, for anybody I may have inadvertently left out, I apologize and thank you for your help and support.

Writing is not a new endeavor for me. Although this is my first published book, I estimate that I have written tens of thousands of pages. Technical manuals and some magazine articles make up the bulk of this work.

As founder and director of Insight Business Solutions, I see my main role as still very much hands-on in the realms of computer security, network design, and technical training. The main business aim for my company is to provide high-quality, focused technical consultancy to both European and U.S. companies. Our client list includes many blue-chip multinationals in the banking, treasury, and manufacturing sectors.

On a personal note, I am a Microsoft Certified Systems Engineer (MCSE) and a Master Certified Novell Engineer (MCNE) and have been working with computers and networks for about 12 years now. Over the years I have worked as a freelance trainer and network consultant in both Microsoft and Novell technologies. My training activities have given way over recent years to seminars, and I have become more tightly focused on system security.

System Security Overview

In this first part of the book we will look at the basics of security in a computer network environment. The two chapters in this part look at security concepts in general, acting as a base from which to form your own ideas and opinions on what security is all about in a computing environment.

Chapter One looks at security concepts in general and how different areas of security can be used together to form a security model.

Chapter Two then takes the general ideas and concepts discussed in Chapter One and looks at these in the context of a Windows NT system, paying particular attention to the security architecture and how this maps to these concepts.

The high-level discussions of security concepts in this part of the book will act as a foundation for the more in-depth coverage contained in further chapters.

Introduction to Security Concepts

Chapter One contains an overview of system security concepts. Anybody who is intent on designing and implementing a secure networked system should be familiar with the concepts covered in this chapter. These concepts form the foundation on top of which you should plan your secure network installation. This chapter also puts forward a suggested definition of a secure system.

This chapter acts as an introduction to concepts that form the foundations for designing and implementing a secure Windows NT environment. Many of the concepts discussed in this chapter are generic and so can be applied to any number of network operating system installations.

For many readers of this book, the concepts discussed in this chapter will be familiar. It is important to have a sound understanding of these concepts before progressing through the text and starting your network security design. Even the most knowledgeable IT professional should take some time to make certain that the importance of the topics discussed is understood.

Introduction

Some people believe that there is little point in spending time securing against small risks; they believe their time and effort are better spent on negating much larger risks. The natural conclusion of an installation built on this belief is to bring all risks to approximately the same level by reducing large risks to the size of the small ones. Another way of thinking would be to reduce all security risks to their lowest possible level whatever the cost. These two examples can be used as the extremes between which a balance must be brokered.

As a general rule, most enterprises will undertake to secure themselves against the major risks to their networks today as a matter of corporate procedure. This leaves the closing of smaller risks as optional. Ultimately, the controls that you implement depend on the risks present at your site, and you should not dismiss any risk no matter how small it may seem until you have evaluated its impact. Even the smallest risk should be countered if an identifiable threat to your business is found.

This chapter discusses the different types of risks that an enterprise may face when implementing a network structure. Objectives for controlling security risks and the different ways in which these objectives can be met are also discussed.

Layered Approach to Securing Your Network

There are many ways in which to apply security restrictions to your network infrastructure. User policies, data encryption, the use of digital signatures and the use of secure communications are some of the methods on which we rely to instill confidence in our security model. In real terms, the only absolutely secure network operating system (NOS) is one that is installed on a machine with no network connections, not switched on, and buried in concrete. Some of the main useful features of an NOS could well be impaired with this type of installation. You must accept that by installing a network you open up your enterprise to some element of risk. A single extreme measure used to counter these risks has a tendency to greatly impact one area of functionality. If you decide to lock the system administrator password in an offsite safe so that nobody could use it, then there could be a severe time impact if the system fails and needs administrator access for recovery.

The layered approach (or *Onion* approach) to securing a network tries to balance the needs for security against the needs for functionality by applying many different techniques to counter known threats. Each specific technique is built on top of a preceding technique and can either rely on its predecessor to aid its own functionality or can counter a security threat by itself. Building up the distinct layers of security around your installation has the advantage of not having to be too restrictive in any one area of functionality. More importantly, the layered approach has the advantage of putting up multiple barriers that need different methods of attack to be breached. If you were to rely solely on extra long passwords to protect your systems, then a sustained attack could be mounted on this one barrier. Eventually, this barrier could be broken. If you couple a medium-length password policy with a policy restricting logons to specific machines, then the attacker needs to find out your machine address before attempting a password break.

The application of several security layers both to address general requirements for system policies and to provide a defense against identified threats is the best way of creating the necessary balance between draconian security models that restrict best business practices and a wide-open network design with little or no defense against misuse, theft, or malicious damage.

Physical Security

The need for physical security is often overlooked in this age of cryptography and 128-bit encryption algorithms. You must remember that for all the people who spend time inventing these algorithms, there are as many people out there inventing countermeasures. One security measure that is very difficult to counter is physical security. As an IT or security professional, your job must include the protection of the business systems for your enterprise (why else would you be reading this?). While you may be tempted to concentrate on the more elaborate and exciting security countermeasures available today to protect your systems, you must spend time considering the more mundane approaches to fulfilling your security needs.

Location

Protection must be provided against both malicious and accidental damage or loss. It can be as costly to a business to lose a critical server because a user spills coffee over it as it is to lose the server by a denial of service attack.

All servers and other important network equipment should be kept in a secure physical location that has the facilities to support computer systems (e.g., UPS power, air conditioning). Access to this location should be both restricted and recorded.

Use of Removable Media

Removable media includes floppy disks, CD-ROM disks, removable hard disks, and backup tapes. Many companies have strict policies on physical location of their data. Custom-built computer rooms are common. People such as yourself go to great lengths to avoid intrusion. And then the backup operator takes a full backup of the systems before an upgrade and keeps the media in an easily accessible desk drawer. This data is generally not encrypted on tape even if it was on disk. The use and subsequent storage of removable media needs to be monitored on all important systems.

Removal of Unnecessary Hardware

You may wish to go one step further and monitor removable media use as well as disable all hardware that can aid intrusion. This could mean disabling COM ports in BIOS as well as CD devices and floppy drives. Remember that you must use the BIOS protection systems (usually password protection on Intel-based machines). Even with BIOS password protection, you must still protect against physical access to the machine because most Intel systems will allow the BIOS protection to be subverted via a motherboard setting.

A good security plan must always be based on balance between extremes. Consider the downside to the removal of this hardware before proceeding. System recovery will generally require floppy drives or CD drives, and their removal could cause extra delay.

Denial of Service

A denial of service attack is used maliciously to prevent a service from being used correctly. Data access is not gained by the attacker. The sole purpose of this attack is to prevent the normal running of a system. In IT realms, a denial of service attack is not generally considered to be a hack because no access is gained directly by the attack. Reasons for this type of attack are numerous. A disillusioned employee may decide to be petty, or a real hacker may plant a bug that needs a system restart to activate.

A common example of a denial of service attack would be the (in)famous *Ping of Death*. The attack is based on the premise that if a large-sized ICMP packet is repeatedly sent to a target, the operating system receiving the packets cannot handle the reassembly of the fragments or the resulting buffer overflow. The net effect of the attack depends on the target OS but can range from no effect, through system freezes and possibly system restarts.

The intention of such an attack is to disrupt the functionality of a system or enterprise, and each type of denial of service problem must be addressed individually.

IT Security Control Objectives

Security control objectives are an integral part of the overall process of implementing a security model. Objectives for your own security model will differ from those of other institutions, depending on the complexity and nature of your business. The following points can help to define your needs and to map out your implementation.

Confidentiality

Data confidentiality is an important consideration for everyone. Whether the case is a business concerned with keeping confidential information from competitors or an internal accounts department trying to keep payroll information a secret, confidentiality is a necessary part of your security model. A good security model should ensure that only authorized people gain access to stored or transmitted information.

If you wish to transfer funds electronically from one account to another, you want to know that the instruction cannot be viewed as it passes over the network. While data is stored on your system, you want to make certain that only the correct people can view or manipulate that data.

The implementation of this part of the security model is accomplished with techniques such as data storage encryption, data transmission encryption, the application of the physical security model, and observance of user and group policies and access controls (all of which are discussed briefly in this chapter and in detail in further chapters).

Integrity

Data integrity is a different issue than confidentiality. The point of a data integrity model is to ensure that data received, stored, or transmitted is from a known and trusted source.

In the preceding fund transfer example, the recipient of the instruction needs to know that the request came from you and nobody else. The implementation of this part of the security model is accomplished with a mixture of electronic signatures and message authentication methods.

Availability

The objective of this part of the security model is to maintain the availability of your business systems by applying the controls necessary to prevent or react to a denial of service attack. These controls can be technical (securing data communications lines from external access) or procedural (regular backup of systems or strictly limiting data access rights). Other considerations such as disk duplexing, RAID, and clustering are not considered to be security issues, although they can impact the availability of your systems.

Legal Notice at Logon

Part of the overall security plan for any computer installation should be to discourage the would-be intruder from progressing in the attempt to break in. Although policies will differ from company to company when it comes to catching hackers and possibly following through with legal action, a legal notice before logon should be used to clearly explain to users that they only have the rights assigned to them by you and that any breach of protocol will be dealt with in the strictest way possible. Even if your company policy would never permit a prosecution, a correctly worded warning may deter a user from malicious computer acts.

The terms used in the legal statement should be devised by your own legal department. Laws change from state to state or country to country, and it would be inappropriate to discuss any specifics here.

 The one warning that is applicable almost worldwide is that your notice should never start with "Welcome." This is considered in many countries to be an invitation to use the computer system, and many would-be prosecutions have failed on the technicality.

Qualities Defining a Secure System

There are many qualities which should be present in a system that has a well-defined security model. The following list is not exhaustive on this subject and can be added to by anybody with a need for extra protection in a certain area. If your system does not possess some of the qualities mentioned below, then you should evaluate the potential security risks and see if they can be covered by another type of control (e.g., the lack of an encrypted file system may be countered by tight physical security and well-implemented discretionary access controls).

Discretionary Access Controls

Discretionary access control involves the use of a number of different ways to limit access to certain objects in the computer environment. Access at a computer level can be controlled with user name and password combinations as well as physical restrictions. Access on a directory or file level can be controlled by user and group policies.

It is important to define the discretionary controls early in the design phase of a system or network.

Audit Capabilities

A secure system should have audit capabilities that can test the integrity of the security model and also track any attempted security breaches. The minimum requirements for an audit system consist of the following:

- Configurable event tracking, which enables you to set your audit policy to suit your business requirements. Examples of event configuration are tracking failed logons, tracking confidential file access, or tracking system rights changes.

- Event viewing and reporting which should allow custom searches to be made for specific events such as logon failures. These failures may indicate an attempted break-in.

- Audit events, which should be logged to separate systems so that logs cannot be tampered with.

- Audit log access, which should be controlled so that even the system administrators cannot amend or change tracked events without being tracked in turn.

Audit capabilities are as important to system security as any other part of the security model. You cannot be sure that your security model works unless you can audit system events. If you audit failed logons and find a persistent attempt to break in to your system, then you can act on the information before the attempt is successful.

Mandatory Identification and Authentication

Mandatory identification and authentication ensure that a user is permitted to access a resource and also apply the discretionary access controls mentioned previously. This essentially means that a user wishing to access any network resources, must provide a unique user ID and prove that she has permission for that ID by providing the password. Systems should not allow access without this authentication. A system that allows anonymous access can still be secured if the user account that provides the access behind the scenes is configured with well-defined access rights to public information only.

Memory Management and Object Reuse

Memory management is an important part of a security model. With the advent of sophisticated virtual memory managers, the risk of having confidential information remain in memory after use is high. The memory manager on a system must be able to separate or partition the memory used by individual processes. After a process has ended and the memory is to be reused, the memory must be flushed of all contents before it can be accessed again.

Encrypted Data Transfer

Data transfer encryption ensures that information that is intercepted during transmission over the network cannot be accessed by unauthorized agents. Encryption keys can provide strong protection against eavesdropping and tampering. Data encryption is covered extensively in later chapters.

Encrypted File System

File system encryption ensures that data is only accessed by users with the correct discretionary access rights. Data encryption and decryption should be completed in a manner that is transparent to the user.

Summary

The security concepts discussed in this chapter can be applied to any networked computer installation. The layered approach to securing a network affords cumulative benefits, making this approach well worth consideration. An administrator must find the correct balance between implementing a secure environment and easing restrictions so as not to impact business processes.

A well-defined security model applied to a system from an early stage on helps a business by supporting its security needs fully while allowing for the range of business activities required by the enterprise today.

There is no substitute for physical security measures. Physical security is part of the layered model and should be considered as important as any other part.

Security control objectives are the foundation of a security model. A definitive list of qualities defining an organization's security systems serves as a baseline measurement tool for an implementation.

NT 4.0 Security Architecture Overview

Chapter Two contains an overview of the Windows NT 4.0 security model and maps the ideas and concepts discussed in Chapter One to their implementation in NT 4.0.

This chapter introduces the security architecture of Windows NT 4.0, acting as a high-level introduction to some of the main security features of Windows NT which are covered in more detail in their own chapters later in the book. It is recommended that you read this chapter to familiarize yourself with some of the terms that are used throughout the book before moving on.

The migration path from NT 4.0 to Windows 2000 provided by Microsoft allows for upgrades to be made at almost any pace. Some companies will want to make a move as quickly as possible, whereas others may take a phased approach. In either case, there will be a period when the two operating systems will coexist on the same network. It is important to understand the security structure of NT 4.0 so that you are in a better position to make an informed choice about your migration strategy. Understanding this security structure will also allow you to appreciate the enhancements to the existing NT 4.0 features and all the new features delivered in Windows 2000.

Introduction

One of your aims as a network or security professional working in an NT environment is to make Windows NT as secure as it can *feasibly* be configured. Identical threats exist in government, financial, and commercial environments, and the techniques for containing them are the same. Hence, the following guidelines are applicable to almost any Windows NT 4.0 environment.

The Windows NT standard software has many available controls for tightening its security. However, even though many of those controls are covered here, I would never rashly recommend the tightest settings for all controls. Implicit in this chapter (and throughout the remainder of this book) is the understanding that any recommendations must be both effective against certain threats and also practical. Some controls impede operational capability and their use must be carefully balanced against the security they offer.

This book does not cover subjects such as regular backups or disaster recovery procedures, although both of these can be a critical part of recovering from a successful system penetration.

Design Goals for Windows NT 4.0 Security

When designing the base Windows NT structure, Microsoft aimed for a strong, robust system with a large amount of built-in security capability. When the base NT 4.0 product is installed from its shrink-wrapped package, the security settings default to minimal values. The idea behind this was that Microsoft felt that the large majority of users would not want to bother with a highly secure system that had too many constraints on usage and a large overhead in management. This assumption has changed as more and more large organizations install and use the product; however it is still thought that it is easier for the enterprise needing security to define and configure this security than it is for the individual customer to turn off the security settings within the operating system.

Modules of the NT 4.0 Security Architecture

Windows NT 4.0 security architecture is made up of several modules that work together to perform authentication, validation of credentials, and audit tracking. The modules that make up the security subsystem of the NT operating system are described below.

Graphical Identification and Authentication (GINA) DLL

GINA is a replaceable portion of the Winlogon component of NT (the component that provides interactive logon support). GINA specifically provides identification and authentication support. It can be replaced with a third-party file to allow access to the system through another means of Secure Attention Sequence. This file would change the authentication method from the traditional user name and password combination to perhaps a smart card with stored credentials or retinal scan technology. Throughout this chapter, the use of the standard Windows NT GINA to provide a format for authentication discussions is presumed.

Trusted System

The NT security subsystem is a trusted system. The security features of NT are built into the base product and do not exist as a separate entity. This makes it impossible for anybody to interfere with the base set of rules for NT security. It is virtually impossible for a programmer to write a program to run on Windows NT that bypasses the credential checks and access control list protection provided for objects within the system.

Objects

The definition of an object in NT is a gray area depending on the context. In the context of security and for the purposes of our discussions, an object is any resource within the NT domain structure. These resources include, but are not limited to, printers, files, directories, security databases, shares, and system components. Objects are protected by the application of ACLs.

Access Control Lists (ACL)

An object within the NT system is protected by an access control list. The ACL is checked when an object or resource access is requested, to determine what rights (if any) a user is granted. When an object is created, a corresponding ACL is created. ACLs contain a header that stores information such as the revision level, size of the ACL, and the number of ACEs it contains.

There are two types of ACL. The discretionary ACL is controlled by the owner of the object and grants or denies permissions to the object. The system ACL specifies audit tracking information for the object and is controlled by the administrator. An ACE in a system ACL may specify that an audit record be generated in the Event log when an access attempt on the object fails.

Access Control Entry (ACE)

An ACE is an entry in an ACL. The ACL is made up of zero or more ACEs (a null ACL contains no entries). An ACE describes the access rights of a user or group to an object. An ACE is made up of a trustee (user account or group), a set of access rights for the trustee, and a flag that indicates whether the rights are granted, denied, or audited.

System Identifier (SID)

A SID is a system identifier. Every computer in a domain except primary and backup domain controllers (PDC, BDC) is statistically guaranteed to have a unique SID within the domain. A SID is a 96-bit identifier that uniquely identifies each individual computer. Domain controllers (PDC and BDC) are treated as one and share a common SID (one reason why a BDC installation requires the presence of a domain controller from which to copy the SID).

User and group SIDs are generated from the machine SID with an extra number set concatenated to identify the unique user and groups of a machine or domain. User SIDs can be seen in the system registry under the key `HKEY_LOCAL_MACHINE\SOFTWARE\Microsoft\Windows NT\Current-Version\ProfileList`. This registry key holds the profile name used by each SID (and so each user). There should be an entry here for each user defined in the systems account database.

Remember to view the registry in read-only mode at all times to avoid possible corruptions. By default, the registry editor opens the registry tree in write mode. Follow the steps outlined below to open the registry in read-only mode and view examples of user SIDs.

1. Select **Run** from the **Start** menu.
2. Enter **Regedt32** and select **OK**. The registry editor opens and cascades the five registry keys.
3. Select the **Options** menu.
4. Select **Read Only Mode**. This places a tick mark next to Read Only Mode.
5. Select the **Options** menu once more to make certain that Read Only Mode is selected. Notice also that the **Confirm On Delete** option is grayed out now because nothing can be deleted from the registry while it is open in read-only mode. Figure 2.1 shows the registry editor options menu after read-only mode is set.
6. Select the **HKEY_LOCAL_MACHINE on Local Machine** window and maximize it.
7. In the tree view (left-hand pane), double-click **Software**.
8. Double-click **Microsoft > Windows NT > CurrentVersion > ProfileList** to produce a list of profiles viewed by user SID.

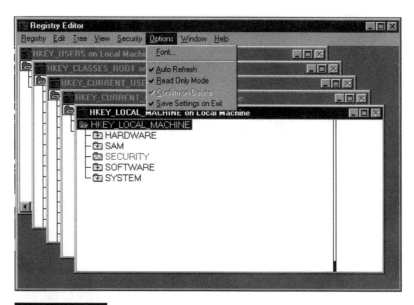

FIGURE 2.1   Registry editor (Regedt32.exe) in read-only mode

All the SIDs listed here represent a different user known on the active system. The number shown before the last "-" represents the unique machine identifier. Several of these identifiers can be listed here if users from other machines or domains have logged on to this machine. The number after the last "-" represents the unique user within each unique machine. This means that if the machine number is the same for two users, the digits representing the user are different.

The suffix digits representing the users on each machine are assigned sequentially, starting at 1000 and moving upward in 1s. The number 500 represents the first user on the system (the administrator).

The SID references a user or group when object rights and permissions are applied or checked. It is because of this method of addressing the permissions issue that you cannot assign permissions to a user, delete the user, create a new user of the same name, and expect the same permissions to apply. Because of the quasi-unique property of the SID (the numbers are assigned sequentially), the new user will have the same name but a different SID. As the SID is the identifier referenced in the ACE when granting or denying permissions, the old ACE entries in the ACL will not apply to the new user.

A sample SID is illustrated in Figure 2.2. This shows the HKEY_LOCAL_-MACHINE registry key and the profile list discussed above.

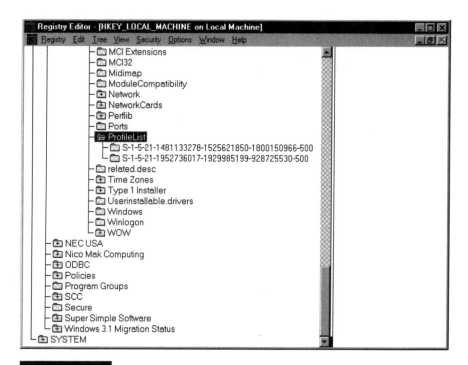

FIGURE 2.2   Sample user SIDs in the system registry profile section

Local Security Authority (LSA)

The local security authority is the function within the security subsystem that validates user credentials when they are supplied at logon time. The LSA is responsible for creating the access token for a user. The LSA is the management entity that controls the policies that define the security subsystem. The LSA also manages the audit policy and is responsible for sending entries to the Event logs.

Access Tokens

Access tokens are created by the LSA at logon time. An access token is created for each user when the user logs on; it survives to the end of that particular logon session. An access token is created once at logon time and is not adjusted after that time.

Access tokens are made up of the following information:

- User SID
- Group SID(s)
- An ACL (every object has an ACL)

- Primary group identifier
- Owner identifier
- List of user privileges

If a user is added to a group that gives extra object rights, then the user will not be able to use those rights until the next logon. At this time, the SID for the new group is included in the user's access token and is available for use.

Access tokens are very small, and they accompany any request for object access. For example, when a user requests a file open, the access token is sent with the request and checked by the security reference monitor (see below), which verifies the access rights against the ACL for the file.

Security Reference Monitor (SRM)

The security reference monitor works on the kernel side of the NT subsystem. This part of the security subsystem actually enforces the control policies managed by the LSA. The SRM sits between the kernel and the hardware abstraction layer (HAL) and protects against unauthorized access to system objects.

Security Account Manager (SAM)

The Security Account Manager controls the user account database that stores all of the user names, passwords, and access rights assigned within the system. For local logons, the SAM verifies the credential call made by the LSA at logon time. It compares the encrypted hash of the password passed through by the LSA to the encrypted hash stored in the database. If the passwords match, the SAM passes back the SID for the user and also any SIDs for the groups to which the user belongs. These are used by the LSA to create the access token needed to define object access rights. This process is discussed in more detail in *Logon and the Authentication Process* later in the chapter.

File and Directory Permissions

File and directory permissions are split into two categories. Special permissions are the individual permissions allowed on a file or directory. Standard permissions are made up from combinations of special permissions and are the most commonly applied.

Mandatory Logon Process

There are many qualities defining a secure system as discussed earlier. One of these qualities is mandatory identification and authentication. It is accomplished in NT with the mandatory logon process. At the end of the boot-up sequence for NT 4.0 workstation and server, the user is prompted to initialize the logon process. This initialization is accomplished with the Secure Attention Sequence (<Ctrl> <Alt> <Del>) keystrokes. User credentials for an interactive logon must be entered through this dialog box, thus ensuring that the mandatory identification and authentication process is used. This process could be circumvented by an administrator changing the GINA to allow automated logon.

With the standard GINA, this mandatory logon process cannot be avoided if the operating system boots up as Windows NT. However if intruders can access your hardware and boot into a different operating system, then they can gain access to your systems' hard drives (including NTFS). The way to avoid this occurrence is to implement the physical security restrictions discussed in Chapter One.

Single Logon

The single logon is an important feature of the NT 4.0 security model. This feature allows the user to log on to the system once; thereafter, the user credentials supplied at logon time are passed across to any remote system where a user has requested a resource. All of this remains transparent to the user as long as credentials are the same on the remote system as they are locally. If passwords are not the same for the corresponding user on the remote system or if the user is unknown to the remote system, then the single logon process is broken and user name or password prompts are provided, depending on the situation.

Security Support Provider Interface (SSPI)

The SSPI is an abstraction layer interposed between the security providers, such as NT distributed security services and the application-level communications mechanisms, such as Microsoft RPC, which may need to use the secure communications methods.

The SSPI is discussed further in Chapter Twelve, *Windows 2000 Overview.*

Intra- and Interdomain Communication

Authenticated RPC and DCOM

RPC (remote procedure call) is a high-level interprocess communications mechanism used as a standard application interface to the SSPI (see above). Authenticated RPCs are used between the workstation and domain controller to establish and maintain a trusted path between the pair. This path is created by the Netlogon service and is maintained throughout the user session. This trusted path is extended by authenticated RPC to other servers in trusted domains. This path is used to pass authentication information between the DC and the workstation such as user name/password combinations and the information returned at logon time used to populate the access token (e.g., user SID, group SIDs).

Authenticated RPC supports distributed application access by using *Impersonation* (see below).

The RPC calls are authenticated by means of the NTLM SSP in Windows NT 4.0 and earlier versions and will be supported by the Kerberos protocol for Windows 2000 domain and Active Directory authentication.

DCOM (Distributed Component Object Model) is an application interface layered on top of RPC. DCOM provides an extra layer between applications and security implementations. The applications themselves need not know what security implementation is used. Security can be provided through the RPC interface, through DCOM, or directly through the SSPI.

NTLM Authentication

NTLM authentication is a challenge/response method of authentication used in Windows NT to provide secure checking of user name, password, and machine credentials. The main advantage of NTLM is that the user password is never openly transmitted to the server. The steps involved in an NTLM challenge/response routine are outlined below.

- The user invokes the logon routine with a <Ctrl> <Alt> <Del> keystroke.
- The user's credentials are entered (plus machine or domain name).
- The machine and user name are transmitted to the security authority (server) if they are not local.
- The server sends back a challenge made up from the received credentials.
- The client receives the challenge and encrypts this with the user password.
- The server encrypts the challenge with the stored password and compares it to the response sent from the client.
- If the two compare successfully, then the authentication is complete.

Note that the password was never transmitted over the network during this sequence. Instead, a hash value is encrypted with the password and transmitted during the NTLM challenge/response routine, which is the main method of authentication used in a Windows NT domain environment.

Impersonation

Impersonation is an important part of using network services to carry out tasks. Impersonation takes place when a network service assumes a user's security context and carries out a task as if it were that user. This is made possible by use of the access token created by the LSA at logon time.

The access token is passed along with any network request made by the user. When the access rights and permissions are verified and access is granted, the network service starts a server thread that carries out the request by using the access token settings to impersonate the user. This means that the task is carried out as if the user were performing it instead of a system service. All of the user's rights and security context settings are used. Impersonation used on distributed applications is supported by use of the Authenticated RPC communications mechanism and the SSPI discussed earlier. When client/server connections are made, the client can define the level of impersonation that the server is allowed to use. Windows NT supports three levels of impersonation.

Level 1. Anonymous. The client does not allow the server to discover information about its security context.

Level 2. Identification. Authentication is allowed by the server. The server cannot use the client's security context for access checks.

Level 3. Impersonation. The client allows the server to perform access checks using the client's security context.

A fourth level of impersonation known as delegation is not supported by NT 4.0 and the NTLM authentication protocol. Support for delegation (where the client allows the server to use the first three levels of impersonation and then to request remote services under the context of the user) will be available in Windows 2000 and will use Kerberos authentication.

Security Implementation Overview

Installation Security Concerns

This section discusses the relevant measures necessary to implement a secure installation of Windows NT.

As with most situations where a layered approach to the work is required (in this case, preparing hardware, installing base OS, installing additional features, adding software and services, etc.), the sanity of the end result will be greatly affected by the strength of the foundation. The security model needs to be applied from the very first stages of design and implementation.

REMOVAL OF NONESSENTIAL HARDWARE

When the removal of nonessential hardware is mentioned, people generally think about floppy drives. However, there are many other devices that could pose a threat to the system security. COM ports, printer ports, and CD-ROM devices can all be used with malicious intent. Where appropriate, these devices should be removed or at least disabled in BIOS. If BIOS is used to control these devices, then a BIOS password is essential.

BIOS: IMPLICATIONS FOR SECURITY CONTROL

A special mention for BIOS is needed at this point to discuss the security implications surrounding this important and often neglected area.

BIOS passwords are commonly used as the method for disabling specific hardware on Intel-based machines. These passwords do not need to be as secure as the NT system passwords, but neither should they be too short or easily guessed (in most BIOS versions these passwords are usually limited to eight characters).

It is important to understand that these passwords can be disabled on most Intel-based machines by direct access to the motherboard. Therefore, physical security measures must be implemented hand-in-hand with BIOS security. See *Physical Security* in Chapter One.

Implementing BIOS security measures is not a replacement for removing any unwanted devices. Consider BIOS security and physical security to be a partnership.

INSTALLING FROM OTHER OPERATING SYSTEMS

Windows NT 4.0 can be installed on a system that already contains other operating systems. Such installations are sometimes used as a shortcut, and the option to upgrade an existing installation can sometimes seem to be very inviting.

Do not install Windows NT from any other operating system or ensure that all disks are re-formatted during installation. Installing over the top of DOS or Windows 95 can lead to system files being left on the hard disk and could aid in circumventing the built-in security features of NT.

BOOTING FROM ALTERNATIVE SOURCES

Ensure that alternative boot devices cannot be used to access your system. Floppy drive and CD-ROM drive booting should be disabled (see *Removal of Nonessential Hardware,* above). Be aware of the physical access restrictions which need to be implemented with BIOS security (see *BIOS: Implications for Security Control*, above).

Further protection of the NT system is afforded by the use of the NTFS file system. (See *NTFS vs. FAT* below.)

INSTALLING ADDITIONAL OPERATING SYSTEMS

Do not be tempted to install more than one operating system on the same machine. Windows 95 and DOS will happily coexist on the same machine as

Windows NT. There are utilities (non-Microsoft) which exist for Windows 95 and DOS that can read NTFS partitions (see *NTFS vs. FAT* below). By preventing these utilities from being run off a floppy disk (by physical security implementations) and by ensuring that Windows NT is the only operating system installed, you will go a long way toward preventing these programs from being used to circumvent NTFS security.

NTFS VS. FAT

NTFS stands for NT file system and is the native file system in use with NT 4.0. Security is implemented with ACLs so that information cannot be read without the correct permission.

The FAT file system is supported for backward compatibility between Windows NT and other operating systems such as DOS, Windows 3.x, and Windows 9x. Security using ACLs and the built-in security mechanisms within NT 4.0 cannot be used to secure files and directories on a FAT partition (although security can be applied to any shares on a FAT partition).

NTFS security is discussed in Chapter Three, *File and Directory Security*.

Logon and the Authentication Process

The way in which NT deals with any request is based on the user account information that accompanies the request. On very few occasions, NT will process a request that it knows came from a trusted source without the benefit of this account information (e.g., WINS replication). These requests would all be system based and are needed for automatic operation.

All other requests must be accompanied by account information before they are processed. The account information (given in the form of an access token) must be valid for the computer accepting the request and is then checked against any access rights or restrictions for the resource requested.

THE LOGON PROCESS

The logon process is started on an NT workstation by the Secure Attention Sequence keystrokes. The user is prompted to enter the security credentials (user name and password) and the SAM to be used to authenticate the credentials. If the user chooses the local SAM based on the workstation, then no authentication takes place within the domain at this time. All authentication is performed locally for local resources only. If the user chooses the domain SAM, then the authentication process is passed to a domain controller for completion.

Logons can be divided into two categories: interactive logon and remote logon.

INTERACTIVE LOGON

Local logon using the local SAM consists of the following steps:

- <Ctrl> <Alt> <Del> keystrokes are used as the Secure Attention Sequence (Winlogon).
- User credentials are entered and a machine or domain is selected.
- <Enter> keystroke is used to confirm these credentials.
- The password is encrypted (hashed) and is sent to the local LSA.
- The credentials are sent to the local SAM for local workstation logons or to the domain LSA for domain logons.
- The credentials are checked and validated.
- Correct password validation results in the user SID and any relevant group SIDs being returned to the LSA.
- The LSA creates an access token containing the returned SIDs.
- A process is created by the Win32 subsystem, the NT explorer shell is started up, and the access token is attached to it.

REMOTE LOGON

A remote logon takes place when a user logs on to a server in a domain. A remote logon consists of the following steps:

- <Ctrl> <Alt> <Del> keystrokes are used as the Secure Attention Sequence (Winlogon).
- User credentials are entered and the <Enter> keystroke is used to confirm these credentials.
- The credentials are sent to the local LSA.
- A call is made to the MSV1_0 authentication package, which initiates a secure RPC session using the Netlogon service.
- A challenge/response sequence is used to send a hash of the password to the server.
- The server's Netlogon process passes the credentials to the server's MSV1_0 authentication package, which checks them against the stored credentials.
- Correct password validation results in the user SID and any relevant group SIDs being returned by the Netlogon processes to the local LSA.
- The LSA creates an access token containing the returned SIDs and any SID information in the local SAM.
- A process is created by the Win32 subsystem, the NT explorer shell is started up, and the access token is attached to it.

SUMMARY

Any user requesting a resource must demonstrate the knowledge of an enabled account name and password valid for the account database scope of the destination computer, whether the attempt to log on is local or remote. A notable exception to this is in an environment where the Guest account is enabled for anonymous access; administrators can set up a machine to automatically log on so that the demonstration of knowledge is not required. This is not recommended in an environment where security is a concern.

The Administrator Account

Every Windows NT computer has an Administrator account created by default at installation. This account cannot be deleted but it can be renamed. On domain controllers, this account is a global one; on all other computers, it is local. The account cannot be locked out after failed access attempts (unless adjusted with the Resource kit) and so can be vulnerable to prolonged attack. Therefore, the user name/password combination for this and any other privileged account needs to be secure.

It is a good idea to increase the integrity of user name/password security for the Administrator account (and any equivalent accounts). The integrity of a user name/password combination is mainly related to the strength of the password. The integrity of the combination also takes into account the locking policy of an installation (how many bad logon attempts before an account is locked and duration of lock). As was mentioned earlier, the Administrator account cannot be locked out by the account policy set for the domain. This immediately reduces the scope of available protection on the password. Prolonged attempts can be made to penetrate the user name/password combination.

 You can apply a program to your installation to force the Administrator user to be affected by your lockout policy, but this practice opens your installation to a denial of service attack and is not recommended.

Microsoft considers user names to be public knowledge and so does not encrypt them in NT 4.0. Passwords, however, are always encrypted. The best way to increase the integrity to an acceptable level would therefore be to increase the size of the password. A 14-character (maximum allowed) password containing random mixes of upper-and lowercase numbers and letters would make a formidable barrier to break through (as well as a very difficult one to remember).

A sound audit policy with regular reviews of the Event logs can highlight repeated attempts to break into a system.

File and Directory Security

File and directory security is one of the mainstays of the NT security model. The NTFS file system allows each individual file and directory to be secured as separate objects. This ability to granulate security settings enables the administrator to be very specific in the application of permissions and rights.

File and directory permissions are applied through graphical interfaces in context-sensitive menus so they are easy to implement and maintain. NTFS permissions are discussed in Chapter Three, *File and Directory Security*.

Registry Security

Registry security is an important part of the overall security implementation for Windows NT. The registry holds settings that control almost all parts of the system. Some of these settings are rather innocuous, but some of them could destroy the system if set wrong.

The registry has some security applied by default, but it requires further fine-tuning to ensure that only the minimum required access is given to the user community. Securing the registry is covered in Chapter Eight, *Registry*.

User Profiles

A user profile is a group of settings that describes the look and feel of a user's environment on a Windows NT or Windows 95 computer. It can be used to control what appears on a desktop or what applications are accessible. User profiles contain settings that can be applied to a user, group, or computer and can be set up so that users can make and save changes or so that users cannot save any changes made.

User profiles were designed in part to answer the need for more control over the ever-growing complexity of the desktop and network systems. Administrators can now deliver and manage from a central point the look and feel required by the enterprise workforce. All users don't have to have the same desktop look. In addition, the profile is capable of travelling with the user (roaming), so that the same look and feel can be provided in different locations with the minimum of administrative overhead.

From the point of view of the IT security professional, the user profile adds an invaluable tool that can be used to clamp down on unnecessary system access and possible security breaches. The creation and implementation of user profiles is covered in detail in Chapter Four, *User Profiles*.

System Policies

System policies are made up from a set of registry entries that control the computer resources available to a user or group of users. These registry entries can be applied to individual users, groups of users, or to anybody logging on to a particular machine.

The system policies can be used to control access to many different resources on the local machine, including access to sensitive system tools such as the registry editor and the task manager. Desktop settings and user access to resources can be controlled easily. Settings such as the contents of the Start menu and which application icons appear on the desktop are examples of the controls that can be applied.

System policies are defined with the System Policy Editor tool, `POLEDIT.EXE`. Poledit is a graphical user tool that saves to a file the settings you wish to apply. This file is then loaded when a user logs on or when a machine is started, and the settings are applied. System policies are covered in more detail in Chapter Five, *System Policies*.

Auditing Capability

The audit capabilities of NT 4.0 are quite strong. All of the auditing capabilities are turned off in NT 4.0 by default because of the overhead in keeping a large Event log. Auditing is discussed more fully in Chapter Nine, *NT Audit*.

New Security Management Tools

Microsoft Management Console

Microsoft Management Console is used as the management platform for all aspects of Windows 2000 system management and is introduced in Windows NT to support the Security Configuration Manager tool, which requires Service Pack 4 support for the Windows NT.

Because this is a relatively new feature in Windows NT 4.0 with only a small amount of functionality and because of its extensive use throughout Windows 2000, available features for both systems and differences in the two formats are discussed in Chapter Ten, *Microsoft Management Console*.

Security Configuration Manager for NT

The Security Configuration Manager for NT 4.0 SP4 is a new system tool that has been released by Microsoft before its full-scale implementation in Windows 2000. The tool brings together most of the system security settings that can be used to protect your NT installation and conveniently packages them within one easy-to-use interface.

This tool is easily the most significant Windows NT release in terms of security for some time. The minimum system requirements for this tool are Windows NT 4.0 with Service Pack 4 loaded. The tool does not work with Windows NT 3.x. All of the individual tools for setting security can still be used on your system if you are unable to use this particular product for some reason.

Even if you do not intend to use the product on your NT 4.0 system, you should familiarize yourself with the concepts involved because later versions of the Windows operating system will use this approach for system management.

Microsoft Proxy Server

Microsoft Proxy Server 2.0 is a firewall package that also provides data caching facilities. It is most commonly used between your private network and any external networks (Internet) to protect your internal environment from unauthorized access, while adding the benefit of increased efficiency for external data requests with its caching feature.

Proxy Server allows configurable Internet access from your private network and offers a fully configurable set of security parameters to protect your internal networks from outside access. Inbound access can be completely closed off or it can be opened up under strict controls and subject to imposed rules.

Windows NT 4.0 Security Components

Chapter Three contains step-by-step guides that address the security concerns surrounding the Windows NT system registry. For both file system security and internal registry access, methods to customize protection to meet the needs of your environment are provided.

Chapter Four introduces the concept of user profiles and includes step-through examples on how to implement them in a Windows NT environment. User profiles are used in an NT environment to control the look and feel of the user desktop and available options at the workstation. This chapter focuses on user profiles defined within the NT workstation and server environment but also includes some information on user profiles applied to Windows 9x clients.

Chapter Five introduces the concept of system policies. These policies are used with the Policy Editor to control the look and feel of a desktop and also to control system settings on a per-machine basis. This functionality complements similar functionality in the user profile setup. The chapter discusses the default values available with the Policy Editor and takes you through each setting in detail. All of the behind-the-scenes portions of the Policy Editor, such as template files, are discussed and the links between these and the various registry values covered by the Policy Editor are exposed.

Chapter Six addresses the topic of cryptography as a general subject and also as it relates to both present and future releases of Microsoft Windows operating systems. Subtopics covered in this chapter include data encryption while data is stored and transmitted, encryption algorithms, authentication, and digital certificate use.

Chapter Seven discusses Microsoft Proxy Server 2.0 with the main emphasis on the security aspects of the product. As a prerequisite for this discussion, the reader should be aware of the general features of a firewall system and how data is passed between secure and nonsecure interfaces.

Chapter Eight looks at the security concerns surrounding the Windows NT system registry and addresses these concerns with a step-by-step guide to securing this important area. Both file system security and internal registry access are looked at with a view to demonstrating how to provide customized protection to meet the needs of your environment.

Chapter Nine discusses the concepts involved in implementing a thorough and sustainable audit policy for NT networks. The chapter takes you through processes, from initial design of an audit policy, through implementation, to managing the defined policy and monitoring the captured audit events.

Chapter Ten introduces one of the newer features of NT 4.0 and a feature that will be at the center of the management and administration of Windows 2000 in the future. Microsoft Management Console will be used as the management tool for all aspects of the Windows 2000 network. This chapter includes some step-by-step instructions for setting up your own security management console, which will accustom you to the look and feel of the MMC. To take full advantage of the step-through examples included in this chapter, you must have access to a Windows 2000 installed machine with Administrator rights. The Windows NT 4.0 MMC requires Service Pack 4 support for the Security Configuration Manager. Because MMC is new to Windows NT 4.0 with only a small amount of functionality and because of its extensive use throughout Windows 2000, this chapter discusses features available for NT 4.0 SP4 and Windows 2000 and points out any differences in the two formats.

Chapter Eleven introduces the Security Configuration Manager for Windows NT 4.0. This is a snap-in tool for the Microsoft Management Console, which is the new host tool designed for managing Microsoft systems. The Security Configuration Manager for NT 4.0 coupled with the MMC moves the management of Windows NT 4.0 networks in the same direction Microsoft has taken in its design of Windows 2000.

File and Directory Security

This chapter discusses file and directory security using both NTFS file permissions and share-level permissions.

Step-by-step instructions take you through the procedures necessary to implement and manage a file and directory security policy including viewing and setting permissions, choosing between share and NTFS permissions, and securing the file system.

Introduction

File and directory security is at the heart of the Windows NT security model. Almost all other security features of the operating system rely on file and directory security to protect access to the control mechanisms.

File and directory permissions are set through context-sensitive menus that allow security to be applied to single files, multiple files, directories, and whole directory structures.

Disk Partitions

Windows NT supports different types of disk partitions.

- **FAT.** FAT partitions are supported for backward compatibility and interoperability with other operating systems.

- **CDFS.** CDFS is the CD-ROM file system and is used as a common file system for CD-ROM support. By its nature, this type of partition is read-only. NTFS permissions cannot be set on a CDFS partition.

- **NTFS.** NTFS partitions are native to Windows NT and are the foundation of Windows NT file and directory security.

FAT

FAT partitions are supported by many disparate operating systems. If you need to dual-boot your machine, you can use a FAT partition as the common disk partition between the two operating systems.

Security using ACLs and ACEs within Windows NT cannot be applied to this partition type. The partition does not support the extended features necessary to apply the security. Whenever possible and certainly whenever you require any level of file and folder security, you should use NTFS-formatted partitions with Windows NT.

Some very specific conditions may give rise to the need for a FAT partition. One example follows.

Your NT server has boot difficulties. If you use software mirroring for the boot device for fault tolerance, then only the first drive in the pair is used to boot into NT. The number of this device is recorded in the BOOT.INI file on the system partition. If the first drive fails, your system will not automatically boot from the second drive. The BOOT.INI file will still have the number of the first drive as the boot drive. As this is software mirroring, the devices will be numbered as separate partitions (unlike hardware mirroring, where two or more drives are mirrored before boot time to form one logical partition). A manual adjustment needs to be made in the BOOT.INI file. If the file system is FAT, then you could start your system from a floppy disk and edit the necessary line in the BOOT.INI file to load from the second drive in the pair. At this time, you can replace the first drive, rebuild the mirror pair, and remirror in NT.

FAT is also used on very small disks because of NTFS performance issues on disks of 250 Mbytes or less. This is rarely an issue today.

CDFS

CDFS partitions are used solely for CD-ROM devices. These devices are read-only by their nature and so are secured by default. NTFS permissions cannot be set on CDFS volumes.

Share Permissions

FAT and CDFS partitions can have some security applied to them within a Windows NT system through share permissions. Network shares give access to a machine's local resources from a network. Users can make connections to the resource through the share name instead of having to navigate through many layers of subdirectories. Security can be applied to these shares in the same way as it can be applied to NTFS shares. If your machine contains a FAT partition and is in a secure location so that the partition cannot be accessed locally outside of the NT operating system, then share permissions could be used to secure network access to the information on the partition. Share permissions are discussed in more detail later in the chapter.

Unless you can identify a situation, such as the one above, which may justify a FAT partition, then NTFS provides far greater benefits.

NTFS

NTFS partitions are native to Windows NT, and so they are fully integrated into the Windows NT security model.

Security is applied in two possible ways to files and directories on an NTFS partition: with share permissions and file and directory permissions.

As mentioned earlier in the book, when you receive Windows NT in a shrink-wrapped package, security is set to minimal values. Users who have little or no interest in security can start using the product immediately without having to learn how to switch security features off. Users who have an interest in security should always define their own security needs according to the requirements of their organization; so, a minimal security installation is a good place to start building from.

File and Directory Permissions

File and directory permissions can only be applied to an NTFS partition. These permissions are divided into two categories: file permissions and directory permissions.

File Permissions

As you would expect, file permissions are applied to control access to files. File permissions can be further broken down into two subcategories: standard file permissions and special access file permissions.

STANDARD FILE PERMISSIONS

The file permissions category contains a standard set of permissions that can be applied to the object of the security implementation. Table 3.1 shows the standard file permissions available and describes their effects.

TABLE 3.1	Standard file permissions	
Name	**Permission Symbol**	**User Has This Access**
No Access	(None)	The user has no access. When this permission is applied, it overrides any other permission gained in other ways, such as from group permissions. It is used to deny access to a particular file without affecting the security of files in the same folder.
Read	(RX)	The user can read files and run applications. The user cannot modify or change the file in any way. This permission is often used for applications or template files that require protection from modifications.
Change	(RWXD)	The user can read files, run applications, delete files and change data in files. This permission gives users all access that they could possibly need to make any modifications at all.
Full Control	(All)	The user receives all of the above plus the ability to take ownership of files and to change permissions on the file.

Standard file permissions are made up of the most common combinations of special access permissions and are defined to make security application and administration that bit easier.

SPECIAL ACCESS FILE PERMISSIONS

As well as the standard permissions offered for file security, a second set of permissions is available. These are known as special access permissions and are really the component parts that go to make up standard permissions.

Table 3.2 shows the available special access file permissions and describes their effect.

TABLE 3.2	Special access file permissions	
Name	**Permission Symbol**	**User Has This Access**
Read	(R)	The user can view the contents of a file.
Write	(W)	The user can change the contents of a file.
Execute	(X)	The user can run a program.
Delete	(D)	The user can delete a file.
Change Permissions	(P)	The user can change permissions on the file.
Take Ownership	(O)	The user can take ownership of the file. This permission is inherent in all files and directories for the Administrators group because of the *Take ownership of files and other objects* user right set in the user rights policy.

As you can see, the individual permissions available here have been put together in convenient groupings to make standard file permissions the easiest way to apply file security. When the convenient standard permissions do not exactly fulfill your security requirements, you can build your own special access grouping and apply this security instead.

File permissions are only applied in rarer cases where a finely grained security approach needs to be implemented. It is more usual to apply directory security, which can be used to protect the directory and all of its contents. File security is only applied when the requirements for a specific file differ from other files in the same location. Examples later in the chapter take you through all of the necessary steps to apply different levels of security, using these permissions.

Directory Permissions

Directory permissions are applied to control access to directories on NTFS partitions. Just as with file permissions, directory permissions can be further broken down into two subcategories: standard directory permissions and special access directory permissions.

STANDARD DIRECTORY PERMISSIONS

Standard directory permissions are built from the available set of special access directory permissions. As well as containing settings for the directory, they contain settings for the files contained in the directory. Table 3.3 shows the standard directory permissions available and describes their effects. The permission symbols are noted in the following format: (Directory)/(File) permissions.

TABLE 3.3	Standard directory permissions	
Name	**Permission Symbol**	**File and Directory Access**
No Access	(None)(None)	No access. Access is denied regardless of rights given in another way.
List	(RX)(Not specified)	The user can see and change location to subdirectories. The user can see files but not their contents. List is used at the top level of a shared directory structure to allow multiple groups to navigate to their own subdirectories. Separate permissions then control access to the group subdirectories.
Read	(RX)(RX)	The user can see and change location to subdirectories. The user can read files and run applications but cannot manipulate file contents or structure.
Add	(WX)(Not specified)	The user can add files and subdirectories but cannot see or manipulate them. Add is used for file drop locations where you may have many respondents to a questionnaire and you do not want to give access to these once they are posted.
Add & Read	(RWX)(RX)	The user can add files and subdirectories and change location to the subdirectories. The user can read and create files and run applications. The user cannot modify existing files.
Change	(RWXD)(RWXD)	The user can add files, add and change subdirectories and delete file and subdirectories. The user can run applications and manipulate the file and directory structure in any way. This permission is used for users' or groups' wholly owned directories.
Full Control	(All)(All)	This permission allows a user to completely manipulate a directory and file structure as in Change. The user can take ownership of a directory or file that he may be denied access to. The user can also change the permissions on a file or directory.

As with the standard file permissions, standard directory permissions are made up of the most common combinations of special access permissions and are defined to make security application and administration that bit easier. In addition, standard directory permissions contain all of the standard file permissions so that you can control file access from the directory level.

SPECIAL ACCESS DIRECTORY PERMISSIONS

Special access directory permissions are used to make up the more commonly used standard permissions. They can, however, be applied as individual permissions should your requirements need this granulated approach to directory security. Table 3.4 shows the available special access directory permissions and describes their effect.

TABLE 3.4	Special access directory permissions	
Name	**Permission Symbol**	**Directory Access**
Full Control	(All)	The user has complete control of the directory.
Read	(R)	The user can view files and subdirectory names.
Write	(W)	The user can add files and subdirectories.
Execute	(X)	The user can change subdirectories.
Delete	(D)	The user can delete the directory.
Change Permissions	(P)	The user can change the directory permissions.
Take Ownership	(O)	The user can take ownership of the directory

Special access directory permissions do not have any effect on file security. Special access file permissions are provided for this purpose.

Viewing File and Directory Permissions

File and directory permissions can be viewed through the context menus available in Windows NT Explorer. The following example shows you how to view permissions for a given directory and explains the results.

1. Select **Programs** from the **Start** menu.

2. Select **Windows NT Explorer**.

3. Navigate to the **Winnt** directory in the folders pane. If your installation did not use default directory names, then navigate to the Windows installation directory.

4. Right-click the **System32** directory in the contents pane and select **Properties**.

5. Select the **Security** tab.

6. Select **Permissions**. Figure 3.1 shows the resulting permissions dialog box for the **Winnt****system32** directory.

Your own directory should have these default settings if you have not yet altered the security. The owner of this directory is Administrators.

The permissions shown consist of a name (e.g., Full Control) and then two permission symbol groups. The first group consists of the symbol(s) representing the individual special access permission used to make up the standard *directory* permission. The second group consists of the symbol(s) representing the individual special access *file* permission.

The permissions shown in Figure 3.1 allow the following access.

■ The *Administrators* group has Full Control permission. This is made up of (All) directory permissions and (All) file permissions.

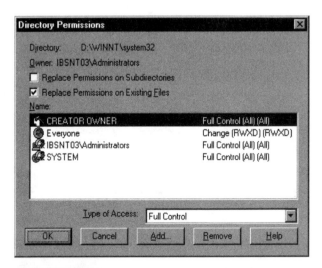

FIGURE 3.1   Permissions dialog box for viewing and setting directory security

- The *Creator Owner* (Administrators, in this case) has Full Control permission. This is made up of (All) directory permissions and (All) file permissions.

- The *Everyone* group has Change permissions. This is made up of (RWXD) directory permissions and (RWXD) file permissions. This means that everyone can read, write, change, and delete files and subdirectories.

- The *System* group has Full Control permission. This is made up of (All) directory permissions and (All) file permissions.

Unlike permissions in some other Network Operating Systems, permissions in Windows NT do not work on a blind inheritance basis, where permissions given farther up the directory structure can influence access at this level without showing it directly. On an NTFS partition, every file and directory stores its own security information within an ACL attached to the object. This means that the security settings shown here are the security settings that apply. Permissions may be set differently above this point, below this point, or for individual files within the directory, but you know that for this specific directory, the settings are those shown. Inheritance is a feature of NTFS security, but when applied, each file or directory in the inheritance path is changed individually and reflects the change when you view security.

The next example views the default security applied to an executable file in the \Winnt\system32 directory. For this example, we use CALC.EXE as the target file.

1. Start **Windows NT Explorer**, following steps 1 and 2 above.

2. Navigate to the **\Winnt\system32** directory in the folders pane.

3. Right-click **CALC.EXE** and select **Properties**.

4. Select the **Security** tab.

5. Select **Permissions**. Figure 3.2 shows the resulting permissions dialog box.

The permissions shown in Figure 3.2 allow the following access.

- The *Administrators* group has Full Control permission. This is made up of (All) file permissions. Note that directory permissions are not shown here because a file is subordinate to a directory.

- The *Everyone* group has Read permissions. This is made up of (RX) file permissions. This means that everyone can read and execute the program.

- The *System* group has Full Control permission. This is made up of (All) file permissions.

So, the default permissions given to this application allow everyone to run the application but not to alter it in any way.

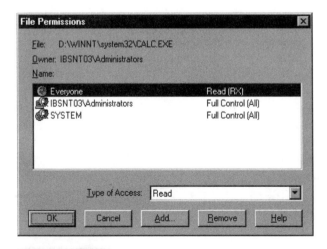

<table>
<tr><td colspan="2">**FIGURE 3.2**</td><td>File permissions dialog box</td></tr>
</table>

Setting File and Directory Permissions

The procedure for setting file and directory permissions is an extension of the procedure for viewing these permissions. Permissions are set through the context menus of Windows NT Explorer. Follow the example below to change permission to a directory and all files and subdirectories contained within it.

1. Start **Windows NT Explorer**.

2. Create a directory structure on the root of an NTFS volume. Include at least one subdirectory and file. Call the root directory **TestDir1**.

3. Follow the procedure in *Viewing File and Directory Permissions* to note the default security settings for the subdirectory and the created file.

4. Right-click the **TestDir1** directory and select **Properties**.

5. Select the **Security** tab.

6. Select **Permissions**. The permissions dialog box is displayed. Unless the volume on which you have created this structure has had NTFS security changes made at the root, the default permissions will be Everyone (Full Control).

7. Select the **Everyone** entry in the permissions list and choose **Remove**. The list of permitted users is now empty.

8. Select **Add** to display a list of users and domains. Select the **Domain Users** group (or **Users** on NT workstation) and select **Add**.

9. In the **Type of Access** box, select **Change**.

10. Select **OK**. The **Replace Permissions on Existing Files** radio button is selected by default.

11. Select the **Replace Permissions on Subdirectories** radio button. Figure 3.3 shows the resulting permissions dialog box.

12. Select **OK** to confirm the changes.

The permissions are now set to those chosen in the dialog box. If this was a large directory structure, it could take some time to complete the task. Also, if any of the files are in use, the procedure will display errors.

The only difference between setting directory security and file security is the two extra options available for directory permissions. These extra options are:

■ **Replace Permissions on Subdirectories** (NOT selected by default).

■ **Replace Permissions on Existing Files** (selected by default).

These two options can be used to granulate the effect of the permission change operation. Using the combination of none, one, or both of these settings, you can define the scope of the operation.

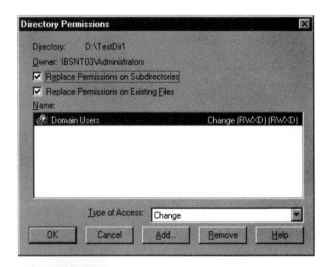

FIGURE 3.3 Setting permissions on a directory structure

REPLACING PERMISSIONS ON SUBDIRECTORIES

Take some time to view the permissions on the subdirectory and file used in the previous example. Note that the permissions were set all the way down the structure because of the *Replace Permissions on Subdirectories* setting. This option enables you to set security from the top of a structure right down to the lowest level. If you need to make further changes, then you can add or remove access at different levels to fulfill your own needs. Remember that the more settings you make at different levels of the directory structure, the harder it is to find a problem and fix it. Try to keep the placement of security settings as high as possible in the directory structure.

REPLACING PERMISSIONS ON EXISTING FILES

This option replaces the security settings on existing files within the directory that is the focus of the operation. This replacement includes files only; it does not include any subdirectories or files contained within those subdirectories.

The "No Access" Permission

The No Access permission takes precedence over all other permissions. If the No Access permission is applied to an object for a user, then the user has no access. This is the case even if extra permissions are granted in another way (e.g., by group membership).

When object access is requested (e.g., a file open request), one of the first steps in granting or denying this is for the ACL of the object to be checked for its No Access list. This list is compared against the SIDs contained in the user's access token. If any of the SIDs in the access token are in the No Access list of permissions for the object, then access is denied.

The No Access permission should not be confused with the *Not Specified* file permission. The No Access permission blocks access to an object. With this permission in place an Administrator can be certain that regardless of any other permissions, No Access takes precedence. The Not Specified permission is simply a way of removing the inheritance feature that would normally transfer permissions from a directory onto the files contained in the directory. A user with this permission applied for an object can still gain access to the object with permissions set in another way (e.g., by group settings).

Implementing File and Directory Security

When you install Windows NT, very little file and directory security is applied. Any drive except for the boot partition will have completely open access for all users by default. Whenever you create a new volume, the default permissions are set for the group Everyone to have Full Control access. This means that if the security is not changed, then anyone who can log on (including Guest if the account is enabled) can delete any files or directories placed on this volume.

A sound strategy needs to be implemented for securing your files and directories. This strategy will depend largely on your individual circumstances, but certain rules should be followed in most installations to limit the risks posed by this fundamental lack of applied security in a new installation.

Securing a New Volume

Whenever you create a new volume on a Windows NT machine, your first task, even before the first file is copied onto the new volume, is to apply security.

When you create a new volume, regardless of the circumstances, you should change the security so that only administrators can access the volume. Follow the steps below to accomplish this task.

1. Start **Windows NT Explorer**.
2. Right-click on the volume you have created.
3. Select **Properties**.
4. Select the **Security** tab.
5. Select **Permissions**. Figure 3.4 shows the default permissions for a new volume.

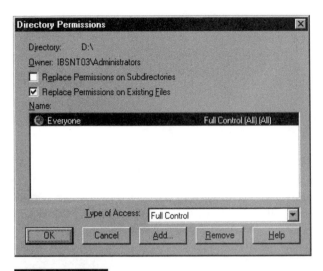

FIGURE 3.4   Default permissions for a new NTFS volume

As you can see, the default permissions allow the Everyone group to have Full Control. Before any data or applications are placed on this volume, you need to secure it.

6. Select the **Everyone** entry in the permissions list and choose **Remove**. The list of permitted users is now empty.

7. Select **Add** to display a list of users and domains.

8. Select the **Domain Admins** global group (Domain) or **Administrators** local group (NT Workstation local volume), and select **Add**.

9. In the **Type of Access** box, select **Full Control.**

10. Select **OK**. The **Replace Permissions on Existing Files** radio button is selected by default.

11. Select the **Replace Permissions on Subdirectories** radio button (although the volume should be empty).

12. Select **OK** to confirm the changes.

This process has set the permissions at the root of the volume to allow only members of Domain Admins or members of Administrators access to any information stored here.

Now you can start placing files onto the volume. All files that are copied onto the volume with drag-and-drop or the copy command, or newly created files and directories will inherit the permission settings from the root of the volume. If you use a backup utility to restore to the volume, then you may have to choose whether or not to replace permissions as well as restoring data.

Securing a volume from the root down at an early stage means that you can now be assured that no unauthorized access is allowed. In a Windows NT installation where security is going to be implemented, it is much more practical to set a restrictive regime early in the process and then to open up access when it is required. If a directory structure has too much security applied, you will find out when applications don't run or user access is denied. If the security is too open, these warnings will not appear and it is much more difficult to ferret out loopholes.

Directory Structure

Most organizations find it practical to mirror their business structure and their IT structure. Where an organization has geographically diverse divisions, you may find this geography mirrored in a multiple domain structure.

The same technique is often used for file systems. The directory structure shown in Figure 3.5 is a typical layout mirroring the business units.

Following the preceding recommendations for securing a new volume, the new volume containing the directory structure shown in Figure 3.5 was secured before the directories were created so that only the Administrators group has Full Control permission. This permission model is inherited by each new directory created, so at this time all directories are secured with the same restrictive permissions. The security that should be applied is shown in Table 3.5.

The permissions given in Table 3.5 are typical within an organization. The two most sensitive areas of data are Human Resources data and Management data. These two areas often need to be secured against access by Administrators who are often given full access to almost all data areas. Experience shows that even if you are sure that access is not granted in another way for these users, it is comforting to be able to show Management and HR personnel that access is actively blocked.

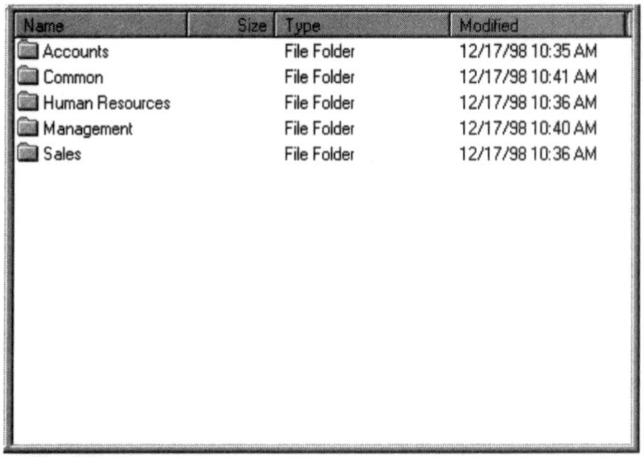

Name	Size	Type	Modified
Accounts		File Folder	12/17/98 10:35 AM
Common		File Folder	12/17/98 10:41 AM
Human Resources		File Folder	12/17/98 10:36 AM
Management		File Folder	12/17/98 10:40 AM
Sales		File Folder	12/17/98 10:36 AM

FIGURE 3.5   Typical file structure mirroring business units

TABLE 3.5	Permissions applied to a typical directory structure		
Directory	**Permission**	**User/Group**	**Level of Access Granted**
Root of volume	List Full Control	Users Group Administrators	All members of Users can see the directories at the root. Administrators can change, delete, and create files and folders.
Accounts	Change Full Control	Accounts Group Administrators	The Accounts team can create, delete, and modify new and existing files and folders. Administrators have full control.
Common	Change Full Control	Users Administrators	All members of Users can create, delete, and modify new and existing files and folders. Administrators have full control.
Human resources	Change No Access	HR Group Administrators	The HR team can create, delete, and modify new and existing files and folders. Administrators specifically are denied access.
Management	Change No Access	Manage Group Administrators	The Manage team can create, delete, and modify new and existing files and folders. Administrators specifically are denied access.
Sales	Change Full Control	Sales Group Administrators	The Accounts team can create, delete, and modify new and existing files and folders. Administrators have full control.

The remainder of the directories are secured so that although all users can see that the directory exists by virtue of the List permission at the root, they cannot access those directories unless they are a member of the respective groups.

Securing an Existing Volume

Securing an existing volume can be much more difficult than securing a new volume. Care must be taken not to affect business processes. As a rule, all security work should be carried out when users are not working in the systems so that files are not in use at the time.

If at all possible, the instructions for securing a new volume should be followed. This would deny access to files, directories, applications, etc.., to all users, but then a sound security policy based on access required can be implemented. This procedure can take some time and may require a large amount of testing to make sure that all access that is required does work.

Once the security has been applied from the root of the volume down, you are in a position to amend the permissions as you work down the directory tree. The following guidelines will help you apply a comprehensive permissions structure to your volumes.

- **Everyone group.** Remove the Everyone group from the permissions list entirely. Membership of the Everyone group cannot be controlled, whereas membership of Users or Domain Users can be controlled.

- **Restrictive permissions.** Set permissions to be as restrictive as possible, then relax them as business needs dictate. It is always more obvious when you need to give more permissions than when a user has too much access.

- **Top-down approach.** Use a top-down approach to secure volumes. Start at the root of the volume, applying the required security, and allow the settings to be inherited throughout the directory structure. Only make changes further down the directory structure when necessary.

- **Simplicity.** Try to keep it simple. Every file and directory object can be secured individually. This is not a good idea. Strike a balance between securing every object exactly as needed and being able to manage and troubleshoot security implementations.

Conflicting Permissions

File and directory permissions are given to users or groups. Users can be a member of many groups, and this could mean that they may have directory permissions that are received from many group memberships as well as directly assigned. To ensure that conflicting permissions are accommodated, a very simple rule governs the application of permissions.

If a user is granted permissions to a directory through group membership and also directly as a user, the most restrictive permissions are applied. This is also the case if a user is given permissions through membership of more than one group.

NTFS Permissions and the Administrator

NTFS file and directory permissions affect the access of all users to files and directories stored on an NTFS volume. *This includes all users and groups without exception.* Access is only given to an object if the user in question has an entry in the ACL of the object or belongs to a group which has an ACL entry giving permissions. Therefore, although the Administrator account is the default superuser on an NT system, the account only gains access to files and directories by virtue of the permissions given directly or by group association. These permissions can be removed, and the administrator can be denied access to any part of the NTFS file structure.

This situation can be used effectively to maintain privacy in certain parts of the file system but could also lead to problems if the one user account with permissions to an important directory is deleted. This would leave a situation where no valid user account has access to the data. To make sure that this doesn't happen, an administrator can always take owner-ship of the directories and files so that they can be recovered. This may seem to circumvent the security that excludes administrators from being able to see all data, but there is no reverse operation to Take Ownership. You can see that ownership of the file structure has changed and that the Admin-istrators group now owns the files. Also, if Take Ownership is tracked in the audit policy, then entries in the Event log show this event taking place.

Default System Permissions

During a Windows NT installation (both workstation and server), the \Winnt\ directory structure has permissions applied that are slightly more secure than the normal Everyone—Full Control permissions applied to new volumes. However, the security applied is still minimal and would benefit from some enhancements. Default permissions for the \Winnt\ directory and selected subdirectories are shown in Table 3.6.

TABLE 3.6 Default permissions for the \Winnt\ directory	
Directory	**Default Permissions**
\Winnt\	Everyone—Full Control
\Winnt\System	Everyone—Change; Administrators—Full Control; Creator Owner—Full Control; System—Full Control.
\Winnt\System32	Everyone—Change; Administrators—Full Control; Creator Owner—Full Control; System—Full Control.
\Winnt\Repair	Everyone—Read; Administrators—Full Control; Creator Owner—Full Control; System—Full Control.
\Winnt\System32\Config	Everyone—List; Administrators—Full Control; Creator Owner—Full Control; System—Full Control.
\Winnt\System32\Repl	Everyone—Read; Administrators—Full Control; Creator Owner—Full Control; System—Full Control.
\Winnt\System32\Repl\Import	Everyone—List; Replicator—Change; Administrators—Full Control; Creator Owner—Full Control; System—Full Control.
\Winnt\System32\Repl\Export	Everyone—List; Replicator—Read; Administrators—Full Control; Creator Owner—Full Control; System—Full Control.

Using the procedures outlined above for setting directory security, set the permissions to match those listed in Table 3.7.

TABLE 3.7 Secured permissions for the \Winnt\ directory	
Directory	**Default**
\Winnt\ and all subdirectories	Everyone—Read; Administrators—Full Control; Creator Owner—Full Control; System—Full Control.
\Winnt\Repair	Administrators—Full Control
\Winnt\System32\Config	Everyone—List; Administrators—Full Control; Creator Owner—Full Control; System—Full Control.

The settings applied above will give Everyone read access to the whole structure from the top down and then amends the access for the two selected subdirectories that require exceptional settings.

Taking Ownership of Files or Directories

From time to time you may find that because of the secure nature of the NTFS file system and the fact that administrators can be prevented from having permissions to access specific files or directories, these files or directories become inaccessible to everyone on the system. An example of how this can happen is as follows.

NTFS permissions are set for DirectoryA so that TempUser1 has Full Control and Administrators are set for No Access. No other permissions are set.

The directory is only accessible by the one user. Permissions are stored in the directory object itself with an entry for the SID belonging to TempUser1, giving Full Control permissions, and an entry for the group SID belonging to Administrators, giving No Access permissions.

The user TempUser1 is deleted. Now there is no valid user with permissions to the directory. Even if a new user called TempUser1 is created, that user has a different SID and it is the SID that is stored as an entry in the ACL to grant permissions.

There needs to be a way to recover the access permissions to this directory. The way to do this is by using the Take Ownership permission, which is granted as a user right to the Administrators group on all Windows NT systems. Follow the example below to remove all permissions from a new directory.

1. Log on as a nonadministrative user.

2. Create the new directory on an NTFS volume called **TempDir1**.

3. In Windows NT Explorer, right-click on the new directory and select **Properties**.

4. Select the **Security** tab.

5. Select **Permissions**.

6. Remove any entries in the permitted users list.

7. Select **OK**. Figure 3.6 shows the warning message that appears when you remove all access permissions to a directory.

8. Select **Yes** to continue.

9. Select **Cancel** to exit the **Properties** dialog screen without an error message.

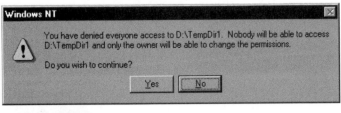

FIGURE 3.6 Warning when removing all access permissions from a directory

If you try to look into the `TempDir1` directory now, you get a permissions error and no access is granted. Permissions can be replaced by the owner of the file, who always has access to the permissions properties. Now we can pretend that the owners' account has been deleted. The permissions property page is now inaccessible to all remaining users. The procedure outlined below can be used to take ownership of the directory and so restore access.

1. Log on as an administrator (or another user who has been given the user right **Take Ownership of files and other objects**).

2. In Windows NT Explorer, right-click on the new directory and select **Properties**.

3. Select the **Security** tab.

4. Select **Ownership**. This would show you the ownership of the directory if you had permissions. A warning appears, as shown in Figure 3.7, because you do not have permission to view ownership.

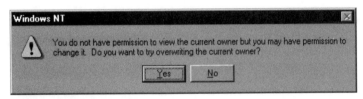

FIGURE 3.7 Warning when trying to view the ownership of a file without the correct permissions

5. Select **Yes**. You are offered the chance to take ownership of the directory.

6. Select **Take Ownership**. Figure 3.8 shows the dialog box appearing as a result of your taking ownership of the directory.

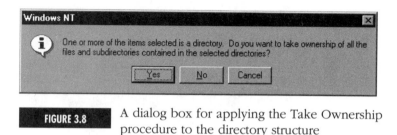

| FIGURE 3.8 | A dialog box for applying the Take Ownership procedure to the directory structure |

7. Select **Yes**. The dialog box shown in Figure 3.9 asks you to confirm the replacement of all permissions.

8. Select **Yes**. All permissions are now replaced, and you have Full Control permissions to the whole directory structure.

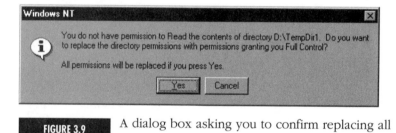

| FIGURE 3.9 | A dialog box asking you to confirm replacing all permissions on the directory structure |

Now that you are the owner of the directory structure and have Full Control permissions, access is restored and permissions can be reset according to your organization's policy.

Share Permissions

Share permissions are applied to a directory shared out on the network. They are applied to the particular directory and subdirectory structure in a similar fashion to file and directory permissions. Share security is applied to access through the network share as opposed to being stored in each individual file and directory object. Network share security only applies to access through the network. An interactive user does not use local shares and so is not restricted by share security.

There are far fewer share permissions than file and directory permissions. Table 3.8 lists the available share permissions and describes their effect.

TABLE 3.8 Network share permissions

Name	Permission Symbol	User Has This Access
No Access	(None)	The user has no access to the shared directory or the files and directories below. When this permission is applied, it overrides any other permission gained in other ways such as from group permissions.
Read		The user can see files and subdirectories. The user cannot modify or change the file in any way. The user can view the contents of the files and run applications.
Change		The user can see files and subdirectories. The user can view the contents of files and change them. The user can run applications. The user can delete files and subdirectories.
Full Control	(All)	The user receives all of the above plus the ability to take ownership of files and to change permissions on the file (NTFS volumes only).

NTFS and Share Permissions Working Together

NTFS permissions and share permissions can be applied to the same directory structure, which means that the settings may conflict. When this happens, the rules governing which permissions are used are simple. The most restrictive permission is used in all cases. If GroupA is given Change permission to a directory through NTFS permissions and the same group is given Full Control access through share permissions, the most restrictive access (in this case, Change permission) is given. If a member of GroupA is given No Access permission directly through NTFS settings, then that one user is denied all access while the other members of the group are unaffected.

The scenario outlined above shows that setting permissions in many places can become confusing to manage. There are very few cases when you are forced to use share permissions. NTFS permissions are more flexible and just as easy to apply.

One case that may call for share permissions would be network access to a non-NTFS volume. A FAT partition cannot be secured with NTFS file and directory permissions, so share permissions are the only alternative. With share permissions, a FAT partition can be secured from unauthorized network access. Remember that share permissions only affect the network access; and so, if users can gain local access to the partition, they can avoid the share permissions set.

Default Shares

The following shares can exist by default on a Windows NT system. Some of the shares cannot be amended; others can.

- **Admin$.** This share points to the `%SystemRoot%\` directory (usually `C:\Winnt`) and is a default administrative share. This share is used for remote administration, and the only permissions are set for Administrators, Backup Operators, and Server Operators groups. These permissions cannot be viewed or changed.

- **C$, D$, etc.** These shares point to the root of the volume and are administrative shares. The same set of user groups (Administrators, Backup Operators, and Server Operators) are allowed access to this share, and, again, these permissions cannot be viewed or changed. These shares are used to give full access to the root of any machine volumes for administrative purposes. The volumes can still be secured with NTFS permissions.

- **IPC$.** This is another administrative share, but this time it does not point to any physical disk area. Instead, it is used for remote administration during communications between programs. This share cannot be modified.

- **Netlogon.** This share points to the `%SystemRoot%\System32\Repl\ Import\Scripts` directory and is used by users when running logon scripts. This administrative share can be modified. As a minimum setting, all domain users need to be able to read from this directory and the Replicator group needs Change access.

- **Print$.** This default share is used as a storage area for print drivers among other print-related information. The share points to the `%System Root%\System32\Spool\Drivers` directory and can be modified. As a minimum, all domain users should be given Read permissions here.

- **Repl$.** This share is only created when the replication service is configured for export. This share is used to house files, such as logon scripts, that are to be exported to other validation servers.

The $ on the end of a share name (as in most of the examples above) hides that share name when shares are browsed on the network. When a user connects to a network resource and browses the list of available network shares for a machine, all of the shares named with a $ at the end will be hidden from view. The share can still be connected to (with the correct permissions) if the exact share name is entered in the path for the network connection. The exact name must contain the $ sign.

Most of the default shares mentioned above are used for administrative or system work and are of little use in the day-to-day business processes of your organization. New shares need to be created so that the correct network resources are offered to your users.

Multiple shares can point to the same directory location and can be set to give different access permissions. This means that depending on which share you connect to, you may have different levels of access to the directory. This practice is not recommended. The only time a directory should have more than one share pointing to it is if a hidden or administrative share already exists and you need to give some access to nonadministrative users. This should rarely be the case because the administrative shares point to sensitive system areas that the general user population should not be connecting to.

Multiple shares can also exist in the same directory structure (as shown with the shares Admin$, Repl$, Print$, etc., above). Suppose your directory structure was \\Directory1\Subdir1\Subdir2 and you shared out Directory1 and Subdir2 at the same time. Access granted to the user would depend on the NTFS file and directory permissions and the share name used to connect to.

User1 and User2 are members of GroupA. GroupA is granted NTFS Change permissions for the entire directory structure described above. GroupA is granted Read permissions for the Directory1 share and Change permissions for the Subdir2 share. User1 connects to the Directory1 share and navigates to the Subdir2 directory. User2 connects to the Subdir2 share.

The access permissions received by the two users would be different. Remember that when NTFS permissions and share permissions are mixed, it is always the most restrictive permission that is applied. User1 will have Read permission in Subdir2 because the most restrictive permission is applied at the share level. User2 will have Change permission in the same directory because the most restrictive permissions are at both the share and NTFS level.

As you can see, complicated share permissions mixed with NTFS permissions can be quite confusing and can lead to difficulty in troubleshooting potential permissions problems.

Applying Share Permissions

Share permissions can be applied through the graphical user interface provided from the Windows NT Explorer context menus. The following procedure takes you through the necessary steps for creating a new share.

SHARING A DIRECTORY FOR THE FIRST TIME

1. Log on as Administrator.

2. Select **Programs** from the **Start** menu and choose **Windows NT Explorer**.

3. Navigate to the directory that you wish to share on the network.

4. Right-click the directory and select **Sharing**. Figure 3.10 shows the sharing dialog box for a directory that has not previously been shared out before.

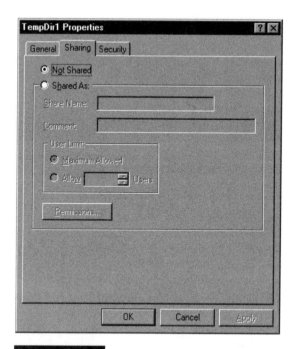

FIGURE 3.10 The sharing dialog box for a previously unshared directory

5. Select the **Share As** radio button. The share name automatically defaults to the directory name. If you do not want the share to be visible, put a $ at the end of the name.

6. Set the **User Limit** to the number of concurrent users you wish to access the share. This option can be useful if you share out an application directory and only have 10 licenses for the application. Setting this value to 10 will only allow the first 10 users to connect and will give the remainder an error message.

7. If the share name has 8 or fewer characters, select **OK**. This creates the share; the shared folder in Windows NT Explorer is denoted with a hand symbol.

8. If the share name contains more than 8 characters or characters that are not valid for DOS file names, select **OK**. The warning message in Figure 3.11 appears. If your circumstances require the use of DOS workstations connecting to this share, consider renaming to make the share name a valid DOS directory name.

9. Select **Yes** to confirm the name or **No** to go back and rename the share.

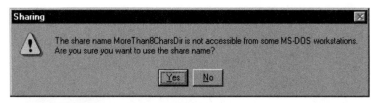

FIGURE 3.11 Warning message for sharing a directory with more than an eight-character name

The share has now been created with the default permission of **Everyone—Full Control**.

SHARING A PREVIOUSLY SHARED DIRECTORY

As stated earlier, there may be a need to share out a directory that has already been shared out previously. One of the main reasons for doing this would be to share a directory that already has an administrative share created. This can be a dangerous practice and should be considered carefully before a system directory is shared out. For the purposes of this next procedure, we will create a share at the root of a volume already shared administratively as C$.

1. Log on as Administrator.
2. Start **Windows NT Explorer**.
3. Right-click the **C:** drive and select **Sharing**. A dialog box similar to the one shown in Figure 3.12 should be displayed. If the Not Shared radio button is selected instead, then a system setting could have been applied to prevent the administrative drive shares from being created, so this would be the first share.

    You can use the Share Name drop down list to see how many times this directory has been shared out.
4. Select **New Share**.
5. Enter a new share name. The same requirements as discussed in step 8 above referring to DOS file names apply here. If you do not want the share to be visible put a $ at the end of the name.
6. Set the **User Limit** if required.
7. Select **OK**.
8. Select **OK**.

The directory (in this case, the root directory of a volume) is shared out under the new share name. This does not affect the previous share names that may apply.

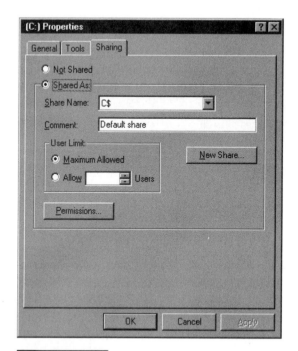

FIGURE 3.12   The sharing dialog box for a previously shared directory

SECURING YOUR NETWORK SHARE

Share permissions are very easy to view and apply. Follow the procedures below to apply security to a network share.

1. Start **Windows NT Explorer**.

2. Right-click the shared directory and select **Sharing**. This brings you to the sharing dialog box.

3. Use the **Share Name** drop-down box to select the share to which you wish to apply the permissions. Remember that shares are independent of each other even if they point to the same directory.

4. Select **Permissions**. If you have selected an administrative share (such as C$) that cannot be amended, you are warned at this point and the operation cannot proceed. Otherwise the **Access Through Share Permissions** dialog box is displayed. The default permission for a share is **Everyone—Full Control**.

5. Use the **Add** and **Remove** buttons to amend the share permission according to your needs. The available permissions were shown in Table 3.8.

6. Select **OK**.

7. Select **OK** to confirm any changes.

The share permissions are now set. Remember that share permissions and NTFS permissions are applied according to the "most restrictive" rule, so any permissions you have set here will depend on the permissions set at the file and directory level.

NTFS Security or Share Security?

Share permissions can be used to secure network access to volumes that are not protected by NTFS security. These can include FAT partitions and CD-ROM drives. Share permissions do not have any effect on a user who logs on locally, so it is important to understand that only network access to the share is protected.

NTFS permissions are far more flexible in the way they can be fine-tuned to the needs of the individual organizations. When a system uses NTFS partitions, the inherent ability to apply security at the source (file or directory) is a great bonus.

You can use a mixture of share and NTFS permissions to protect your systems. The overhead in management and possible delay in troubleshooting permission-related problems must be considered when deciding how to apply file and directory security.

Consider the following rules of thumb when you are deciding how to secure your file systems.

- Use NTFS partitions where possible.

- Use NTFS permissions to secure these file systems, following the guidelines discussed earlier in this chapter.

- Do not mix NTFS permissions and share permissions on the same directory structure. Observing this rule will minimize the overhead in management and troubleshooting. If you are forced to mix the two, then make it an exception to the rule.

- When you cannot use NTFS, such as with a CD volume, then use share permissions to secure access to the data. Again, this would be an exception to the rule.

■ Shares are still required by the users to access network file systems, but the permissions can be left at their default settings (Everyone—Full Control) so that there is no confusion when it comes to management and troubleshooting. This approach can work well as long as you secure your systems methodically with NTFS permissions.

These guidelines do not suit all configurations but should be referred to when you are deciding between NTFS and share permissions.

User Profiles

This chapter introduces the concept of user profiles and includes step-through examples on how to implement them in a Windows NT environment.

User profiles are used in an NT environment to control the look and feel of the user desktop and available options at the workstation.

This chapter focuses on user profiles defined within the NT workstation and server environment but also includes some information on user profiles applied to Windows 95 clients.

Introduction

Client/server technology has long been heralded as the way forward for large IT infrastructures. The days of the centralized mainframe supplying the computer power for an enterprise have passed!

Now, anybody who has worked in the IT business for any number of years knows that this is not strictly true. The promised yield of the client/server environment has never quite come to fruition. The lower costs, ease of maintenance, less costly hardware, and lower administrative overheads have been very difficult to spot.

Total cost of ownership (TCO) is a phrase that has been used more and more over the last few years. One of the main claims made all those years ago when the salesmen were trying to convince us to move away from the centralized mainframe systems was that client/server would lower the cost of owning and running an IT infrastructure.

Client/server technology certainly had a large impact and brought with it some major benefits, including distributed systems, distributed management, well-known GUI interfaces, and applications that were much more user friendly. It also brought with it the unforeseen costs. The difference in costs between distributed and centralized hardware has been reduced dramatically. Where once users had a terminal and were able to run one program interactively at a time, they are now faced with a desktop and many available applications. Training is not only needed now to run the applications but also to run the operating system that used to be hidden from users. IT infrastructures are growing to huge proportions, and administrative costs escalate in proportion. In all, the cost of distributed systems is not quite as small as it may have been portrayed to be some years ago.

Recent studies show that a large amount of the TCO goes to providing user support. This is hardly surprising considering the technology available to the average user at the moment. Of these costs, a high proportion is used fixing problems caused by user interference with the computer services due to lack of understanding or to the complex nature of the systems today. After all, users may be faced with a desktop with ten or more applications. Those users may only need to run two applications for their particular job but policy may dictate that a uniform desktop is required to make administrative duties that bit "easier."

Some sort of control is needed to reduce the apparent complexity of the computer systems. Average users performing an accountancy role don't need to know how or why a system works. They need to know where their applications and resources are and how to use them. An investment in training so that everybody understands something about the computing environment is rarely wasted, but controls are needed to make sure that a little knowledge doesn't cause a lot of damage.

User Profile Overview

One of the two main controls in a Microsoft Window NT network environment that helps lower the cost of administration and management is user profiles. The second control is *system policies*. System policies control availability and access to resources for a user or group and can be set either for users/groups or for the computer. System policies are discussed in Chapter Five.

What Is a User Profile?

A user profile is a group of settings that describe the look and feel of a user's environment on a Windows NT or Windows 95 computer. It controls what appears on a desktop or what applications are accessible. User profiles contain settings that can be applied to a user, group, or computer and can be set up so that users can make changes and save them or so those users cannot save any changes made.

User profiles were designed in part to answer the need for more control over the ever-growing complexity of the desktop and network systems. Administrators can now deliver and manage from a central point the look and feel required by the enterprise workforce. All users don't have to have the same desktop look. In addition, the profile can travel with the user (roaming profile) so that the same look and feel can be provided in different locations with a minimum of administrative overhead.

From the point of view of the IT security professional, the user profile adds an invaluable tool that can be used to clamp down on unnecessary system access and possible security breaches. User profiles can be used to control access to sensitive system tools such as the registry editor and the task manager.

Types of User Profiles

Three types of user profiles are available on Windows NT machines.

- **Local profiles.** These profiles are local to a given machine and are only available to users when they log on to that one machine.

- **Roaming profiles.** Roaming profiles, as the name suggests, are available from a central source to users within the domain. They are used by the particular user or groups of users whenever they log on to a machine within the domain. If the roaming profile is not available, users can be logged on with a copy of the profile saved the last time they accessed the machine or with a default profile available to them. When users make changes to the desktop appearance or other objects stored in the profile, the changes are saved to the central copy of the profile at logoff time and are then provided the next time the user logs on. Roaming profiles give users a uniform base look on their desktop and then allow them to make changes as necessary.

- **Mandatory profiles.** Mandatory profiles are similar to roaming profiles except that the user *must* use the profile to log on to the network. The two main differences between roaming and mandatory is that if the mandatory profile is not available, then the user is refused permission to log on or cannot make changes to the mandatory profile. Mandatory profiles offer the greatest security and if implemented correctly can reduce the TCO by reducing the number of support incidents caused by inadvertent system changes. These profiles are restrictive and could impact business (by not letting users log on when the profiles are unavailable), so you should consider both business and security needs when looking at this option.

User Profile Location

Parts of the user profile are stored in two separate places. Some of the settings are stored in a set of directories on either the local machine (local profile) or the validating server (roaming and mandatory profiles). The remainder of the settings are stored in system registry format in a file called ntuser.*xxx* (.dat or .man) in the profile directory structure.

The profile settings are split along two distinct lines. The profiles directory holds settings such as desktop icons, icons representing shortcuts to applications, user links (generally as icons), and any other settings represented by visual objects such as folders, icons, files. The registry hive that stores user profile settings is HKEY_USERS (ntuser.*xxx* file); and it holds less tangible environmental preferences such as wallpaper and background settings, international settings, and keyboard/mouse settings. Security-related settings such as the ability to run applications and access to system tools are also stored here. Tables 4.1 and 4.2 list the settings available in the two locations and briefly describe their use.

TABLE 4.1   `%SystemRoot%\Profiles\%Username%` directory contents

Directory Name	Description
Application Data	Content defined by application programmers.
Desktop	Any items to be displayed on the desktop such as shortcuts.
Favorites	Shortcuts to the user's favorite locations. Used with Internet Explorer.
NetHood	Shortcuts to Network Neighborhood objects. A hidden directory by default.
Personal	Default storage location for files created by the user. Applications are specifically designed to save files here by default.
PrintHood	Shortcuts to printer objects. A hidden directory by default.
Recent	Shortcuts to the most recently used files and objects.
SendTo	Shortcuts to locations required for placing files into. Referenced by the Explorer context menu for files.
Start Menu	Shortcuts to applications. Newly installed applications should place shortcuts here.
Templates	Shortcuts to template objects. A hidden directory by default.

TABLE 4.2	`ntuser.xxx` registry hive contents
Item	**Description**
NT Explorer	Persistent network connections and user-defined explorer settings.
Taskbar	Taskbar settings and personal program groups and properties.
Printers	Networked printer connections.
Control Panel	User-defined settings made in Control Panel.
Accessories	User-defined settings for all applications within the Accessories group.
Help Bookmarks	All bookmarks placed in Windows NT help.

User accounts are mapped to profiles by means of a registry entry in the local registry for every user who has logged on locally. Entries do not exist for users who only log on remotely.

The registry entry is held in the `HKEY_LOCAL_MACHINE` registry hive under the key `\SOFTWARE\Microsoft\WindowsNT\CurrentVersion\ProfileList`. Listed under this key are the system identifiers of all users who have logged on interactively to this machine. One of the values stored under each SID key is the `ProfileImagePath`, which holds the location of the profile used by that user. This value can be edited to point the user account to a profile in another location.

The profile directory can sometimes have a three-digit suffix appended to it. This usually means that more than one user with the same user name has logged into this machine (perhaps from two different domains). The second user profile is created in the `Username.000` directory, and subsequent users with the same account name use directories `.001`, `.002`, etc.

Figure 4.1 shows the registry entries for users on an NT workstation. The three users who have logged on interactively each have an entry listed here under their System Identifier key.

Creating a Roaming User Profile for NT 4.0

This next section takes you through all of the steps necessary to create a roaming user profile for users within your enterprise. The process consists of the following steps.

- Define the location.
- Create the network share.
- Create a template user.
- Use the template user to create a base profile.
- Distribute the base profile.
- Set up users to access the copies of the base profile.
- Amend the copies of the base profile as necessary.

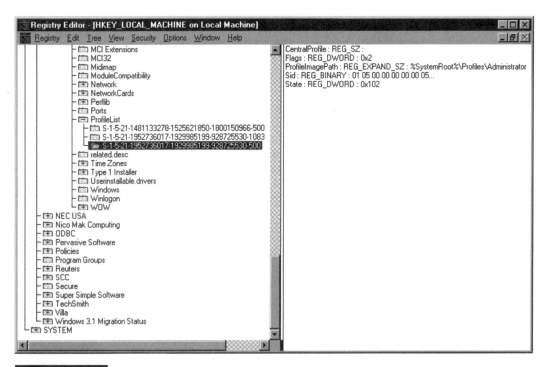

FIGURE 4.1 Registry entry that maps user accounts to profile directories

Define the Location

The user profile should be stored on a network share accessible to the user. Consider two main factors when deciding where to locate the user profiles for your organization:

- **Storage space.** Users profiles can range in size from hundreds of kilobytes to many megabytes. If a user copies a file to the desktop and then saves the roaming profile when logging off, the file is then transferred with the rest of the profile information up to the network share and back down when the user logs on again. The location needs to have enough free disk space to be able to store all of the profiles used in your organization.

- **Link speed.** The link speed between the network share location and the workstation affects user perception of system performance. A profile can be quite large, and it needs to be downloaded at logon time and uploaded at logoff time. This can cause severe delays for the user at these times if the link speed is slow. Slow link speeds can be accommodated in system policy settings as described in Chapter Five, *System Policies*.

Create the Network Share

When you have chosen the location for the centrally stored profile, you must prepare the network share. For this example and in the remainder of this chapter, we will place the profiles on a network share called NetProfs on the domain controller. Profiles must reside on an NTFS partition so that correct permissions for them can be applied. We use the following information for the examples in this chapter.

- The profiles directory resides on a domain controller named IBSNT03.
- The network share used to house the profiles is called NetProfs.
- A user account named Tempusr1 is created to use the profile.

You can substitute more relevant information from your own organization for any of the information listed above.

1. Use Microsoft Explorer to create a folder called **NetProfs** on the domain controller.
2. Right-click the new directory to bring up the context menu.
3. Select **Sharing**.
4. In the sharing dialog box select the **Shared As** radio button. Figure 4.2 shows the Network Share dialog box.

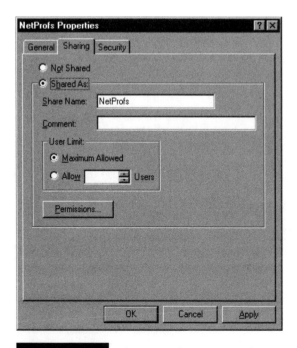

FIGURE 4.2   Sharing a directory on the network

5. Accept the default share name of **NetProfs**.

6. Select **OK**.

The directory is now shared on the network with the default share permissions of Everyone—Full Control. Ensure that the NTFS permissions on the directory are set to Everyone—Full Control as well. You can adjust these permissions to fit your own situation if you want to limit access to profile directories.

Create a Template User Account

This step-through example takes you through the processes involved in creating a new user account to be used to set up the look and feel for the new profile.

1. Start up **User Manager** on a workstation that can be used to build the profile.

2. Select **New User** from the **User** menu.

3. Enter the username **Tempusr1** and password details for the new user.

4. Select the **Profiles** button.

5. Ensure that the **Profiles Path** remains empty. When the user logs on for the first time, a directory will be created in the local \%System-Root%\Profiles\ directory named after the new user.

6. Select **Add** to add the user.

7. Select **Close**. The user **Tempusr1** is added to the SAM of the local workstation.

Create a Base Profile

It is often useful to create a base profile that is common to all users. IT policies within large organizations often dictate requirements for everybody to use the same basic application. E-mail, word processing and spreadsheet applications are often licensed per enterprise and all staff have access automatically. A base profile supports a common desktop look that could include shortcuts to all of these applications.

Other applications such as graphics applications for the Marketing department and number-crunching applications for the Accounts department are less widely used and would not necessarily appear on the base profile.

Now that the template user is set up, it can be used to create a base user profile.

1. Log on locally as **Tempusr1** to the workstation used in the previous step. Allow the default user profile on the machine to populate the desktop at this time.

2. Make any changes to the desktop look and feel that you find necessary. This should include shortcuts to all applications that are common to everyone, as well as any other desktop settings common to all.

3. Log off. The new profile is saved to the `%SystemRoot%\Profiles\Tempusr1` directory when you log off.

The base profile is now created and is ready to be copied to the Net-Profs share for use by different users. At this point, make a copy of the base profile (`Tempusr1` directory) to keep it safe. To do this, you must be logged on as a different user with sufficient permissions to the source and destination directory. If you attempt to copy the profile while you are logged on and using it, you will get a sharing violation error.

Distribute the Base Profile

You should be able to use the base profile in its present state as the starting point for all user logons within the enterprise. By making copies of the profiles for the different users or groups, you can have this profile loaded as a starting point and then amended to fit the more specific requirements of individual users or groups. Remember that although you have created shortcuts to all of your base applications, they still need to be installed and available to all of the required machines in the same directory and drive structure that is used in the shortcuts.

There are two main methods used for distributing a base profile: manual distribution and Default User distribution.

MANUAL DISTRIBUTION

To manually distribute the base profile to one or more users, follow these instructions.

1. Log on locally as Administrator on the machine that stores the base profile.

2. Select **Settings** from the **Start** menu and choose **Control Panel**.

3. Double-click on the **System** application.

4. Select the **User Profiles** tab.

5. Select the **Tempusr1** profile and choose **Copy To**.

6. Enter the path to the NetProfs share created earlier and append the individual directory information for this copy of the template. This information can be in UNC form or can be a previously hard-coded drive letter. For this example, we use **\\IBSNT03\NetProfs\Accounts**. This procedure will copy the profile to an accounts destination directory.

7. Select the **Change** button in the **Permitted to use** box.

8. Select the user or group permitted to use this profile in the final location. These permissions are difficult to change and so unless you have a good reason for protecting the profiles at this point, choose **Everyone**.

9. Select **Add > OK**.

10. Select **OK** to begin copying the profile.

You can repeat this method to make multiple copies of the base profile that can then be amended to cater to individual or group preferences. However, the easiest way to make multiple copies of this profile is to simply copy the whole Accounts profile directory created above, using Windows Explorer. As security is already set to allow the Everyone group to use the profile, then this is all you have to do to make multiple separate copies of the base profile.

DEFAULT USER DISTRIBUTION

You can use the default user distribution method to supply the base profile as the first profile downloaded by new users logging on to the system. The users can then make changes as permitted and save the profile when they log off. Follow these instructions to set up the base profile as the default user profile.

1. Log on locally as Administrator on the machine that stores the base profile.

2. Select **Settings** from the **Start** menu and choose **Control Panel**.

3. Double-click on the **System** application.

4. Select the **User Profiles** tab.

5. Select the **Tempusr1** profile and choose **Copy To**.

6. Enter the path to the **NETLOGON** share on the domain controller and append the directory name Default User. This can be in UNC form or can be a previously hard-coded drive letter, for example, **\\IBSNT03\NETLOGON\Default User.**

7. Select the **Change** button in the **Permitted to use** box.

8. Select the user or group permitted to use this profile in the final location. These permissions are difficult to change and so unless you have a good reason for protecting the profiles at this point, choose the **Everyone** group.

9. Select **Add > OK**.

10. Select **OK** to begin copying the profile.

11. Repeat steps 5 through 10 for each validating server (backup domain controllers) or use the Replication service to replicate the profile to the BDCs.

User Setup

Users need to be assigned a profile before they can load it. Profiles are assigned to users only. They are not assigned to groups. Follow these steps to assign the Accounts copy of the base profile to an already existing user named SmythJ. This procedure can be performed for any user.

1. Start up **User Manager for Domains**.
2. Double-click the user **SmythJ**.
3. Select the **Profiles** button.
4. In the **Profile Path** box, enter **\\IBSNT03\NetProfs\Accounts**. Figure 4.3 shows the Profiles dialog box.

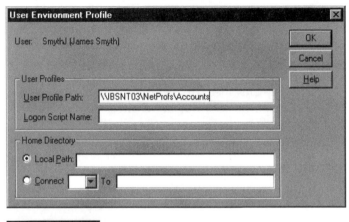

| FIGURE 4.3 | User profiles dialog box |

5. Enter login script and home directory information if you wish, and select **OK**.
6. Select **OK** to confirm the changes.

The next time James Smyth logs on, he will receive the new roaming profile. The profile can be used by many people; set up all users of the profile in the same manner.

Amend the Roaming Profile

The new roaming profile called Accounts can now be amended to reflect any required differences between the base profile and a profile for the Accounts department. If there is an application for sole use by the Accounts department then a shortcut can be created on this desktop for user SmythJ; it will be uploaded at log off to be included in the profile. In this way, the profiles can be amended to more closely suit the needs of the user community.

The basic way to amend a roaming profile is simply to log on as the user who is using the profile and make any changes at the desktop that are required. For example, you may wish to add a program to the Start menu by using the Taskbar editor, or you may wish to create a shortcut on the desktop pointing to a particular application. When you have amended the desktop you simply log off the machine. At logoff time, the roaming user profile is copied to the central location where you store user profiles and overwrites the stored copy. The locally stored copy is also updated at this point. When the user next logs on (or when any user authorized to use this profile logs on), the saved changes are downloaded to the desktop and used.

This ability to change the roaming profile as easily as changing the desktop look can cause problems with desktop management. Imagine the scenario where you set the whole of the Accounts department to use a single roaming profile. The positive aspect of this would be that any of the Accounts users could log on at any machine and get the same desktop look. Everything goes well for a while and then one user, when he is working late, decides that he doesn't require a shortcut to one of the accounts packages on his desktop because his job responsibility doesn't require him to use it. He deletes the icon. He is the last person in the department that night, and when he logs off, the changes he has made (deleting the icon) are copied to the roaming profile used by everybody in Accounts. When the users arrive the next day, they all download the profile, which is missing the icon, and nobody knows how to access the package anymore.

This can be a common problem when a roaming profile is shared among multiple users. All users have the same rights to the profile folder, and any changes made to the local desktop are replicated to the centrally stored (single) copy. Even when you intend to make a change, you could make the change locally and log off to replicate the change to the central copy. However, if another user is logged on using that profile when you do this, the change you made will be overwritten when that user logs off and automatically copies the profile to the server.

This problem has two resolutions. You can create a profile for every user, based on a profile template. This template is simply a saved copy of a basic template, which everyone can use and to which you add extra facilities, depending on the users needs. The overhead in managing this type of installation is quite large and it is not recommended for anything except the smallest of installations. The second way of tackling the problem is to use mandatory profiles. These are profiles that can be shared among many users and are basically read-only for these users. These profiles are discussed in the next section.

Making a Profile Mandatory

The new roaming profile called Accounts, which is being used by SmythJ, can be shared among many users. The whole of the Accounts department could use the same roaming profile.

As described above, the one real drawback of this approach is that if one person makes a change to the desktop and logs off, then the profile is overwritten at the central storage point and the new settings are downloaded when the next person logs on. This can quickly negate all of the benefits of a common desktop.

This is where the mandatory profile comes in. A mandatory profile is simply a roaming profile that is set so that the user cannot save any changes to the settings contained in the profile and must use the profile to log on. These two restrictions are placed on a roaming profile in two separate stages.

To change a roaming profile to a mandatory profile so that the user cannot save changes to the profile, follow these instructions.

1. Using Windows Explorer navigate to the folder represented by the **\\IBSNT03\NetProfs***profilename.*

2. Double-click the **Accounts** directory.

3. Select **Folder Options** from the **View** menu.

4. Select the **View** tab.

5. Make sure that the **Hide file extensions for known file types** button is *not* selected. This will ensure that all file extensions are shown in Explorer.

6. Select **OK**.

7. Right-click the file **ntuser.dat** and select **Rename**.

8. Change the file extension from **.dat** to **.man**. The profile is now a mandatory profile.

Follow the instructions below to change a roaming profile into a mandatory profile so that the user must load this profile in order to log on (i.e., if the server holding the mandatory profile is unavailable, the user cannot log on). This is a separate stage from the one above, which makes the profile read-only and does not have to be set if not required.

1. Using Windows Explorer, navigate to the folder **IBSNT03\NetProfs*profilename.***

2. Right-click the directory **Accounts** and select **Rename**.

3. Add the file extension **.man** to the directory name. The resulting directory name is **IBSNT03\NetProfs\Accounts.man.**

4. Start **User Manager for Domains**.

5. Double-click user **SmythJ**. This could be any user that you wish to apply this profile and restriction to.

6. Select the **Profiles** button.

7. In the **Profile Path** enter **\\IBSNT03\NetProfs\Accounts.man.**

8. Select **OK** and then **OK** again to confirm.

A cautionary note. Mandatory profiles can be useful if you need to use a common desktop for many users and the users do not need to make changes of their own. However: some application programmers write their applications to hold user-dependent information in the registry. An example of this could be a word processing application that stores the user's preferred settings (file locations, etc.) in the registry. Because the user cannot save any of the settings stored in a mandatory profile an error occurs when you try to save these settings (usually at program exit). This error can lead to loss of functionality, so you must be careful to fully test all applications to be included in a mandatory profile before a widespread rollout.

Profile Permissions

User profiles are protected by up to three sets of permissions.

- **Network share permissions.** Although network share permissions can protect user profiles, they can add difficulty to troubleshooting if you need to find out where permissions are being derived. If at all possible, you should avoid using share permissions in favor of NTFS file and folder permissions.

- **NTFS file and folder permissions.** When you copy a user profile and set the Permitted to Use flag, you are actually setting NTFS permissions on the destination directory structure. NTFS permissions can be changed easily to further restrict access to a profile if necessary. We discussed NTFS permissions in Chapter Three, *File and Directory Security*.

- **Encoded permissions contained in the ntuser.xxx file.** The permissions set with the Permitted to Use flag when a user profile is copied are also set in the ntuser.xxx file, which is a binary representation of a registry hive. These permissions can only be changed with the registry editor, so if permissions need to be made more restrictive, it is easier to use just NTFS permission. If permissions need to be made less restrictive or need to be set for extra users, then they must be set in the ntuser.xxx file as well as at the NTFS level. The steps required to change permissions for the registry portion of the profile are described below.

Amending the Profile with Regedt32

You can easily adjust the portion of the profile stored in the directory structure by simply adding shortcuts to the folder representing the functionality you wish to achieve. To place an application icon on the desktop, you simply add the icon to the Desktop folder within the profile structure. The next time the profile is loaded, the new icon will appear.

The profile attributes held in the binary `ntuser.xxx` file are a little more difficult to get to. To make changes to these settings, you must use the registry editing tool `REGEDT32.EXE` for Windows NT 4.0 profiles. Remember that you should not make profile changes while the user is logged on unless the profile is mandatory. Roaming profile changes will be overwritten when the user logs off if the profile is already in use when the changes are made. The example below takes you through some sample changes to the Accounts user profile created previously.

1. Log on to a machine with Administrative rights and Full Control permission to the **Accounts** profile directory on the **NetProfs** share.

2. Select **Run** from the **Start** menu.

3. Enter **Regedt32** and select **OK**.

4. Select the **HKEY_USERS** hive.

5. Select **Load Hive** from the **Registry** menu.

6. Navigate to the **IBSNT03****NetProfs****Accounts** directory (or the directory holding the profile that you wish to amend).

7. Choose the **ntuser.xxx** (**.dat** or **.man**) file and select **Open** to display the Load Hive dialog box. The **Key Name** being asked for is a unique name that can be used by you to distinguish it as the loaded hive. This is important because the hive needs to be unloaded after the changes are made.

8. Enter a unique key name. For this example, enter **Accounts**.

9. Select **Open**. The Accounts hive is added to the **HKEY_USERS** hive. Figure 4.4 shows the Accounts registry hive.

   Now you can make any changes that you wish to make. Take care whenever you use the registry editing tool not to make any changes in any registry hive unless you are certain of the outcome. When you have finished making the changes, unload the profile hive.

10. Select the root of the **Accounts** hive.

11. Select **Unload Hive** from the **Registry** menu to unload the hive and to save the settings to the original **ntuser.xxx** file.

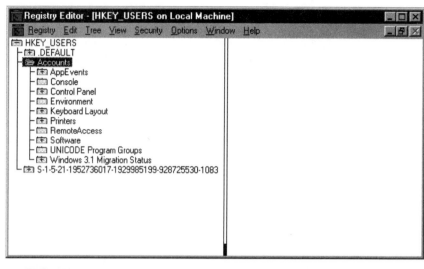

Registry Editor - [HKEY_USERS on Local Machine]

Registry Edit Tree View Security Options Window Help

HKEY_USERS
 .DEFAULT
 Accounts
  AppEvents
  Console
  Control Panel
  Environment
  Keyboard Layout
  Printers
  RemoteAccess
  Software
  UNICODE Program Groups
  Windows 3.1 Migration Status
 S-1-5-21-1952736017-1929985199-928725530-1083

FIGURE 4.4   The `ntuser.xxx` registry file opened as a hive in `Regedt32.exe`

Ntuser.xxx Registry Permission Changes

Permissions are set in the registry portion of the user profile in two ways. First, NTFS file and directory permissions need to be set so that the required users can gain the correct access. Second, there are permissions set by the registry editor in the same way as for any other registry hive. To view or change the permissions set in the registry file, follow these instructions.

1. Load the required registry hive following the instructions in steps 1 through 9 above.

2. Select the root of the **Accounts** registry hive or the hive that you have loaded.

3. Select **Permissions** from the **Security** menu.

4. Change the permissions to match your requirements.

5. Select **OK** to confirm the changes.

6. Unload the registry hive following steps 10 and 11 above.

When the registry hive is unloaded, it is written back to the `ntuser.xxx` file that opened during the *Load Hive* process. Further details on registry permissions can be found in Chapter Eight, *Registry*.

Default User Profile

During Windows NT installation, a generic user profile called the Default User profile is created. This profile exists in the local `%SystemRoot%\Profiles` directory as the subdirectory `Default User`. Users who log on locally and who are not set up to receive any other profile will store a copy of the Default User directory under their own user name as their locally cached profile.

Windows NT 3.5x Profile Upgrades

When a user who is set up to use a Windows 3.5x profile (a `\\server\share\profilefolder.usr` directory) logs on to an NT 4.0 workstation, the NT 4.0 machine recognizes an earlier profile version and creates an NT 4.0 profile in the same share directory and with the same directory name except for a `.pds` suffix. This profile contains the same settings that the earlier version contains.

The format of the Windows NT 3.5x and 4.0 profile interaction is such that users on a mixed network can log on from either version of workstation and receive a profile. The older Windows 3.5x profile is not overwritten; it is copied to a new directory and updated to NT 4.0 format. Once the NT 4.0 version of the profile is created, it is used as a separate profile and changes made in one of the profiles are not reflected in the other.

If the Windows NT 3.5x profile is mandatory, then the automatic copy and conversion process will not work. To make the copy and conversion work, you must remove the mandatory file extension from the NT 3.5x profile directory and then log on from an NT 4.0 workstation. This procedure starts the copy and conversion process for the now nonmandatory profile. After the conversion process has completed, you can then make both the NT 3.5x and NT 4.0 profiles mandatory again.

Creating a Roaming Profile for Windows 95

Windows 95 users can use roaming profiles similar to those in use on Windows NT machines. Follow the instructions below to set up a Windows 95 roaming profile held on a central server.

Client Workstation Setup

There are two stages in the client workstation setup. First, enable profiles for the workstation and then set the default Primary logon to *Client for Microsoft Networks*. The following steps are carried out on the Windows 95 client workstation.

TO ENABLE PROFILES:

1. Select **Settings** from the **Start** menu.
2. Select **Control Panel**.
3. Run the **Passwords** applet.
4. Select the **User Profiles** tab. By default, profiles are turned off.
5. Select the radio button beginning **Users can customize their preferences** to switch on profiles. Figure 4.5 shows the profiles dialog box with profiles enabled.

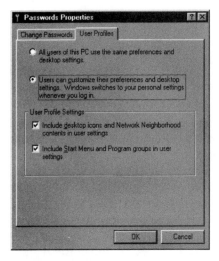

| FIGURE 4.5 | Windows 95 Passwords applet

6. In the **User Profiles Settings** box, choose the options that you wish to enable.
7. Select **OK** to confirm the settings. You must reboot the system before profiles are enabled.

TO SET THE PRIMARY LOGON:

1. Select **Settings** from the **Start** menu.
2. Select **Control Panel**.
3. Run the **Networks** applet.
4. Ensure that the **Primary Network Logon** is set to **Client for Microsoft Networks**, as in Figure 4.6.

5. Double-click the **Client for Microsoft Networks** service and ensure that the radio button **Log onto a Windows NT Domain** is checked and the correct domain name is entered.

6. Make any necessary changes and choose **OK** to confirm. If changes were made, you must reboot to enable them.

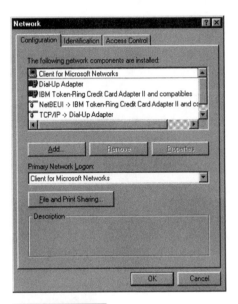

FIGURE 4.6   Windows 95 Networks applet

Domain User Setup

The next step in enabling a roaming profile for Windows 95 users is to create the user account in the domain and set it up with a home directory. The example below uses the account name BrownJ and a home directory under the previously created NetProfs share.

1. Log on to the domain as an administrator and start up **User Manager for Domains**.

2. Select **New User** from the **User** menu.

3. Enter the username **BrownJ** and password details for the new user.

4. Select the **Profiles** button.

5. Ensure the **Profiles Path** remains empty. Windows 95 users store their profiles in their home directory.

6. In the **Home Directory** section, select a drive letter for a home directory and enter the path to the network share. Append the user name to the end of the path. Figure 4.7 shows the completed profiles page for this user.

```
User Environment Profile                                    [X]

User:   BrownJ (Jim Brown)                            ┌──────────┐
                                                      │    OK    │
                                                      ├──────────┤
┌─User Profiles──────────────────────────────────┐   │  Cancel  │
│                                                 │   ├──────────┤
│ User Profile Path:  [                        ]  │   │   Help   │
│                                                 │   └──────────┘
│ Logon Script Name:  [                        ]  │
│                                                 │
├─Home Directory─────────────────────────────────┤
│                                                 │
│  ○ Local Path: [                            ]   │
│                                                 │
│  ⦿ Connect [Z:] [▼] To [\\IBSNT03\NetProfs\BrownJ]│
│                                                 │
└─────────────────────────────────────────────────┘
```

┌──────────────────┐
│ **FIGURE 4.7** │   Windows 95 user profile destination folder setup
└──────────────────┘

7. Select **OK**.

8. Select **Add** to add the user. The home directory should be created automatically. Under certain circumstances, this will not happen and a message will ask you to create it manually. Remember to give the correct permissions if you create the directory manually.

9. Select **Close**.

Create the Profile

The next stage in the process is to create the profile for the Windows 95 user. This stage is accomplished on the Windows 95 workstation.

1. Log on to the Windows 95 workstation as the user concerned (BrownJ). A message stating "You have not logged on here before [since the profile settings were enabled], would you like to retain individual settings for use later" is displayed.

2. Answer **Yes**. A yes answer creates a directory called Profiles as a subdirectory to the %Windir% directory if it is the first profile on the machine and also creates a subdirectory below Profiles named after the user. In this case, it creates C:\Windows\Profiles\BrownJ and populates it with the default profile information.

3. Enter the password confirmation if this is the first time this user has logged on to this machine.

4. Make any required changes to the profile.

5. Log off. The changes will be saved to the local profiles directory.

The profile will be copied to the network share when the user next logs on and is then used as a roaming profile. The profile in its entirety exists as the directory structure and files within `%Windir%\Profiles\%username%`. This directory structure is copied to the network share that was entered as the user's home directory in *User Manager for Domains*.

When the user next logs on, he will receive the copy of the profile stored on the network share; any changes made to the profile will be saved back to the network share.

Making the Windows 95 Profile Mandatory

The Windows 95 roaming profile that has just been created can be made into a mandatory profile in a manner similar to that for the Windows NT profiles. A file called `User.dat` exists in the users profile directory, and you simply change the extension of this file from `.dat` to `.man` to change to a mandatory profile.

When changing file extensions, always make sure that the *Hide file extensions of known file types* is turned off, to ensure that you can see the file extension and replace it properly without placing a double extension on the file.

System Policies

This chapter introduces the concept of system policies. These policies are used with the Policy Editor to control the look and feel of a desktop and also to control system settings on a per-machine basis. This functionality complements similar functionality in the user profile setup.

The chapter discusses the default values available with the Policy Editor and takes you through each setting in detail.

All of the behind-the-scenes portions of the Policy Editor such as template files are discussed, and the links between these and the various registry values covered by the Policy Editor are exposed.

Introduction

System policies are made up from a set of registry entries that control the computer resources available to a user or group of users. These registry entries can be applied to individual users, groups of users, or to anybody logging on to a particular machine.

The system policies can be used to control access to many different resources on the local machine. Desktop settings and user access to resources can be controlled easily. Settings such as the contents of the Start menu and the application icons that are to appear on the desktop are examples of the controls that can be applied.

System policies are defined with the System Policy Editor tool, POLEDIT.EXE. This program is not installed on an NT system by default and needs to be loaded (see the instructions in the next section). Poledit is a graphical user tool that presents you with an easy-to-use browser list of available settings.

You may be forgiven for wondering about the differences between user profiles and system policies. In reality, many of the settings that can be controlled by user profiles can also be set in system policies. The main difference between the two methods of system control is the way in which they are applied.

User profiles are applied when the user logs on and reads in the settings from the profile directory. User profiles are applied before the user portion of the system policy. System policies are applied either at system startup (for machine settings) or as the user logs on. These settings are copied from the policy file and permanently change settings in the local registry. The user portion of the system policy is applied to the user after the user profile and overwrites any settings that may have already been applied. In this way an administrator can allow user profiles to be amended by the user but, by means of the system policy, can apply settings that should not be changed (system policy settings cannot be changed by the user).

When a user profile is applied, registry settings are changed in the HKEY_USERS registry hive for any portions relevant to the user. System policy settings are made to the same registry hive, and computer-specific settings are made in the HKEY_LOCAL_MACHINE registry hive, so when you apply a system policy which contains settings that may conflict with profile settings, the policy settings overwrite the profile settings in the registry. This gives the ultimate control of the available settings back to the Administrator.

System policies can be applied to all users, individual users, groups of users, all computers, and individual computers.

Policy Editor Installation

The System Policy Editor is made available on all Windows NT 4.0 Server CDs, although it can be installed on Windows NT 4.0 workstation as well. A Windows 95 version of the System Policy Editor is provided on the Windows 95 CD. The following sections describe the installation procedures for each type of machine.

Windows NT Server

Follow the procedures below to install the System Policy Editor on a Windows NT server machine.

1. Log on locally as Administrator or attach to a network share connected to the %SystemRoot% drive of the server.

2. Load the **NT Server CD** into an available drive.

3. Copy the files Common.adm, Windows.adm, and Winnt.adm to the server's %SystemRoot%\inf directory (which is hidden by default). Set your view option to **Show all files** to see this directory.

4. Copy the Poledit.exe file to the %SystemRoot% directory.

5. Copy the Poledit.cnt and Poledit.hlp files to the %System-Root%\Help directory.

6. Create a shortcut to the Poledit.exe program in the Administrative Tools folder.

The System Policy Editor is now ready for use on the NT server machine.

Windows NT Workstation

1. Log on locally as Administrator or attach to a network share connected to the %SystemRoot% drive of the workstation.

2. Load the **NT Server CD** into an available drive.

3. Copy the files Common.adm, Windows.adm, and Winnt.adm to the servers %SystemRoot%\inf directory (which is hidden by default). Set your view option to **Show all files** to see this directory. Copy the Poledit.exe file to the %SystemRoot% directory. Copy the Poledit.cnt and Poledit.hlp files to the %SystemRoot%\Help directory.

   or

   Run the \Clients\Srvtools\Winnt\Setup.bat file. This will install the client-based server administration toolkit, which includes the System Policy Editor.

4. Create a shortcut to the Poledit.exe program in the Administrative Tools folder.

The System Policy Editor can now be used from the Windows NT workstation.

Windows 95

The Windows 95 Policy Editor installation is slightly more involved than the previous two. Follow exactly the procedure outlined below to make sure the programs are installed correctly. Do not copy the file as in the examples above; otherwise, you risk damage to your system when trying to use the Policy Editor.

1. Make sure the machine has a CD-ROM drive available (or you can attach to a network shared CD-ROM drive).

2. Run the **Add/Remove Programs** applet in **Control Panel**.

3. Select the **Windows Setup** tab.

4. Select **Have Disk**.

5. Enter `Z:\Admin\Apptools\Poledit`, where `Z:` is the drive letter mapped to your CD-ROM drive.

6. Select **OK**. Figure 5.1 shows the resulting dialog box with the two possible program choices.

7. Select both **Group Policies** and **System Policy Editor**. Both of these choices are required for full operational benefit of system policies on a Windows 95 machine.

8. Select **Install**. The required system files are copied.

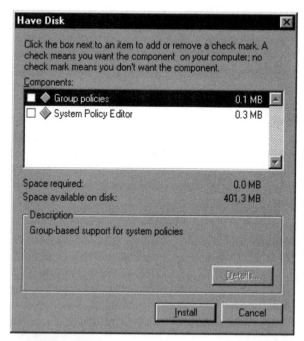

FIGURE 5.1 Available selections for installation of System Policy Editor on a Windows 95 machine

System Policy Editor Modes

The System Policy Editor works in two modes. These are Registry mode and File mode. The settings exposed in both modes are the same. These settings are controlled by administrative template files (.adm) loaded at program initialization time. These files are used to expose only those parts of the registry required for this operation.

Registry Mode

Registry mode allows you to open the local registry and make changes to the settings presented to you through the System Policy Editor. In this mode, the System Policy Editor acts as a user-friendly registry editing tool. Only the settings made available by the templates are exposed making this tool a safe way to implement registry changes.

File Mode

File mode allows you to change registry settings in the same manner as above but does not implement the changes in real time. Instead, the changes are saved to a policy file that can be applied to any number of machines at a later date. A default policy file can be saved on a domain controller (and replicated to all other validating servers) so that it is loaded as users log on to the domain. Windows 95 machines have a different registry format, which is not compatible with Windows NT machines. The Windows 95 policy file is saved in ASCII format, and the Windows NT 4.0 policy is saved in Unicode format. Therefore, any policy file created on a Windows 95 machine cannot be applied to a Windows NT machine (and vice versa) and you must use the Policy Editor natively to manipulate policy files on each of the two systems.

Registry Mode vs. File Mode

The interface options available to you with the two different modes are exactly the same. The main difference between the two modes is that one of them (Registry) is used to make changes directly to the registry either on the local machine or directly to the registry on a machine to which you can make a remote connection. In either case, the change is made to the registry on that specific machine. The other mode (File) is used on any machine to make registry changes that are then saved to a file. It doesn't matter which machine you use to create the file (other than remembering that Windows NT 4.0 and Windows 95 machines are not interchangeable) because the settings are not implemented locally as they are in Registry mode. The changes are saved and implemented when a user logs on to the domain from a networked PC.

In summary, Registry mode is used for instant changes to the registry on a single local or remote machine; File mode saves the changes for later implementation, possibly on all machines within the domain.

Available Settings Groups

As well as there being two modes for setting registry entries, there are two available groups of entries that can be set. These groups are defined as *computer* and *user*.

Computer Settings

Computer settings manipulate registry entries that control such things as the creation of default drive shares, SMMP settings, remote access settings, and logon banner settings. These entries are all made on a computer-by-computer basis and are not affected by the user logging into the machine. These registry settings are applied before the user gains control of the system and so cannot be affected by the user.

User Settings

User settings manipulate registry entries that control such things as system display settings, control panel availability, wallpaper settings, and the ability to use the registry editor. These settings can be applied for all users, for a single user, or for groups of users. The settings are applied after the computer-specific settings.

Windows NT 4.0 Policy Editor Interface

The System Policy Editor in Windows NT 4.0 is a simple graphical tool that simplifies the difficult task of changing registry settings. To use the Policy Editor, ensure that you have installed the necessary files according to the instructions above. The remainder of this chapter presumes that a shortcut to the Policy Editor has been added to the Administrative Tools folder on the NT workstation or server.

To start the Policy Editor, simply double-click on the shortcut created earlier. The Policy Editor starts up but no policy is loaded. Figure 5.2 shows the System Policy Editor at startup and the available File menu options.

Figures 5.3 and 5.4 show the available options in the Edit and Options menus, respectively.

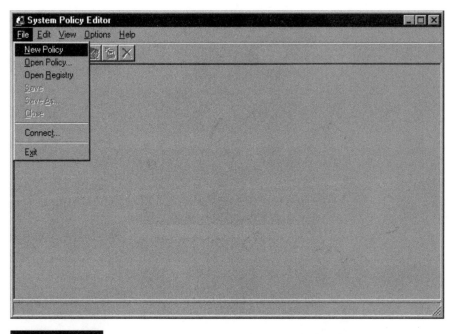

FIGURE 5.2 System Policy Editor and the available File menu options

FIGURE 5.3 System Policy Editor available Edit menu options

FIGURE 5.4 System Policy Editor available Options menu options

Categories

When you configure a policy (either directly in the registry or in file mode) a list of available settings is offered. These groups of settings are known as Categories. Each main category contains one or more subcategories or a set of policies. Figure 5.5 shows the default user policy with the system category expanded to show one subcategory (Restrictions) and two policy settings.

Policy Settings

The policy settings contained within the categories described above actually map to a registry key where the setting of registry values takes place.

You enable the policy value by selecting the square check box preceding the policy description. The three available settings are:

- **Checked box.** This activates the setting in the policy that you are configuring. The registry key is activated (or added if it does not already exist).

- **Blank box.** This deactivates the setting from the policy that you are configuring. The registry key is added if it is needed and set to off.

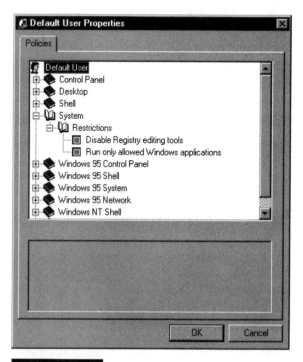

Default User properties page in the System Policy Editor

■ **Grayed box.** This excludes the setting from the configuration. The current setting in the registry (at the time that the policy is implemented on a machine) remains the same. If the key does not exist, it is not created. If the key exists, the setting is not changed.

It is important to understand the difference between deactivated and excluded. When policies are applied, a user may take settings from many different sources. If a user belongs to a group that has a defined policy and to a second group with a defined policy, then settings may conflict. If this happens, the policies are applied in a specific order, as described later in the chapter. If a key in the first applied policy is set as activated and the second applied policy has the key set to deactivate, then the key will be deactivated, overriding the first setting. If, however, the second policy had the key set as excluded, the setting is left as activated because the excluded setting leaves the key untouched. Remember this distinction and think about what you are trying to achieve. Do you care what a key value is set to? If not, leave it as excluded. If you do, set it to activated or deactivated as necessary.

Template Files

The categories, subcategories, and policy keys discussed above appear in the Policy Editor because they are included in a template file automatically loaded at program startup. These template files have a .adm extension and usually exist in the %SystemRoot%\inf directory (which is hidden by default). The template file should have been copied into this directory by you at installation. The three standard template files are Common.adm, Winnt.adm, and Windows.adm.

WINNT.ADM

The Winnt template file contains computer and user categories and keys that can be set only for a Windows NT 4.0 system. This file is loaded by default when you first start up the Windows NT version of the Policy Editor. This template file and the ability to create custom template files are discussed later in this chapter.

WINDOWS.ADM

The Windows template file contains computer and user categories and keys that can only be set for a Windows 95 system. This file is not loaded by default in the Windows NT version of the Policy Editor and is not covered in any more detail in this chapter.

COMMON.ADM

The Common template file contains computer and user categories and keys that are common to both of the operating systems mentioned above. To be included in this template file, a registry key must have exactly the same name in both systems and have the same supported values.

It may seem strange that there is a common template file when the system policy file cannot be shared between the two operating systems because of the difference in registry structure. It *is* strange. There seems to have been a plan at some point in the design of the two operating systems to bring the registry structures in line with each other. This never happened.

This `Common` template file is loaded by default the first time you start up the Windows NT version of the Policy Editor. This template file and the ability to create custom template files are discussed later in this chapter.

Policy File

When you choose to use the program in file mode, you must eventually save the settings to a file. Windows NT 4.0 systems and Windows 95 systems both receive policy updates by default in what is known as Automatic mode. This means that the systems automatically look for a policy file on the Netlogon share of the validating server with a file name of `NTCONFIG.POL` for NT systems and `CONFIG.POL` for Windows 95 systems. If you are using any of the standard domain structures, this setting will work well. All Windows NT or 95 workstations that belong to a domain will go to this network share by default to look for a profile. It is only under certain circumstances, such as when the machines are part of a workgroup and so cannot see a Netlogon share, that you may need to set the update mode to Manual. Setting the mode to Manual and amending the location and file name are discussed later in the chapter.

REPLICATION

If you choose to leave the policy update mode as Automatic, then you must ensure that the policy file is replicated either automatically, using the Replication service, or manually to all validating servers. If the policy file is not available for some reason, you may find that a user profile overrides a previously set policy definition and the resulting user access could cause problems.

Default Computer Policy

Computer policies consist of settings that affect the machine regardless of who logs on to that machine. They include network share settings, remote access settings, the placement of customized shared folders such as the Start menu, and how user profiles are downloaded.

Computer settings are configured with the Policy Editor in either Registry or File mode. Your first decision is whether you need to make changes on one single machine, in which case Registry mode is available, or whether the changes will have to be implemented on many machines, in which case File mode will be used to save the changes for later implementation.

Of the two available modes for implementing system policies, File mode is the most commonly used. The ability to make the settings changes and store them for later user, coupled with the ability to implement the settings uniformly throughout the domain, make this the sensible choice for managing access to resources on the machine and administering security there. The procedure below uses the System Policy Editor in File mode to amend registry settings for the computer. Almost all policy work carried out in a domain is done in this mode.

1. Start the **Policy Editor** (use the shortcut created earlier in **Administrative Tools**) to open a blank policy sheet.

2. Select **File > New Policy** to open a new policy file containing the Default Computer and Default User icons.

3. Double-click **Default Computer**. Figure 5.6 shows the eight standard categories available for the default computer.

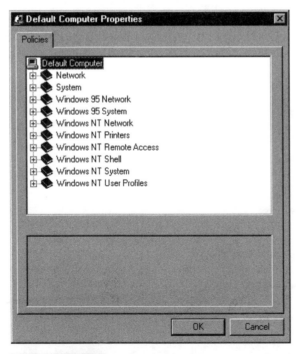

| **FIGURE 5.6** | Eight standard categories of computer settings available in the Policy Editor |

The eight categories shown in Figure 5.6 above are defined in the two template files that are loaded by default at Policy Editor startup. These are `Common.adm` and `Winnt.adm`. Each of the categories is described in more detail in this next section.

Network

The Network category comes from the `Common.adm` template file. Figure 5.7 shows the available settings for this category. Only one key value is set here, although up to four registry keys are affected.

You can use the setting for Remote Update to change the update type from Automatic to Manual and back again. You can also set the path to the remote location from which the system policy file should be downloaded.

This is a valuable setting if you do not intend to use the default policy file name or location. By default, the workstations are set to use Automatic mode and only look in the Netlogon share for the default policy file name. If you are set up in a workgroup instead of a domain, the Netlogon share will not necessarily exist. To overcome this problem, you can set the update mode to Manual and set a different path and file name to be downloaded. Follow the procedure below to do this.

1. Ensure there is a check mark in the **Remote update** check box. The **Settings for Remote update** dialog box is now available for use.

FIGURE 5.7   Network category settings for the Default Computer policy

2. Set the Update mode to **Manual**.

3. Enter a UNC path for the new policy file. Remember to include both the path *and* file name.

4. Select **Display error messages** and **Load balancing** if necessary (see below).

5. Move on to the next category, or select **OK** to finish editing the computer settings.

The Load balancing check box allows the policy download to come from the same path on another domain controller. This feature is used in Automatic mode where the downloading workstation is a domain member. If the validating server that is being used is busy then the workstation looks for another domain controller from which to receive the policy.

To cause the Manual update setting to take effect you must do one of two things:

- Set the policy locally on the machine through Registry mode. The next time the machine reboots, the new setting is read from the registry and the new location and file name are downloaded.

  Or

- Set the Manual update in the NTCONFIG.POL file and place the updated file on the Netlogon share. All of the workstations will be set to Automatic mode by default and so will look at this policy file the first time they are started. They will then have the registry setting changed and will look at the manual update path and file from then on. Even if the manual update policy file is deleted, the workstations will simply fail to load the profile. They will not change back to Automatic update mode until another policy change is made and implemented.

System

The System category comes from the Common.adm template file. Figure 5.8 shows the available settings for this category.

SNMP manipulates information about a TCP/IP host on a network. It is generally used for status and error message logging but can also be used to set parameters on the host.

The Run key is a useful setting; it can be used as a replacement for the Startup folder on the system so that any program listed is definitely run. The problem with the Startup folder is that users could interfere with the running of a program. This registry key is inaccessible to the users (with the correct registry security) and so cannot be altered. Programs such as anti-virus suites or system audit suites that look for unauthorized software are likely candidates for this setting. You can look at the list of programs or add or remove programs from the list by selecting the **Show** button.

FIGURE 5.8   System category settings for the Default Computer policy

Figure 5.9 shows the Show Contents dialog box for this option.

The Run key setting is split into two sections. The Value is the path and program name that you wish to run at startup. The Value Name is used as a label for the program if it is still in memory after the Explorer shell starts.

 Any programs placed here run before the Explorer shell.

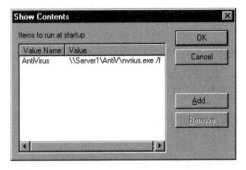

FIGURE 5.9   Show Contents dialog box for the Run option in the System category

Select the **Add** button to place more programs in the list, or highlight an entry and select the **Remove** button to delete an existing entry. An entry in the list should contain the full path and file name for the program as well as any parameters needed to run the program successfully.

Windows NT Network

The Network category comes from the `Winnt.adm` template file. Figure 5.10 shows the available settings for this category.

This category controls the creation of some of the administrative shares on an NT workstation and NT server. Some administrators consider the `<drive_letter>$` administrative shares to be a security risk. I personally use them for administrative ease on workstations and do not create them on servers. Use your own judgement, bearing in mind that the share permissions cannot be changed on these administrative shares and are secured as described in Chapter Three, *File and Directory Security*.

Windows NT Printers

The Printers category comes from the `Winnt.adm` template file. Figure 5.11 shows the available settings for this category.

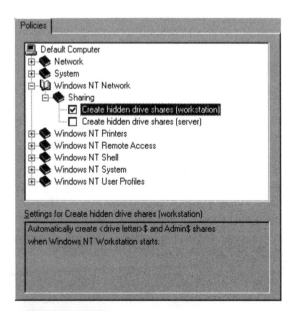

FIGURE 5.10 Windows NT Network category settings for the Default Computer policy

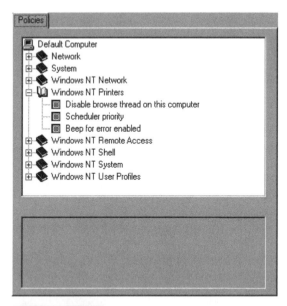

FIGURE 5.11 Windows NT Printers category settings for the Default Computer policy

Use the first setting to remove from the browser list the printer share that exists on the target machine. The share will not appear in the browser lists from then on, but the share can still be connected to if a user knows the exact name. Use second setting to change the priority of print jobs in relation to other tasks running on the machine. The choices here are Above Normal, Normal, and Below Normal. Setting this key to Above Normal can increase printing speed but usually to the detriment of other running threads. The third and final setting in this category enables a beeping sound every 10 seconds when a remote job error occurs on a print server. Use your own judgement as to whether this is a bonus or a real pain.

Windows NT Remote Access

The Remote Access category comes from the `Winnt.adm` template file. Figure 5.12 shows the available settings for this category.

This category can help secure your RAS access and should be set on the RAS server only.

Use the first setting to set a maximum number of logon attempts before the service is disconnected.

Use the next setting to set the maximum time that the RAS service will wait between a dial-in connection being made and the authentication details being passed through. The default setting is 20 seconds; you can lower it to approximately 10 seconds before real users start having problems entering their credentials. The rationale for this setting is that somebody trying to break in will hesitate when trying to decide which password to use.

Use the third setting to set the time interval between disconnecting the incoming call and starting the dial-back procedure.

Use the last setting as a time-out interval for auto-disconnect on an unused line. This feature is useful if your modems are highly utilized or to ensure that unattended client machines are not left connected for too long.

Windows NT Shell

The Shell category comes from the `Winnt.adm` template file. Figure 5.13 shows the available settings for this category.

This category centralizes the look and feel of the Start menu and Startup folder. The registry settings changed under this category point by default to the local All Users profile directory. If you want to provide the same icons and shortcuts for many users on just one machine, then it is simpler to just place the appropriate icons and shortcuts in their relevant place in the All Users folder structure. The procedure below shows you how to change the settings so that the folders can be centrally stored and used on many machines.

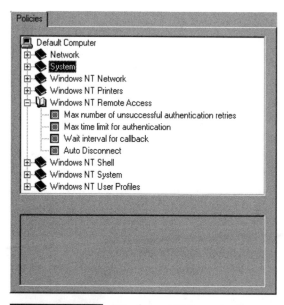

FIGURE 5.12   Windows NT Remote Access category settings for the Default Computer policy

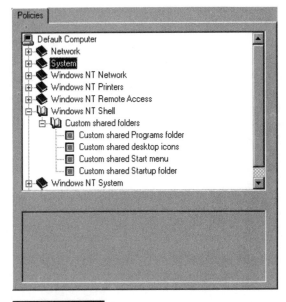

FIGURE 5.13   Windows NT Shell category settings for the Default Computer policy

CUSTOMIZED SHARED PROGRAMS FOLDER

The first setting controls the items that appear in the Programs folder. To control the items that appear here, follow these steps.

1. Create a centralized folder and set the correct access permissions for your users (Read should be enough).
2. Share the folder out and set the correct share permissions if necessary.
3. Place shortcuts to your applications in this folder.
4. Install the necessary applications either centrally on the server or locally. The location must be correctly defined in the shortcut.
5. Select the **Custom shared Programs folder** check box and enter the path to the shared folder.

This procedure can be useful if you have a strict set of available programs that should appear in the Programs folder. By combining policies for different groups and this setting, you can give each group a different Programs folder. Even if users have access to the registry to undo this setting, it will be redone the next time the system is started.

CUSTOMIZED SHARED DESKTOP ICONS

The second setting controls the icons that appear on the desktop. To make the same icons appear on many desktops, follow this procedure.

1. Create a centralized folder and set the correct access permissions for your users.

2. Share the folder out and set the correct share permissions if necessary.

3. Place in this folder the icons that you want to appear on the desktop.

4. Install the necessary applications either centrally on the server or locally. Remember that these icons are usually just shortcuts to programs in another location.

5. Select the **Custom shared desktop icons** check box and enter the path to the shared folder.

CUSTOMIZED SHARED START MENU

The third setting controls the items that appear on the Start menu. To make the same icons appear on everyone's Start menu, follow this procedure.

1. Create a centralized folder and set the correct access permissions for your users.

2. Share the folder out and set the correct share permissions if necessary.

3. Place in this folder the icons that you want to appear on the desktop.

4. Select the **Custom shared Start menu** check box and enter the path to the shared folder.

CUSTOMIZED SHARED STARTUP FOLDER

The fourth setting controls the programs that start automatically at logon time. To add a program to the Start folder, follow this procedure.

1. Create a centralized folder and set the correct access permissions for your users.

2. Share the folder out and set the correct share permissions if necessary.

3. Place in this folder the icons that you want to appear on the desktop.

4. Install the necessary applications either centrally on the server or locally.

5. Select the **Custom shared Startup folder** check box and enter the path to the shared folder.

Those who think that this setting is similar to the earlier Run setting in the System category are right. The only differences between the two are that this setting causes the program to run after Explorer starts up and the setting is visible to the user (a shortcut exists in the Start menu). The visibility may be important if the program is closed during the user session and the user wants to run it again.

Windows NT System

The Windows NT System category comes from the `Winnt.adm` template file. Figure 5.14 shows the available settings for this category.

There are two subcategories in this section: Logon and File System.

LOGON

The Logon category allows you to change registry settings that affect the choices available to users when they attempt to log on to a machine.

LOGON BANNER • The Logon banner displays a message after the Secure Attention Sequence (<Ctrl> Alt> <Del>) is used. To create a banner, follow this procedure.

1. Place a check mark in the **Logon Banner** check box. The **Settings** dialog box is now available.

FIGURE 5.14   Windows NT System category settings for the Default Computer policy

2. Enter the **Caption** header. This header will appear above the main text of the message.

3. Enter the text of the message in the **Text** box.

This setting can be used as an informational message for all users or as a legal notice before logon.

ENABLE SHUTDOWN FROM AUTHENTICATION DIALOG BOX • This setting allows you to set a registry key that either enables or disables the shutdown option that appears as you press <Ctrl> <Alt> <Del> on a machine. By default, this setting is enabled on a Windows NT Workstation and disabled on an NT server.

If you disable this selection, then a user must log on to the machine successfully before being able to shut it down. This option is of little use if a user can access the power switch or electrical outlet for the machine. In these cases, a genuine user may well be tempted to power off the machine if he has difficulty logging on, and a malicious individual who wants to deny access to a service on the machine will welcome the chance to power off and possibly cause more damage than denial of service.

The option is of more use on systems that are locked away or have the power button and electrical feed protected in some way. If you have a showroom with machines open to the public, you could consider this option.

This setting also gives some protection against an individual booting into another operating system and possibly using that OS to circumvent the NT file and directory security. Again, the setting is of little use on its own, and you should consider physical protection in the form of a lockable cabinet for the machine base.

DO NOT DISPLAY LAST LOGGED-ON USER NAME • By default, a Windows NT system displays the user name of the last user to log on. If a hacker decides to break into your system and is able to gain access to the screen, then he has part of the information required to break in, namely, a valid username. This can also be a problem if you use an administrative equivalent user name for troubleshooting a user machine. Your user name is left behind when you leave.

If you enable this setting, the username field in the logon dialog box is left blank after every logout or reboot. This option is useful if machines are constantly used by different individuals.

RUN LOGON SCRIPTS SYNCHRONOUSLY • This setting defines the order of logon script processing and shell activation. When enabled, user logon scripts must complete before the shell starts to run applications in the Startup folder. Use this option to ensure that all required drive mappings are available to run the applications.

FILE SYSTEM

The File System category only affects the Windows NT file system. These are the available settings in brief.

DO NOT CREATE 8.3 FILE NAMES FOR LONG FILE NAMES • This setting disables the creation for an old-style DOS 8.3 file name for every long file name created on the system. The old file names are only used by programs that require DOS format name. The Win16 subsystem does not use these file names but rather has equivalent file names created as they are needed. Unless you have an application that requires these file names to already exist, then turning off this option saves system effort at file creation time.

ALLOW EXTENDED CHARACTERS IN 8.3 FILE NAMES • Whenever an 8.3 file name is created on a Windows NT system, an extended character set is available. Enabling the use of the extended character set may make a file name unreadable on a system that does not have a character code page available containing the item used. If the setting is disabled and the 8.3 file names are created, you are limited in the extended character range that you can use.

DO NOT UPDATE LAST ACCESS TIME • This setting only affects files when they are read. Every time a file is accessed for read or write, the Last Accessed flag is set by default. Changing this setting disables the update of that flag whenever a file is accessed for read-only. If the file is accessed in any other way, the flag is still set. Setting this option speeds up disk access time on read-only jobs because the overhead of writing to the disk is minimized.

Windows NT User Profiles

The Windows NT User Profiles category comes from the `Winnt.adm` template file. Figure 5.15 shows the available settings for this category.

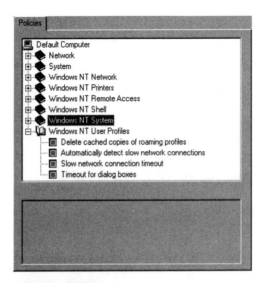

| FIGURE 5.15 | Windows NT User Profiles category settings for the Default Computer policy |

This category contains some settings that affect the way user profiles are downloaded and cached.

DELETE CACHED COPIES OF ROAMING PROFILES

The first setting saves disk space by deleting the locally cached copy of the user's profile when they log off. The locally cached copy of the profile is used if the roaming profile that is stored on the network is unavailable (because of a slow network connection or some other reason). Unless your workstations are running very low on disk space, you should not use this setting.

AUTOMATICALLY DETECT SLOW NETWORK CONNECTIONS

The second setting detects a slow network connection. Your authentication server may be on the other side of a bridge or router and there may be a delay in downloading your profile. If your profile is large, the problem will be more apparent. In this case, the NT system defines the network as being slow and asks if you would like to use the locally cached version of your profile. This setting is turned on by default, and you can use this option to turn it off if you do not require system intervention for slow networks.

SLOW NETWORK CONNECTIONS TIMEOUT

Here is how the NT system decides that you have a slow connection: A timeout limit of just 2000 milliseconds is set by default. If you are using the slow network detection setting, then this is how long the system will wait before giving you a message asking whether you want to wait or use the locally cached profile.

TIMEOUT FOR DIALOG BOXES

The dialog boxes that appear as part of the slow network detection process and user profile date checking process are on a timer. The default time setting is 30 seconds, after which one of the choices is implemented. You can increase this timeout value to give the user more time to consider the question, or you can decrease it if you are happy with the default answers and just want the process to finish as quickly as possible.

Individual Computer Policy

Policy settings can be applied to single computers instead of to all machines. Follow the steps below to configure settings for an individual user on your domain.

1. Start the **System Policy Editor**.

2. Open the domain policy file that you have already created, or select **File** > **New Policy** to start a new policy file.

3. Select **Add Computer** from the **Edit** menu.

4. Enter the netbios name of the computer that you want the policy to apply to. You can type the name or browse for the name. If you type the name, make sure it is spelled correctly. There is no error checking to make sure a user exists.

5. Select **OK**. An icon is added to the policy file desktop named after the computer.

6. Double-click the new icon.

The registry settings exposed here are exactly the same as they are for the Default Computer policy. All settings are defined in the same way, and the only difference is that settings defined here only apply to the one named computer (regardless of user).

Repeat the steps above for as many computers for which you need to define separate policies.

Default User Policy

As with Default Computer policies, when configuring user settings, you must first decide whether to make changes on one single machine, in which case you will use Registry mode, or whether to implement the changes on many machines, in which case you will use File mode to save the changes for later implementation.

Of the two available modes for implementing system policies, File mode is also the most commonly used for implementing user settings. To start configuring the user portion of the system policy, follow this procedure.

1. Select **OK** in the **Default Computer Properties** policy screen, as shown in Figure 5.6 in the *Default Computer Policy* section previously, and skip to step 3

   or

   Start the **Policy Editor**, using the shortcut created earlier in **Administrative Tools**, to open a blank policy sheet.

2. Select **File** > **New Policy** to start a new policy file;

   or

   select **File** > **Open Policy** to open a previously saved policy file.

3. Double-click **Default User**. Figure 5.16 shows the six standard categories available for the default user.

FIGURE 5.16 Six standard categories of user settings available in the Policy Editor

The categories shown in Figure 5.16 are described in more detail in the next section.

Control Panel

The Control Panel category comes from the Common.adm template file. Figure 5.17 shows the available settings for this category.

This category restricts changes of some potentially harmful display-related settings and enables you to be extremely pedantic in your control of user activities.

When you choose to implement a restriction, you should look at why it is implemented. Because a function "is not required for business reasons" does not mean that it should be restricted. Putting restrictions in place simply because the ability exists may make your users feel like they are being treated like children.

The five available restrictions are described below.

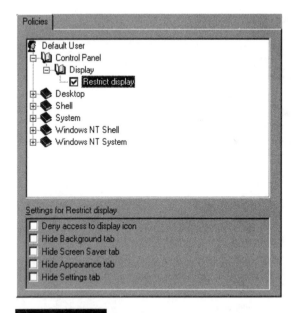

FIGURE 5.17   Control Panel category settings for the Default User policy

DENY ACCESS TO DISPLAY ICON

This restriction will still allow the display icon to be seen in Control Panel, but when users try to run the applet, a message will inform them that the Administrator has disabled this function. Unless you have a very good reason for this restriction, such as a public machine with a shared user ID, then this is not a security issue.

HIDE BACKGROUND TAB

Here is a prime example of being overzealous in restricting users. Short of a corporate standard requiring the organization's logo as a background, then this setting can do no harm. User's ability to remind themselves during those long work hours that they do have a family may be the only thing keeping them sane.

   If the selection is checked, the Background tab will not appear as a selection in the display properties.

HIDE SCREEN SAVER TAB

This restriction is slightly more useful. Some screen savers can consume large amounts of CPU time, while other third-party screen savers can damage the system.

A screen saver set to Blank Screen can be password protected and set to come on after a specific time delay after inactivity. This should be enough to protect systems while allowing programs that are running on the machine to continue using the CPU without interference.

Selecting this check box removes the Screen Saver tab from the display properties screen.

HIDE APPEARANCE TAB

Again, this is a restriction that is usually set just for the sake of setting it. I have come across only one problem in the past that would justify this setting. A user once set the font color and the background color to be the same (both white instead of black on white) and could not understand why all of the writing disappeared in the windows. If you have never had to fix a problem caused by users changing color schemes, then this option is one to ignore.

Selecting this check box removes the Appearance tab from the display properties screen.

HIDE SETTINGS TAB

This setting is also useful. There should be no need for the users to change their own screen size and display settings. Programs may need a particular minimum color palette size. The display driver can be changed using this setting. This is a system function and should be controlled.

Selecting this check box removes the Settings tab from the display properties screen.

Desktop

The Desktop category comes from the `Common.adm` template file. Figure 5.18 shows the available settings for this category.

The two items controlled by this category are *Wallpaper* and *Color scheme*. As mentioned earlier, these are not sensitive settings and can give the user some feeling of freedom. The procedure for setting both of these items is self-explanatory.

Shell

The Shell category comes from the `Common.adm` template file. Figure 5.19 shows the available settings for this category.

The Shell restrictions category contains some important settings. You can enable any of these settings by placing a check mark in the appropriate box.

FIGURE 5.18   Desktop category settings for the Default User policy

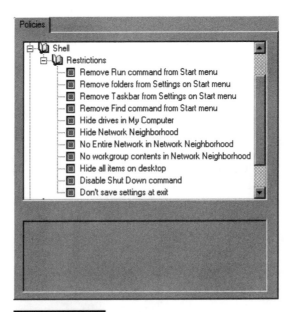

FIGURE 5.19   Shell category settings for the Default User policy

REMOVE RUN COMMAND FROM START MENU

The Run command on the Start menu can be used to start nonstandard applications, which may cause some damage or bring into question licensing issues. You can help to avoid this problem by selecting the check box for this option. Remember that as long as the users can get to an Explorer screen, they can still run the application from there.

REMOVE FOLDERS FROM SETTINGS ON START MENU

This setting limits the access a user has to system settings. Placing a check mark in this check box removes the Control Panel and Printers folders from the Settings menu. Users can subvert this limitation by selecting the Run option mentioned above and entering `Control.exe` to run the control panel that gives access to the Printers applet. If used in conjunction with the setting for the Run option, this option can place slightly more security on the use of your systems. Again, if users know where the `Control.exe` file resides, then they can navigate to the directory and run the program with a simple double-click.

REMOVE TASKBAR FROM SETTINGS ON START MENU

The taskbar menu can be used to set taskbar options and Start menu options as well as to browse the profile storage folders. To restrict users from accessing this system tool, simply place a check mark in the appropriate box. Again, users can still browse the profiles directory with Explorer if they can find it.

REMOVE FIND COMMAND FROM START MENU

This setting removes the Find option from the Start menu and from Explorer, including context-sensitive menus. This makes it difficult for users to find files on the system. If you implement correct permissions on the files and directories, then you can leave this setting to be used as it was intended— as a file and directory navigational aid.

HIDE DRIVES IN MY COMPUTER

This setting removes the drives from view in Explorer and My Computer. There is not much point to either of these views if the drives are removed. This is an extreme measure that may be useful on a public system that has shortcuts to all of the allowed programs.

Programs can still be run from shortcuts or with the Run command if the user knows the exact path and file name.

HIDE NETWORK NEIGHBORHOOD

As you would expect from the name, this setting removes the Network Neighborhood icon from view on the desktop. This setting could be used in a situation where you wish to restrict network browsing (for bandwidth issues or some other purpose), but unless you are sure that all connections that are necessary for the user are already mapped, it can be a pain.

NO ENTIRE NETWORK IN NETWORK NEIGHBORHOOD

This setting is a less drastic step than the previous one but still of little benefit. The restriction here stops browsing on the wide area. Only the local domain or workgroup is accessible. Remember that this is a browser setting and as such will not prevent a drive being mapped to an unseen host with the correct permissions and network connectivity.

NO WORKGROUP CONTENTS IN NETWORK NEIGHBORHOOD

Again, a browser setting. It prevents nondomain machines from appearing in the browser list in Network Neighborhood. Members of workgroups do not appear here. This could prevent a small security loophole where workgroup members are not protected by the domain security policy and so may be slightly exposed if they can be browsed.

HIDE ALL ITEMS ON DESKTOP

Well, what can I say about this one? I've never had use for this setting and find it difficult to envisage when I ever will. A public machine set up to demonstrate one program or feature may benefit from fewer distractions on the desktop and no ability for the public to make alterations. Apart from that, definitely one to stay away from.

DISABLE SHUT DOWN COMMAND

This setting removes the ability to shut down the machine except through the Secure Attention Sequence. As any administrator knows, the temptation for users to power down NT machines without a proper shutdown is already quite strong.

If you disable the shutdown routine for some reason, then the machine needs to be protected against powerdown from the power switch or electrical outlet.

DON'T SAVE SETTINGS AT EXIT

When you log off your machine, Explorer remembers the status and position of certain programs and windows (Explorer windows, Control Panel etc.) This can be useful or it can be a pain. In the good old days of Windows 3.x, this feature was a menu setting. You can switch this off so that no windows are opened by default when you log on again. This can speed up the logoff and logon process and aid in the appearance of a common desktop.

System Restrictions

The System Restrictions category comes from the Common.adm template file. Figure 5.20 shows the available settings for this category.

Two options are available in the System Restrictions category.

DISABLE REGISTRY EDITING TOOLS

The registry editors (Regedt32.exe and Regedit.exe) are available to all users by default. The registry itself should be protected by the correct security settings, but as another precaution, this setting can be used to withdraw all access to this sensitive area. This withdrawal also prevents the user from using the tools to access a remote registry that may not be as well protected. With this setting enabled, the registry editing programs will not run. Renaming the programs will make no difference.

Tools such as Poledit.exe and Control Panel applets are types of registry editing tools in that they can make changes directly into the registry. These tools are not affected by this setting.

RUN ONLY ALLOWED WINDOWS APPLICATIONS

Of all the settings available here, this one gives the tightest security. With this setting enabled, the user can only run the executables that are listed in the table accessed through the Show button. When entering programs here, you should only put in the program name and extension as shown in the example in Figure 5.20.

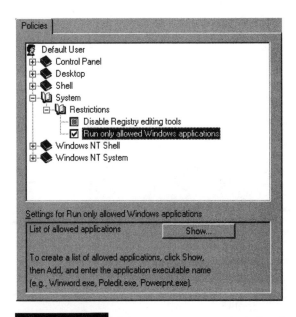

FIGURE 5.20   System category settings for the Default User policy

Remember that this setting works on file names, if users can rename an executable, they may be able to run it.

This setting is very restrictive and could possibly restrict business activities if used unwisely. Again, the setting is generally reserved for a situation where you must restrict access to the machine such as a public-use workstation.

Windows NT Shell

The Windows NT Shell category comes from the `Winnt.adm` template file. Figure 5.21 shows the available settings for this category.

There are two subcategories under this heading.

CUSTOM FOLDERS

The Custom Folders category contains settings that are similar in nature to those configured in the Default Computer properties for the Windows NT Shell category. The main difference is that the settings discussed below are set for a user or groups of users regardless of where in the domain they log on and the similar settings (discussed in the previous sections) are set for the machine(s) that are defined to use the policy regardless of the user.

The benefit of the settings contained in this category is the centralized management and standard desktop look that can be provided.

FIGURE 5.21   Windows NT Shell category settings for the Default User policy

CUSTOM PROGRAMS FOLDER • Custom programs folders give the same Program folder look to a group of users. This setting can be implemented on a departmental basis. Follow these instructions to implement this setting.

1. Create a centralized folder and set the correct access permissions for your users.

2. Share the folder out and set the correct share permissions if necessary.

3. Place shortcuts to your applications in this folder.

4. Install the necessary applications either centrally on the server or locally. The location must be correctly defined in the shortcut.

5. Select the **Custom Programs folder** check box and enter the path to the shared folder.

When assigning a policy setting like this one, it makes sense to assign it via group membership instead of using the Default User. This subject is covered later in the chapter.

CUSTOM DESKTOP ICONS • The custom desktop icons setting is similar to the one above. The process for implementing this setting is the same as the one above. The desktop icons are placed in a shared central location for all defined users to access.

HIDE START MENU SUBFOLDERS • This setting removes from view the subfolders contained in the Start menu. This just leaves shortcuts to applications for the user. This can be a little restrictive for the advanced user. The setting is used in conjunction with the previous two and is enabled with the check box.

CUSTOM STARTUP FOLDER • This setting provides a mechanism for customizing the startup applications for various groups of users. It is implemented in a similar fashion to the Custom Programs folder mentioned above.

CUSTOM NETWORK NEIGHBORHOOD
This setting allows you to use a set of shortcuts that point to various network resources. This setting can replace the normal Network Neighborhood and remove the need for browsing. It is only useful if you can define all of the resources that will be required for the group of users that you apply this setting to. Again, this is achieved by a process similar to that in the Custom Programs folder section above.

CUSTOM START MENU • This setting allows you to create a Start menu that can be shared among a particular group of users. You can create many start menus and assign them to particular user groups through the group policy settings. Again, the same process as above is used. This time, the folder structure as well as the items should be created, and the path should point to the root of that folder structure.

RESTRICTIONS

ONLY USE APPROVED SHELL EXTENSIONS • This setting forces you to only place shortcuts to known document and file types in the Start menu and Desktop folder structure. The approved extension list is held in the registry and can be seen as a registered file type if you start Explorer and choose the View > Options > File Types tab. All shortcuts will have the appropriate program registered locally to run successfully.

REMOVE COMMON PROGRAM GROUPS FROM START MENU • This setting removes the Common program groups from the Start menu. The programs still exist and can be run if the user knows their location or the programs in the system path. This setting may remove some temptation to explore, which is a good thing, but it does not replace the need for proper file and directory security.

Windows NT System

The Windows NT System category comes from the `Winnt.adm` template file. Figure 5.22 shows the available settings for this category.

PARSE AUTOEXEC.BAT

This setting forces the `Autoexec.bat` file to be parsed so that any new entries since the last time it was parsed (possibly at installation) are checked and possibly removed if unneeded. One example is environment variables set by an older installed program. These can be removed and added to the user's environment variables.

FIGURE 5.22   Windows NT System category settings for the Default User policy

RUN LOGON SCRIPTS SYNCHRONOUSLY

This setting forces the logon script for a user or group of users to finish before shell loading can continue. This setting can be used to allow time for a network connection to be made or drive mapping in a lengthy logon script to finish. It can also be set in the Computer section; if it is, that value takes precedence.

Individual User and Group Policies

Policy settings can be applied to individual users and groups of users instead of to all users.

Single User

Follow the steps below to configure settings for an individual user on your domain.

1. Start the System Policy Editor.
2. Open the domain policy file that you have already created, or select **File** > **New Policy** to start a new policy file.
3. Select **Add User** from the **Edit** menu.
4. Enter the user name of the person to whom you wish to apply the policy. You can type the name, or browse for the name. If you type the name, make sure it is spelled correctly. There is no error checking to make sure a user exists.
5. Select **OK**. A single-person icon, which is named after the user, is added to the policy file desktop.
6. Double-click the new icon.

The registry settings exposed here are exactly the same as they are for the Default User policy. All settings are defined in the same way, and the only difference is that settings defined here only apply to the one named user.

Groups

Follow the instructions below to configure settings for a group of users on your domain.

1. Start the System Policy Editor.
2. Open the domain policy file that you have already created, or select **File** > **New Policy** to start a new policy file.
3. Select **Add Group** from the **Edit** menu.

4. Enter the name of the group to which you wish to apply the policy. You can type the name or browse for the name. If you type the name, make sure it is spelled correctly. There is no error checking to make sure a user exists.

5. Select **OK**. A multiperson icon, which is named after the group, is added to the policy file desktop.

6. Double-click the new icon.

Again, the settings exposed with the new icon are the same as above and for the Default User policy. These settings are applied to any member of the group as defined in User Manager for Domains.

Additional group settings can be defined in the same way as above. As you can see, a user may well be receiving settings from different policies now. Figure 5.23 shows a system policy file with multiple groups, users, and computers defined.

Group Priorities

Group priorities can resolve conflicts that may arise when a conflicting setting is made in multiple groups and a user belongs to some or all of those groups. To set priorities you must arrange the groups that have policies defined in some sort of hierarchical order. Follow these steps to arrange the groups.

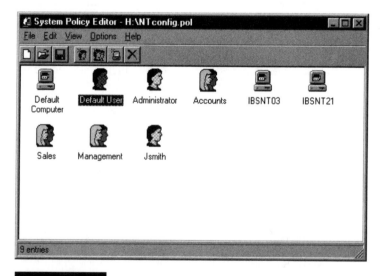

FIGURE 5.23   System Policy containing multiple policy entries

1. Start the **System Policy Editor** and open your policy file.

2. Define the group policies that you want to place in this policy file (or at least create the icon for each group).

3. Select **Options** > **Group Priority** to open the dialog box shown in Figure 5.24.

4. Rearrange the order of the defined groups. Policy settings that conflict are applied from the bottom up. In this case, a conflicting setting applied in the Sales group would be overwritten by the setting in the Management group if the user belonged to both.

5. Select **OK**.

The groups have now been prioritized.

Saving the Policy

You can save the system policy that you are creating at any time. The procedure for saving the policy is the same whether you are setting user configurations, computer configurations, or both, because the one policy file holds all of the policy settings for both computer and user. There are two possible ways of saving the policy for future use.

Automatic Update Mode

Follow these steps to save the policy so that it can be used in Automatic mode by each machine.

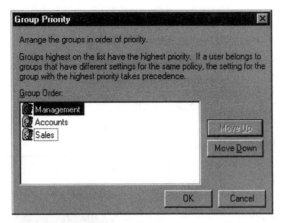

FIGURE 5.24   Defining Group priorities to help resolve conflicts in user settings

1. On the **Default User Properties** screen shown in Figure 5.16 in the *Default User Policy* section, or the **Default Computer Properties** screen shown in Figure 5.6 in the *Default Computer Policy section*, select **OK** to confirm any entries made in that portion of the policy.

2. Select **Save As** from the **File** menu.

3. Navigate to the **Netlogon** share of the domain controller set as the replication export server. Enter the file name **NTconfig.pol**. If the file name is different or the policy location is not the Netlogon share, then Automatic policy mode will not work for the workstations. No error message is given; the workstation simply does not find a policy and cannot be set to expect a policy.

Manual Update Mode

If you wish to use Manual mode for policy updates instead of Automatic mode, then follow the instructions above, substituting the file name and path for your own required details. Then, set up an Automatic policy file as described above with the single computer setting entered, as shown in Figure 5.7 in the *Default Computer Policy* section. The setting should be configured for Manual Update and should contain the path and file name for the new policy. When each machine is used, the Automatic policy setting will change the registry to pick up policy updates from the new location from then on.

Policy Implementation Rules

Settings available for manipulation within the system policy are also set in other ways. A user can change his wallpaper on his own local machine by using *Control Panel > Display*. As an administrator, you can set the wallpaper in a roaming profile or you can set it in a mandatory profile. The system policy also allows this setting to be implemented. Where there are conflicts in system or user settings, you need to set a hierarchy to resolve any problems.

The order in which these settings are implemented is defined in Windows NT. Figure 5.25 shows a graphical representation of the implementation of these settings.

The order of precedence is as follows:

■ Original registry settings and any user-defined registry settings are applied to the machine.

■ Registry settings defined in user profiles are applied to the machine when the user logs on. These settings can come from a local profile, a roaming profile, or a mandatory profile. The settings contained in the profile overwrite any existing registry settings.

- The system policy is applied next and overwrites any conflicting settings in the registry. This means that even if the user were to set preferences for wallpaper settings locally and save them to their roaming profile, the introduction of a system policy stipulating that all users must display the company logo as wallpaper would overwrite the local settings. If the profile is a roaming profile then these settings would be uploaded and overwrite the profile settings. If a mandatory (read-only) profile is in use, then the settings would not be saved to the profile but would still be overwritten every time the policy file is read. The user could change these settings (if the policy allows), but the next time the user logs on, the policy settings appear.

Policy Conflict Resolution

When using system policies, you have a great deal of choice on how and where to apply settings. Certain settings exist in both the user and computer configurations. You can apply settings to individual users, to groups (possibly containing the same users), and also to all users. You may apply settings to individual computers or all computers. It is understandable therefore that there may be conflicts when the policies are applied. A user may receive a settings for an individual registry key from the Default User policy and also through multiple group membership. There must be a hierarchy here to resolve any conflicts in settings that may arise from these possibilities.

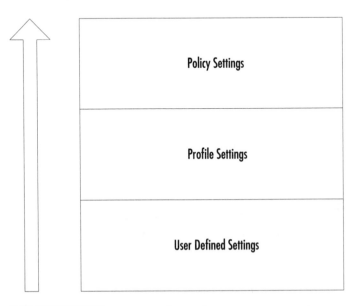

| FIGURE 5.25 | Sequentially applying computer and user settings depending on where they were set |

Computer Policy Conflicts

When conflicts arise because of multiple registry settings for a computer (i.e., a setting exists in the Default Computer policy and the setting exists in the named computer policy), there is more than one possible outcome, depending on the value of the setting. To illustrate the example, we use the setting shown in Figure 5.26.

The setting shown in Figure 5.26 is applied in the Default Computer properties sheet. This setting will be applied to all domain machines. An entry in the policy should be made for all servers in the domain. A single computer entry is made in the policy for the machine IBSNT03, as shown in Figure 5.23 in the Individual User and Group Policies section. The setting described above is made in this policy, but it is set to be disabled (white check box but with no check mark).

When the policies are applied, they are applied in the priority order shown in Figure 5.27.

The computer policy settings contained in Default Computer are applied if a named computer policy does not exist. This is not the case so the settings contained in the individual computer policy are applied; any defined settings in this policy overwrite already existing settings. In this particular case the server IBSNT03 will have a setting applied so that shutdown from the authentication box is not allowed.

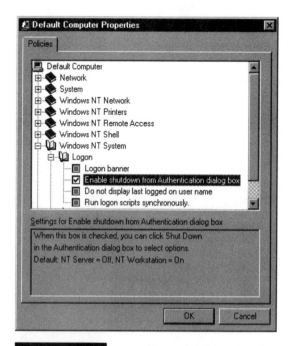

FIGURE 5.26 Example setting for resolution of computer policy conflicts

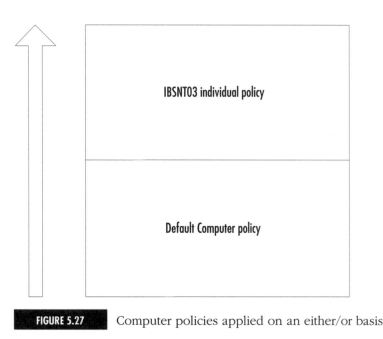

FIGURE 5.27   Computer policies applied on an either/or basis

This order is accomplished because of the definite setting in the IBSNT03 policy disabling the registry key. If the setting had been grayed out instead of white with no check mark, then any setting already applied would be left untouched.

User Policy Conflicts

When conflicts arise because of multiple registry settings for a user (i.e., a setting exists in the Default User policy, in multiple group policies, and in the individual user policy), there is more than one possible outcome, depending on the value of the setting.

To illustrate the example, we use the setting shown in Figure 5.28.

The setting shown in Figure 5.28 is applied in the Default User properties sheet, meaning that this setting will be applied for all users. The same value is grayed out in the Accounts group policy, and is set as disabled (white box but with no check mark) in the Management group policy. User Jsmith is a member of Accounts and Management groups in the domain. He does not have an individual user policy. The group priorities have been set in the order shown in Figure 5.24 in the *Individual User and Group Policies* section. These priorities (from highest to lowest) are Management, Accounts, Sales.

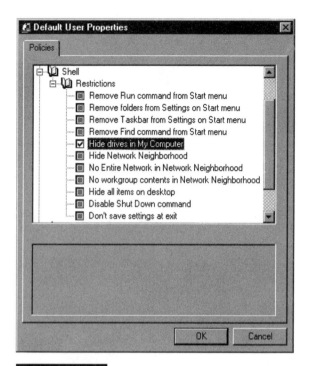

FIGURE 5.28 Example setting for resolution of user policy conflicts

When the policies are applied, they are applied in the priority order shown in Figure 5.29.

The settings applied in the Default User policy are applied first if no individual user policy exists. If an individual policy exists, then it is applied and the Default User policy and group policies are skipped. Group policies are applied in the order defined by their respective group priorities.

For the example shown in Figure 5.28, the Default User policy is set to hide the drive in My Computer. This setting is ignored in the two group policies. The Accounts group policy is applied next and the setting is grayed out so the active setting remains in force. The Management group policy is applied last and the setting is also grayed out. The net result is that this user can see the drives in My Computer.

When an individual user policy exists the Default User policy and Group polices are NOT applied. Only the named policy is applied. Therefore a named policy takes precedence over all other user related policies.

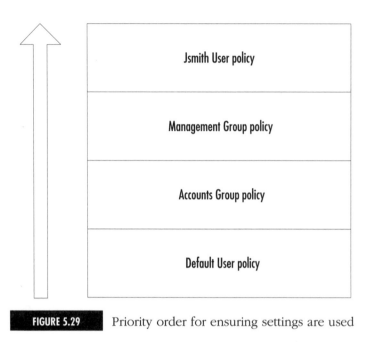

FIGURE 5.29 Priority order for ensuring settings are used

The Dangers of Conflicts

The main danger when applying conflicting settings is that you may leave a setting ignored (grayed out) in the higher-priority policy, expecting the existing setting to remain in place. If one of the interim stages of policy application (such as from group membership) alters the existing setting, then this new setting is passed through the higher-priority policy and the result is not what you expected. If a setting is important to you, set it as enabled or disabled. Do not leave it grayed out unless you are certain of the underlying logic of policy structure (including group membership).

This same warning does not apply to computer policies. For these policies, you can only receive settings from one of two places (Default Computer and named computer), so the chances for confusion are eliminated.

Policy Template Files

The policy template files expose areas of the registry that should be configured by the Policy Editor without allowing any other registry changes to take place through the tool.

Template files are flat ACSII files that can be opened and edited with a text editor such as Notepad. The exposure of registry keys is defined in the template file structure, which is checked every time you try to load a template (and at Policy Editor startup). If you make a syntax error in the file structure, the template will not load and an error similar to that in Figure 5.30 is displayed.

The error message gives you the file name and location as well as the line number that contains the syntax error and the text that is invalid. You cannot get much more helpful than this.

Appendix A contains the listings of the two Windows NT-related template files; Common.adm and Winnt.adm. The third template file supplied is for use with Windows 95 only.

Template File Structure

The file listing that follows is an edited extract from the Winnt.adm template file. This extract inserts the Windows NT Printers category into the Computer properties screens in the Policy Editor. It is placed in the Computer policy screen as opposed to the User policy screen because of the CLASS statement type which is set to MACHINE.

```
CLASS MACHINE


CATEGORY !!Printers
KEYNAME System\CurrentControlSet\Control\Print
        POLICY !!PrintManager_Browser_Restrict
        VALUENAME DisableServerThread
        PART !!Disable_Server_Tip1              TEXT
        END PART
        PART !!Disable_Server_Tip2              TEXT
        END PART
        END POLICY


        POLICY !!Scheduler_Thread_Priority
        PART !!Scheduler_Priority              DROPDOWNLIST
        VALUENAME SchedulerThreadPriority
             ITEMLIST
                   NAME "Above Normal"    VALUE NUMERIC 1
                   NAME "Normal"          VALUE NUMERIC 0
                   NAME "Below Normal"    VALUE NUMERIC -1
             END ITEMLIST
        END PART
        END POLICY


        POLICY !!Beep_Enabled
        VALUENAME BeepEnabled
    VALUEOFF NUMERIC 0
        PART !!Beep_Tip1                        TEXT    END PART
        PART !!Beep_Tip2                        TEXT    END PART
        END POLICY
END CATEGORY
```

```
[strings]
Printers="Windows NT Printers"
PrintManager_Browser_Restrict="Disable browse thread on this computer"
Disable_Server_Tip1="When this box is checked, the print spooler does not"
Disable_Server_Tip2="send shared printer information to other print
     servers."
Scheduler_Thread_Priority="Scheduler priority"
Scheduler_Priority="Priority"
Thread_Priority_Above_Normal="Scheduler priority above normal"
Thread_Priority_Below_Normal="Scheduler priority below normal"
Thread_Priority_Normal="Scheduler priority normal"
Beep_Enabled="Beep for error enabled"
Beep_Tip1="A check in this box enables beeping (every 10 seconds)
     when a remote"
Beep_Tip2="job error occurs on a print server."
```

The first part of the template files is made up from keywords and values. While discussing the different sections of the template, we will refer to the screen shot in Figure 5.11 previously shown. This screen shot of the Default Computer policy shows the Windows NT Printers category expanded. This category is the entry represented by the file extracts above. The next sections explain how the file sections and keywords correspond to the Policy Editor interface and the registry setting. Figure 5.31 repeats Figure 5.11 for convenience.

CLASS

The first entry in the file is the class. The class is always set to one of two options. MACHINE is used as the class when all of the entries that follow are to be part of the Computer policy. USER is the class when all of the entries that follow are part of the User policy. All entries that follow a class statement are placed in the corresponding policy until the next class statement changes the focus to the other policy type.

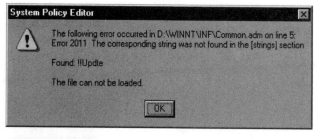

FIGURE 5.30   Error message warning that a template file contains invalid syntax

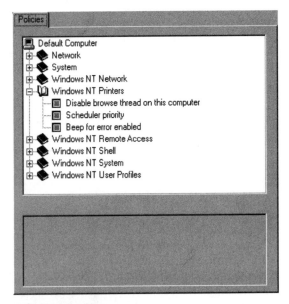

FIGURE 5.31   Repeated Figure 5.11 showing the Windows NT Printers category

CATEGORY

The Category keyword opens a new section in the policy properties screen or further subdivides a section already opened. Referring again to Figure 5.11, the category keyword in the listing above corresponds to the Windows NT Printers category.

You can have many layers of categories. They should simply be nested within the parent category. This structure will be familiar to anyone with programming experience.

All category statements should have a corresponding `END CATEGORY` statement.

TEXT STRING

If you look at the text string that immediately follows the Category keyword in the listing above, you will see that it is `!!Printers`. The `!!` symbols indicate that there is a string definition for this entry in the `[strings]` section. If you follow the listing down to the `[strings]` section, you see the entry `Printers="Windows NT Printers"`. This is where the Windows NT Printers category title comes from (see Figure 5.11).

Text string variables are defined so that short variable names appear in the category design and can represent much longer text strings that are substituted when the policy editor is run. The short variable name only has to be defined once, and it can be used many times throughout the file.

KEYNAME

The KEYNAME statement points to the registry key that will be amended within this category. Because the class has been defined already, there is no need to put the registry hive name here.

POLICY

POLICY is the actual change that can be made with this selection. It is identified with another text string that should translate in the [Scripts] section to a meaningful label describing the type of change that can be made with this selection. Policy statement requires a corresponding End Policy statement.

VALUENAME

The value name is the name of the registry value that should be amended for this option. If the value needs to be set in the lower part of the Policy Editor screen (where value input is required), then the value name must be contained within a Part statement.

PART

The PART statement places text information, drop-down lists, or dialog boxes in the lower part of the Policy Editor screen. These can be used to convey context, sensitive help or for user input when registry values are required. The PART statement comes before the corresponding value name statement and must finish with a corresponding End Part statement.

PART VALUE

The value is a flag that is placed on the end of a Part statement and denotes the type of information contained in Part. The several options are listed.

TEXT • The Text flag only displays text and can be used as context-sensitive help. The text can be displayed when the option is highlighted.

NUMERIC • The NUMERIC flag causes the value to be written to the registry with the data type of REG_DWORD. You need to know what data type the registry value can hold before setting this flag.

DROPDOWNLIST • The DROPDOWNLIST flag provides exactly what you would expect. The list syntax is shown below in an extract from the fuller listing provided at the beginning of this section.

```
PART !!Scheduler_Priority                    DROPDOWNLIST
VALUENAME SchedulerThreadPriority
        ITEMLIST
                NAME "Above Normal"     VALUE NUMERIC 1
                NAME "Normal"           VALUE NUMERIC 0
                NAME "Below Normal"     VALUE NUMERIC -1
        END ITEMLIST
    END PART
```

The text for the drop-down items is defined by the Name statement. The data values that would be entered into the registry are associated with each option: in this case, the numbers 1, 0, and –1.

EDITTEXT • The EDITTEXT flag denotes that the data type for the selected registry value is REG_SZ.

REQUIRED • The REQUIRED flag does not allow the option to be selected without a corresponding value being entered. An error message is generated if no value is entered and the user must either enter a value or deselect the option.

EXPANDABLETEXT • The EXPANDABLETEXT flag denotes that the data type for the selected registry value is REG_EXPAND_SZ.

MAXLEN • The MAXLEN flag specifies the maximum length of a text input.

DEFAULT • The DEFAULT flag specifies the default value for numeric or text input.

MIN AND MAX • The MIN and MAX flags denote the minimum and maximum values allowed for a numeric field.

VALUEOFF

The VALUEOFF statement places a specified value in the registry if the option is set as OFF.

VALUEON

The VALUEON statement places a specified value in the registry if the option is set as ON.

[STRINGS]

The last part of the template files is made up of the string definitions. For every entry in the file preceded with !! symbols, there should be a corresponding entry in the [strings] section.

Hints for Building Custom Template Files

You can build your own template files to expose registry settings that are not normally available to the Policy Editor. You may want to do this so that you can include extra security related settings in a policy that can be implemented domainwide. An outline of instructions for creating your own template files is presented below. Make sure you are comfortable with the layout of the template files and the keyword uses before proceeding.

- Make a list of the registry key that you want to include in your template, along with all supported values and data type involved.

- Start a new template file in Notepad or open a *copy* of an existing file and remove most of the entries, leaving just enough information to help you lay the file out properly.

- Enter the required information in the proper format. This instruction is only eight words but is the most difficult part of the whole exercise.

- Test the template file by trying to load it into the Policy Editor. Do this often and fix problems before adding more functionality.

- Build up the functionality of your policy template step by step with testing at each stage.

- Test the finished, loaded policy on the local registry of a machine that you can afford to destroy. This is no idle warning. Mistakes in syntax are found by the Policy Editor at load time. Mistakes in registry settings are not found until they are applied and possibly kill the system.

- Last but not least, make sure you understand the registry before attempting this type of exercise. A custom-made policy can bring great benefit to your organization by allowing you to apply controlled measures to restrict unwarranted activity. If it exists as a registry key in the HKEY_LOCAL_MACHINE or HKEY_USERS registry hives and it can be amended with Regedt32.exe, then it can be controlled by this program with a custom template file. Take some time to browse through these registry hives and look at the number of entries here.

Summary

Take some time to look at the template files and get used to the layout before trying to build custom files of your own. The syntax can be quite tricky, and you should test any changes on a registry that you can afford to trash. Remember to make copies of the template files and only work from the copies.

Cryptography

This chapter addresses the topic of cryptography as a general subject and also as it relates to both present and future releases of Microsoft Windows operating systems. Subtopics covered in this chapter include data encryption while stored and transmitted, encryption algorithms, authentication, and digital certificate use.

What Is Cryptography?

Of the many challenges faced by the security professional today, surely one of the most important is how to secure data storage and communications. While standard connectivity protocols such as TCP/IP and IPX/SPX allow for efficient widespread communications, they were never designed to incorporate high levels of security in their structure. Another level of protocols was needed to bring security to the transmissions without affecting the underlying transport protocols. These protocols must be inherently robust, and they must be platform independent because of the nature of the large heterogeneous networks installed today (Microsoft, Apple, NetWare, Unix).

Cryptography is a grouping together of technologies, generally in the form of security protocols, that provide the solution to many of the security-related problems we face when implementing data communications networks. People ask many questions about data communications networks such as;

- How can I replace insecure username and password combinations for authentication?
- How can I be certain that the single logon process is secure?
- How can I be sure of the identity of a user or entity on the network? (When I send my credit card details to a trusted online shop, how do I know those people are operating the site?)
- How do I know when I receive a message that it is from the correct person?
- How do I know if a message I send or receive has been tampered with?
- How can I make sure that messages I send are kept private?

The answers to these questions and many more like them lie in the implementation of cryptography. Cryptography can be loosely divided into the following categories.

- **Encryption and decryption.** Encryption technology turns readable data into a form that would be unreadable to anybody who should not see the contents. This is a necessary technology in today's large networks where Internet connectivity and use is common. Decryption is the opposite of encryption.
- **Authentication.** This technology guarantees an entity's ID.
- **Verification.** This technology verifies the source of a message and verifies that the contents of the message have not been altered after leaving the source. It is similar to written signatures at the end of a document. You use the signature to guarantee the identity of the sender.

Each of the categories listed above is discussed in detail later in this chapter.

The word *message* in this chapter refers to any body of data, including documents, database files, emails, etc., that you want to encrypt or verify.

Encryption and Decryption

Within Windows 2000, encryption is based mainly on key pairs as a replacement for simple username and password technology. The following sections discuss the encryption and decryption technology used in Windows 2000.

Asymmetric (Public Key) Cryptography

The basis of asymmetric or public key cryptography is the generation of a key pair. One of the keys (the public key) is published for all to use. The second key (the private key) is kept secret. This scheme facilitates a secure one-way encryption. If Mary wants to send confidential information to a service provider, she encrypts the data with the public key of the service provider. The public key can only be used to encrypt data. Data encrypted by the public key cannot be decrypted by the same key. Now the service provider is the only person who can decrypt the data with the (secret) private key.

One of the added strengths of this encryption method is never having to transmit the private key at any time. The transmission of passwords or keys has always been a weakness in a distributed security model.

Symmetric (Shared Key) Cryptography

Symmetric key encryption uses the same key at both ends to encrypt and decrypt the data. This version of encryption is faster and less CPU intensive than public key but is more prone to problems. A large security issue arises when you try to decide on the transfer method for the key that must be known to both parties. How do you agree on the key that will be used? Do you send it on floppy disk? Do you confirm it over the telephone? However it is done, it can be difficult to complete in real time and is less secure than public key encryption. Anybody who intercepts the key can use this information to interfere with communications.

So, how do you get the speed advantage of symmetric key encryption and the security of public key encryption? You use the slower public key encryption to pass the agreed symmetric key between the two parties. You now know that the parties hold secure symmetric keys. The remainder of the transaction can be completed with these symmetric keys.

In the real world, secure transmissions are completed by a method close to the scenario above. SSL, which is one of the most popular secure channel encryption protocols, uses both public key and symmetric key encryption when establishing and using a communication session.

Shared Key vs. Public Key

As discussed, one of the main advantages of public key encryption over shared key encryption is that public key encryption relies on a key pair, one of which is never transmitted or revealed (the private key), whereas, the shared key system needs the parties involved to agree on a key at some point. Either this is done together or one party decides and sends the key to the other. In either case, there is a period when the key is vulnerable and can be disclosed to third parties.

Public key systems have the advantage of firmly placing responsibility on key holders for their own key safety. At no time should the private key be disclosed. If it is, then that disclosure would be the sole responsibility of the private key holder. With the shared key method, there is a period of vulnerability in which a key could be disclosed. It would be easy for either party to deny sending data and blame an incident on key disclosure by the other party.

Public key systems are generally slower than shared key systems. So, many secure channel protocols use both systems to communicate. Public key systems are used to securely transmit the shared key so that a faster communication channel can be used for the main part of the transaction. Figure 6.1 shows the interaction between shared key and public key technology when used together for maximum security and speed. The interaction is described below.

1. Both Stations exchange public keys. Private keys are kept secret at both stations.

2. Station 1 defines a shared key according to a predefined protocol.

3. Station 1 encrypts the shared key with the public key of Station 2.

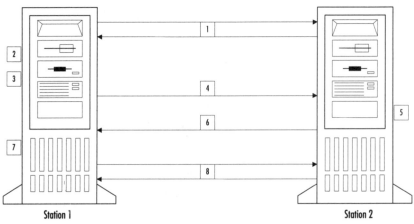

Station 1   Station 2

FIGURE 6.1   Shared key and public key technology for the best of both worlds

4. Station 1 transmits the encrypted key to Station 2. If this transmission is intercepted it doesn't matter because the transmission can only be decrypted with the private key held by Station 2. This method provides a secure means to exchange private key information.

5. Station 2 decrypts the message, using its own private key.

6. Station 2 sends an acknowledgment message to Station 1. This message is encrypted with the shared key.

7. Station 1 receives the message and decrypts it, using the shared key.

8. Two-way communications are now possible, using the shared key for encryption. This method provides fast, efficient, and secure communications between the two hosts.

As you can see from the description above, the slower but more secure method of encryption (public key) is used to securely transmit a shared key which allows faster communications. The higher level of security afforded by the public key technology is fully utilized, yet the majority of the communications take place using the shared key technology, which has less overhead and greater efficiency. When you make a secure channel connection over the Internet via SSL (perhaps to send credit card information) your system will go through steps similar to those outlined above to safely set up a connection that can be encrypted by a shared key system. SSL is described later in this chapter.

Encryption Algorithms

Encryption algorithms are the actual mathematical formulas applied to a data stream to turn it into an indecipherable and therefore safe communication. Many different algorithms are in use today on many different systems. The algorithms and encryption functions discussed below are used by Microsoft in Windows NT and Windows 2000 to protect message transmissions.

One-way Functions

One-way functions are functions that are far more difficult to perform in a reverse direction. For example you can say with relative certainty that 50 * 100 = 5000. It is much more difficult to break down the function into its original parts when you only have the result. There are many original functions that could create the result of 5000.

When these functions are used for encryption, they make up *one-way encryption protocols*. This is the basis of *public key* encryption. One-way encryption is based on the premise that it would be infeasible to decrypt a data stream, given only the encrypted output and the encryption key. Note that the premise is based on *infeasibility* and not *impossibility*. You cannot prove the impossibility of the action. You can prove the possibility of the action by breaking the encryption code. Until this happens, the protocol strength is measured by the feasibility of breaking the code.

The decryption takes place with a trapdoor mechanism (contained in a private key). The trapdoor mechanism is known to the recipient of the encrypted data. Knowing the trapdoor allows the decryption process to take place. It is important therefore that the decryption trapdoor mechanism is not stored or transmitted in a manner in which it is likely to be intercepted.

RC4

The RC4 algorithm is a shared key cipher used for data encryption. It is generally used in a session after the initial handshake and the shared key creation has been completed by a public key cipher. Uses of the RC4 algorithm in Windows NT and Windows 2000 include PPTP session encryption (after handshaking and authentication), RAS connectivity, and secure data communications using Microsoft Explorer and SSL.

The RC4 algorithm is restricted for export outside the United States. Inside the United States, a 128-bit encryption system is available. The higher the encryption bit level, the harder it is to break the code. Only 40-bit RC4 is allowed to be exported from the United States at the moment. This encryption level provides significantly less security than does 128-bit encryption. One important point to remember is that when one party uses 128-bit encryption key strength, then the other party must be capable of this level of key strength. Key strengths are generally negotiated at the time of initial handshaking. Just because your system has the capability of 128-bit key strength, don't automatically assume that all communications channels are secured to this level. If you allow key strength negotiations on your system, then they will be negotiated to the highest *common* level.

Data Encryption Standard (DES)

The DES algorithm is also a shared key cipher used for data encryption. This algorithm is often used to encrypt data on hard disks and is the first supported encryption algorithm for the *Encrypting File System* in Windows 2000. Future releases of the EFS will support more algorithms. DES is also used to encrypt messages before transmitting them (digital envelope), while a public key algorithm is used to encrypt the DES key and send it to the recipient.

DES using a 56-bit key is implemented in the SET (Secure Electronic Transfer) payment system developed by Microsoft and Visa International.

The DES variants provided with Windows 2000 are DES-CBC-MD5 and DES-CBC-CRC. These are used as the main encryption algorithms for intra- and interdomain authentication using the Kerberos protocol.

RSA

RSA is a public key cipher used for both encryption and authentication. With RSA, anyone who holds the public key can encrypt a message or verify a signature on a message, but only the holder of the private key can decrypt the message or sign a message.

RSA is widely used in Internet connectivity models today. SSL, S/MIME, secure email, PCT, and S-HTTP all support the RSA cipher.

Authentication

As Windows NT installations grow in both size and complexity, the need for trusted, secure communications protocols is increasing. There are two main security protocols in use with Windows NT for authentication; these will be joined by a third with Windows 2000. These protocols are NTLM, DPA, and Kerberos version 5. Windows 2000 uses the Kerberos authentication protocol for all credential authentication within the active directory, including interdomain connections.

NT LAN Manager (NTLM)

NTLM is the authentication protocol with Windows NT 4.0 and previous versions of the operating system and will be supported by Windows 2000 for backward compatibility. Any connectivity with Windows NT or Windows 95/98 operating systems will still use the NTLM protocol for authentication. All connectivity between Windows 2000 nodes and the directory tree is carried out with the Kerberos authentication protocol described below.

Distributed Password Authentication (DPA)

DPA is a shared key authentication protocol used in many large Internet-based organizations for shared client authentication. The same password can be used to authenticate to many organizations such as MSN and CompuServe. The different sites need only be a member of the same membership organization. This protocol is part of the Microsoft Commercial Internet System (MCIS) and provides transparent authentication to many sites after the initial credentials are entered.

Kerberos v5

The Kerberos authentication protocol will be the replacement for NTLM in Windows 2000. It is used for all connectivity across domains where Windows NT or Windows 95/98 are not involved.

Kerberos installations are based upon the building of *realms*. These realms are analogous to Windows domains, and the words are generally interchangeable when reading about Kerberos in Windows 2000 documentation.

Kerberos v5 is an industry-standard protocol developed by MIT and is well-known for its security features. It is based on the RFC 1510; the NT implementation will support any client that is RFC 1510-compliant, including Windows 9x.

Kerberos relies on symmetric (shared) key encryption algorithms [see *Symmetric (Shared Key) Cryptography* in this chapter]. The implementation of this encryption method relies on the central storage of users' keys, so if this central storage area is insecure, then all users' keys could be found. This is a drawback of any key storage system. Kerberos authentication is used within the Active Directory structure in Windows 2000, including interdomain communication, but is not used beyond that scope.

X.509 Standard

X.509 is the standard specification for security and authentication services for an X.500 directory. Microsoft's Active Directory is based on the X.500 specification (but is not a true X.500 directory). X.509 version 3 certificate syntax specifies the following fields.

- Version
- Serial number
- Signature algorithm ID
- Issuer name
- Validity period
- Subject name
- Subject public key information
- Issuer unique ID
- Subject unique ID
- Extensions
- Signature on all fields

The X.509 standard is based on key pair security. It does not specify any particular algorithm to be used for encryption.

The X.509 standard is based on either public or symmetric key encryption technology. When public keys are used in the X.509 standard, they are in the form of certificates. All X.500 directory authentication can be carried out with protocols written to the X.509 standard.

Smart Cards

Support for Smartcard technology has been built into Windows NT for some time now. This relatively new and rapidly evolving technology will help to reduce the reliance on username and password technologies as well as making it easier to transport a users' digital credentials from PC to PC. A smart card can hold all different types of information such as personal details and bank information. The technology is used in conjunction with card readers, so for the foreseeable future the implementations are likely to be made in the public arena.

Microsoft has been a strong advocate of the development of Smartcard technology and has included a standard API kit for Smartcard implementation in their SDK forum since 1997. These APIs are device independent and so relieve the programmer of the need to write interfaces to the many different Smartcard and card reader devices.

Kerberos in Windows 2000

The Windows 2000 distributed security model is supported by Kerberos authentication for single logon functionality and trusted path building within the Active Directory. Kerberos is one of the four main protocols implemented as a Security Support Provider (SSP) within the SSPI model.

Kerberos in Windows 2000 is implemented as a network authentication system service known as a Key Distribution Center (KDC) on all domain controllers within the Active Directory.

The protocol defines the interaction between the KDC and client requests for security approval. The Kerberos implementation can act as a KDC for non-Microsoft clients and hosts as long as they conform to the Kerberos v5 model. These systems can authenticate to the KDC by using the same encryption algorithms as native Windows 2000 clients. Further interoperability is achieved with the implementation of the GSS-API token mechanisms defined in RFC 1964. Again, the standard format used in this implementation lends itself to easy compatibility for authentication, using the Kerberos SSP provided in Windows 2000.

Kerberos authentication and the logon process are discussed in more detail in Chapter Thirteen, *Active Directory*.

Kerberos vs. NTLM

Kerberos has some major benefits over NTLM as an authentication protocol. Kerberos can handle delegation as a means of client impersonation. This means that a server can impersonate a client after the initial credential check.

If the client then wishes to connect to another server to access a service, Kerberos allows full delegation to take place. The first server can make the connection to the second server, using the security context of the client. NTLM can also perform this service. The difference is in the next stage. If the second server needs to connect to a third server to perform a requested task on behalf of the client, it cannot do so when using NTLM authentication. Kerberos, however, allows this extra stage of impersonation, known as delegation. The second server can use the credentials of the client passed on from the first server to carry on the impersonation to the third server.

A benefit arising partly from this delegating ability and partly from the transitive trust nature of Kerberos within the Active Directory is authentication speed. Back-end servers do not need to go back to a domain controller to authenticate the client when network services are requested. This means that the authentication process for network activity is much faster than with NTLM.

Domain management is simplified using Kerberos and the KDC for authentication because transitive trust relationships can be used for interdomain connections. KDCs implemented in one domain of the Active Directory can trust other KDCs in the same tree, and so the management overhead is reduced.

Verification

Being able to trust the origin of a message and being able to trust that the message has not been tampered with in transit are an important part of data communications over the Internet today. Origin verification is addressed by the implementation of digital signatures.

Hash Function

Digital signatures rely on hash functions for their implementation. Hash functions take in a variable-length message and output a fixed-length hash value that does not resemble the original message yet is a precise representation of the original message. This hash value is also known as a digital fingerprint because of the precise way in which it represents the original message.

Hash functions are said to be *one-way* when it is infeasible, given the hash value, to find the original message. The benefit of this method is that the hash input key cannot be determined from the hash result.

Hash functions are said to be *strongly collision-free* if it is computationally infeasible to produce the same output values from any two input messages to the hash function. That is, when x is not equal to y but $F(x) = F(y)$. The benefit of this approach is that a message cannot be altered after the hash value is calculated and encrypted. Any alteration to the original message results in a different hash value.

Digital Signatures

Digital signatures are the main cryptography mechanism to use hash functions. They are created by a public key algorithm, to encrypt a fixed-length hash value that is transmitted along with the message. The sender's own private key encrypts the hash created for the message. The message is not changed or encrypted by this process (although encryption can take place after the signing if required). The sender's public key decrypts the hash value for the message. The hash value is then calculated for the received document and is compared to the decrypted hash. If the two hash values are the same, this verifies the signature and also confirms that the message has not been altered in transit.

Anyone attempting to intercept and change the message would not be able to use the original sender's private key to encrypt a new hash value. The old hash value could not be used to represent the changed message because of the collision-free nature of the algorithm.

As you can see, digital signatures are used to prove the source and validity of a message and its contents. Figure 6.2 shows the digital signature process flow.

Digital Envelopes

Digital envelopes are sometimes discussed in Microsoft literature in connection with digital signatures. Although they are based on the same public key technology, they are different implementations of this technology.

A digital envelope encrypts a message so that only the intended recipient can read it. Whereas digital signatures use the sender's own private key for encryption (and therefore verification of the source), digital envelopes use the recipient's public key for encryption. This means that only the recipient can decrypt and therefore read the message. Figure 6.3 shows the digital envelope process flow.

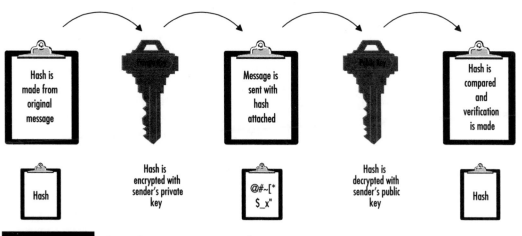

FIGURE 6.2   Digital signature process flow

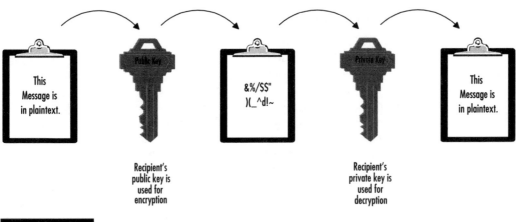

This Message is in plaintext.

Public Key

&%/$$")(_^d!~

Private Key

This Message is in plaintext.

Recipient's public key is used for encryption

Recipient's private key is used for decryption

FIGURE 6.3   Digital envelope process flow

Digital (Public Key) Certificates

When you use digital signatures to verify the identity of the sender, you assume that this identity has already been established beyond all doubt. When you need to communicate securely over the Internet with a well-known vendor, how do you know that you are actually connected to that particular vendor's site? How do you know somebody is not impersonating that vendor on the Internet? How do you know that the public key you ask for actually belongs to this well-known vendor?

Digital or public key certificates are used as a secure means of identification. The way around the problems outlined above is for the interested parties to apply to a Certificate Authority (CA) for a digital certificate. It is then up to the CA to verify that applicants are who they appear to be. This means that the identity of a party is established by a CA on your behalf (and on behalf of anybody else who wishes to perform secure communications with them). Digital certificates often contain the level of authentication used by the CA to establish the identity of the holder. Two of the most popular CAs at the moment are VeriSign and GTE.

When the CA is satisfied that the request for a certificate is verified, the CA responds with a dataset that contains a digital certificate listing, among other things, the requester's new public key. This certificate is signed with the private key of the CA. Now the vendor can supply the certificate to their clients, and its clients trust the CA. You know that the certificate is genuine because you compare the hash signature by using the public key of the CA.

This still leaves one last link in the chain of events concerning certificate distribution. How do you know that you have the correct certificate from the CA containing the correct public key?. At some point you must still find a secure means of sending this information. Software vendors often ship these certificates with their software. Microsoft ships CA certificates for many CAs with Internet Explorer.

Certificate revocation lists are an important aspect of digital certificates. All certificates should have a finite life span like any other type of identification. The CRL is a way for people to validate the life span of certificates. CAs publish these lists regularly, so that they can be downloaded by validation agents.

Secure Channel Services (SCS)

Secure Channel Services is the software implementation that enables users to form secure end-to-end channels for communications, using Windows NT and Windows 2000. SCS is implemented as a DLL (schanell.dll) and provides encryption services and digital signature verification. Many protocols are supported by SCS, including SSL, PCT, and TLS (in future releases).

Windows NT/2000 and Internet Explorer 4.0 support SSL and PCT as providers for secure channel communications over the Internet. These security protocols are application independent, and therefore Internet protocols such as HTTP can be layered on top of them. Sessions are generally set up with public (asymmetric) key encryption to perform a handshake routine and shared (symmetric) key encryption for the remainder of the secure session.

Secure Sockets Layer (SSL)

SSL was developed by Netscape to address the need for secure channel connectivity over the Internet. It is now an industry-standard protocol supported by all of the major manufacturers with networking and Internet interests. SSL 3.0 is used by Windows NT/2000 and Internet Explorer 3.0 and above to provide secure channel communication between browsers and Web servers. It facilitates both server and client authentication.

When SSL is used by Internet Explorer to implement a secure channel, the first stage in the process is for the client to make the request (possibly by selecting an online payment button on a Web page). The request is sent to the server, which replies with its own certificate containing the public key. If client authentication is required, then the client also sends its own certificate to the server. The server's certificate is verified and the client sends back a shared session key encrypted with the server's public key. The server receives the client's message and uses its own private key to decrypt the shared key message. If the client certificate needs to be verified, this verification is completed as well. The server replies to the client, using the shared key.

The public key exchange is encrypted by the RSA public key algorithm discussed earlier. The public key encrypted session negotiates the details of the shared key. After the initial negotiation phase is completed, the secure channel communications are encrypted with the shared key, using protocols such as RC4 or DES.

All of the session is encrypted from the handshake phase onward. All HTTP traffic, all form data (useful if sending credit card), all URL requests, and all other information are encrypted end-to-end. The only way to decrypt is with the secret shared key.

The SSL protocol supports many encryption algorithms. When a session is started using SSL, the RSA public key algorithm can be used. Once the public key part of the process has finished, the RC4 or DES algorithms can be used for the remainder of the session.

Private Communications Technology (PCT)

PCT was developed in a joint venture between Microsoft and VISA International to challenge the domination of Netscape's SSL. In basic functionality, the two are very similar; however, PCT has lower overheads than SSL and so is more efficient. PCT also supports a wider range of encryption algorithms. SSL uses the same algorithm for encryption as it does for authentication. Therefore, when it is exported from the United States, the authentication algorithm cannot be as strong as it can within the United States. PCT uses separate encryption and authentication algorithms, and because the export laws only apply to the encryption side, PCT can take advantage of full 128-bit algorithms for authentication.

TLS is being proposed as a future standard for this type of communication. It combines the robust features of SSL and the best extensions of PCT.

Proxy Server

This chapter discusses Microsoft Proxy Server 2.0 with the main emphasis on the security aspects of the product. As a prerequisite for this discussion the reader should be aware of the general features of a firewall system and how data is passed between secure and nonsecure interfaces.

This chapter concentrates on the security aspects of the Proxy Server and does not include installation instructions, which are available in the product documentation.

Introduction

Microsoft Proxy Server 2.0 is a firewall package that also provides data caching facilities. It is most commonly interposed between your private network and any external networks (Internet) to protect your internal environment from unauthorized access while adding the benefit of increased efficiency for external data requests with its caching feature.

Proxy Server allows configurable Internet access from your private network while offering a fully configurable set of security parameters to protect your internal networks from outside access. Inbound access can be completely closed off or it can be opened up under strict controls and subject to imposed rules.

Caching allows frequently requested Internet data to be stored locally so that users receive the information faster and with fewer visits to external sites.

In this chapter we will concentrate on the firewall aspects of Proxy Server which provide the necessary security services.

Microsoft Proxy Server 2.0 is administered using Internet Information Server as a host for the administrative tools. Internet Information Server runs as a snap-in to the Microsoft Management Console. See Chapter Ten, *Microsoft Management Console,* for more information on this host platform package.

Proxy Server security is closely linked with IIS security, and both applications need to be configured to properly control user access to the Internet and external partner sites.

Services Overview

Proxy Server is made up of three distinct system services.

- **Socks Proxy**—This service provides a means of securing communications between two nodes, independently of platform type. The service supports Socks version 4.3a and part of the TCP/IP protocol suite. UDP-based applications and the IPX/SPX protocol are not supported. The Socks Proxy service is dependent on the Web Proxy service being started.

- **Web Proxy**—This service provides HTTP, FTP, and Gopher connectivity for TCP/IP nodes on your network.

- **Winsock Proxy**—This service provides support for applications based on Windows Sockets and supports both TCP/IP and IPX/SPX protocols. Winsock Proxy allows client-side authentication, using Windows NT challenge/response authentication.

The three system services are administered from the IIS snap-in tool, as shown in Figure 7.1.

The Default Web Site node in the scope pane is not part of the Proxy Server installation and is not covered here.

Benefits of Proxy Server

Microsoft Proxy Server can bring many benefits to your LAN environment if you intend to connect to external services such as the Internet. The benefits discussed below revolve around security. Proxy Server provides many other benefits that are not discussed here.

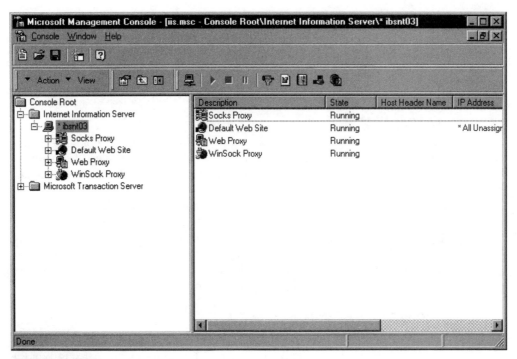

FIGURE 7.1   IIS node in the scope pane with the three Proxy Server system service nodes

Single External Contact Point

Microsoft Proxy Server sits between your internal network and external network. There is an obvious clue in the product name as to the base functionality and purpose of this tool. A proxy is defined as a person authorized to act on behalf of someone else. The proxy in this case acts on behalf of clients on the internal network.

One of the benefits of this approach in a properly configured proxy design is that only the one external interface is revealed to the outside world. Any attack on your network from an external source must now come through this one heavily fortified interface. Knowing where the only external point of entry is allows you to concentrate efforts in preventing the breakdown of this one defense.

The installation of Proxy Server does not mean that you can discard all other protective measures. It merely concentrates the point of attack from an external source in this one area. It relies on a well-designed proxy setup with no "backdoor" entries.

Concealing Internal IP Addresses

Following from the single point of contact mentioned above is the fact that the only IP addresses visible to the external world are the addresses belonging to the Proxy Server (when IP forwarding is switched off). Again, this limits the scope for spoofing attacks from external sources.

Packet Filtering

Packet filtering is a method of looking at the incoming or outgoing data on a packet level and comparing the results to a set of defined rules. If a match is made between the data packet and a defined rule, the specified action is taken.

Proxy Server allows dynamic packet filtering to take place, using packet type and ports as the main comparison item. Packets can be enabled or disabled for different packet types, different ports, or combinations of both. The dynamic element of the packet filtering means that a port is only opened after the filtering rules have been checked and the packet is deemed to be OK. The port is closed whenever it is not in use, thus limiting the chances of an attacker using an open port for entry.

Protection of Published Data

When using IIS for Web publishing, you could run the risk of opening up your local network to outside influences. This could mean that you build a separate publishing network to your own internal network. Proxy Server allows you to publish from your own internal network while securing the data and network from unauthorized access.

Reverse Proxy impersonates the internal Web server so that the external users do not make contact directly with your internal nodes. This protection is a follow-on from the single point of contact provided to your internal network by Proxy Server.

Administering Proxy Server

Microsoft Proxy Server is administered through the Internet Information Server MMC snap-in to provide an interface to the three proxy services supported by the product. To start an administration console for the Proxy Server, follow these steps.

1. Select **Programs** from the **Start** menu.
2. Select **Microsoft Proxy Server** > **Microsoft Management Console** to open the IIS console for administering the Proxy Server.
3. Expand **Internet Information Server** in the scope pane.
4. Double-click the Proxy Server machine name in the scope pane. The resulting view can be seen in Figure 7.1 in the *Services Overview* section.

The results pane shows the installed IIS options as well as the three defined proxy services. The State column shows whether the individual services are started or stopped. Any work that needs to be carried out on the proxy services can be done through the context-sensitive menus for each of the services. This includes stopping and starting the services. For further details on Proxy Server administration, see the product documentation.

Permissions

Once the Proxy Server is installed on your Windows NT 4.0 server, you will need to configure permissions for users and groups to use the system services associated with the Proxy Server. The Web Proxy permissions are set similarly to setting Winsock Proxy permissions, but each one must be set separately.

A firm recommendation is to use User Manager (for Domains) to create groups of users to apply these permissions to. You should avoid configuring individual user rights when possible. Follow these instructions to open the permissions dialog screen for the any of the three proxy services.

1. Start the Proxy Server management console (IIS) as described in the *Administering Proxy Server* section.
2. For Web and Winsock Proxy service permissions, right-click **XXX Proxy** in the scope pane; **XXX** is either **Web** or **Winsock**.

   or

   For Socks Proxy service permissions, right-click **Socks Proxy** in the scope pane.
3. Select **Properties**.
4. Select the **Permissions** tab. Figures 7.2, 7.3, and 7.4 show the resulting screen for the Web Proxy service, Winsock Proxy service, and the Socks Proxy service, respectively.

Web Proxy

The *Grant access to* box is empty by default. The *Protocol* dropdown list contains four available protocols for this service.

- **FTP Read.** Standard FTP client-side protocol.
- **Gopher.** Standard Gopher protocol.
- **Secure.** This protocol facilitates secure communications channels using SSL but cannot be used for HTTPS. This protocol is reserved for protocols using all secure ports except port 443.
- **WWW.** Web browser protocols (HTTP and HTTPS). This protocol gives access to the HTTP protocol and its secure version HTTPS.

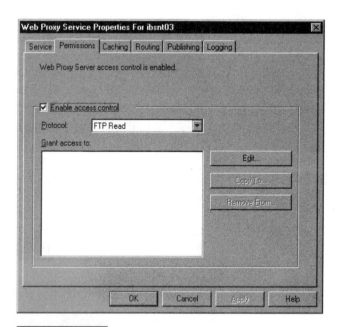

FIGURE 7.2 The permissions screen for the Web Proxy service

FIGURE 7.3 The permissions screen for the Winsock Proxy service

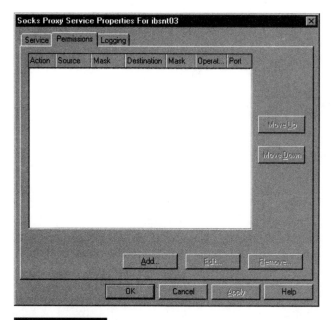

FIGURE 7.4 The permissions screen for the Socks Proxy service

The *Enable access control* check box is selected by default, and the scope of this check box is all protocols. This means that all four protocols are subject to access restrictions as configured in this section. No Web access is allowed through the Proxy Server by default—the *Enable access control* check box is marked and the *Grant access to* list is empty.

ADDING USERS TO SINGLE PROTOCOLS

Follow these instructions to add permissions to the local administrators group for the WWW protocol only.

1. Select **WWW** from the **Protocols**.
2. Ensure that the **Enable access controls** check box is selected.
3. Select the **Edit** button.
4. Select **Add**.
5. Select the Administrators group.
6. Select **Add**. The **Type of Access** is always **Full Access** for this protocol.
7. Select **OK**.
8. Select **OK** to confirm. The Administrators group appears in the **Grant access to** box.
9. Select **OK** to exit the **Properties** dialog screen.

REMOVING USERS FROM SINGLE PROTOCOLS

Removing users from a protocol is similar to adding them.

1. Follow steps 1 through 3 above.
2. Highlight the user or group you wish to remove.
3. Select **Remove**.
4. Select **OK** to confirm.
5. Select **OK** to exit the **Properties** dialog screen.

ADDING OR REMOVING USERS FROM MULTIPLE PROTOCOLS

1. Select **WWW** from the **Protocols**.
2. Ensure that the **Enable access controls** check box is selected.
3. Select the Administrators group in the **Grant access to** box. The **Copy To** and **Remove From** buttons become available.
4. Select either the **Copy To** or the **Remove From** button. Figure 7.5 shows the resulting dialog box, which is the same regardless of the choice made.
5. Select the target protocol(s). Hold the <Ctrl> key down to select multiple protocols.
6. Select **OK**. The permissions are copied to or removed from the target protocols.
7. Select **OK** to save the permissions changes and exit the **Properties** dialog screen.

Winsock Proxy

The permissions structure for the Winsock Proxy service is similar to that of the Web Proxy service. The *Grant access to* box is empty by default. The *Protocol* drop-down list contains the more than 30 default protocols available for this service. Protocols can be added to this list with the *Protocols* tab in the *Winsock Proxy Services Properties* sheet. The default protocols defined are:

- **AlphaWorld**
- **AOL**
- **Archie**
- **DNS**
- **Echo (TCP)**
- **Echo (UDP)**
- **Enliven**
- **Finger**
- **FTP**

- **Gopher**
- **HTTP**
- **HTTP-S**
- **ICQ**
- **IMAP4**
- **IRC**
- **LDAP**
- **MS NetShow**
- **MSN**
- **Net2Phone**
- **Net2Phone Registration**
- **NNTP**
- **POP3**
- **Real Audio (7070)**
- **Real Audio (7075)**
- **SMTP (client)**
- **Telnet**
- **Time (TCP)**
- **VDOLive**
- **VXtreme**
- **WhoIs**

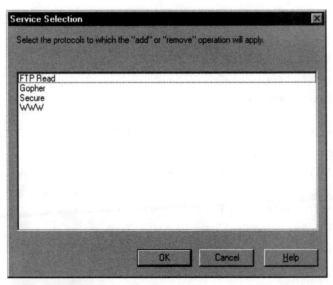

| FIGURE 7.5 | Dialog box for adding or removing users from protocol permissions |

The *Enable access control* check box is selected by default; the scope of this check box is all protocols. No access is allowed through the Winsock Proxy service by default as the *Enable access control* check box is marked and the *Grant access to* list is empty.

ADDING USERS TO SINGLE PROTOCOLS

Follow these instructions to add permissions to the local administrators group for the Telnet protocol.

1. Select **Telnet** from the **Protocols**.
2. Ensure that the **Enable access controls** check box is selected.
3. Select the **Edit** button.
4. Select **Add**.
5. Select the Administrators group.
6. Select **Add**. The **Type of Access** is always **Access** for this protocol.
7. Select **OK**.
8. Select **OK** to confirm. The Administrators group appears in the **Grant access to** box.
9. Select **OK** to exit the **Properties** dialog screen.

REMOVING USERS FROM SINGLE PROTOCOLS

Removing users from a protocol is similar to adding them.

1. Follow steps 1 through 3 above.
2. Highlight the user or group to remove.
3. Select **Remove**.
4. Select **OK** to confirm.
5. Select **OK** to exit the **Properties** dialog screen.

ADDING OR REMOVING USERS FROM MULTIPLE PROTOCOLS

1. Select **Telnet** from the **Protocols**.
2. Ensure that the **Enable access controls** check box is selected.
3. Select the Administrators group in the **Grant access to** box. The **Copy To** and **Remove From** buttons become available.
4. Select either the **Copy To** or the **Remove From** button.
5. Select the target protocol(s). Hold the <Ctrl> key down to select multiple protocols.

6. Select **OK**. The permissions are copied to or removed from the target protocols.

7. Select **OK** to save the permissions changes and exit the **Properties** dialog screen.

As you can see from the example above, the Web Proxy permissions and the Winsock Proxy permissions are set in a similar fashion with only the number of available protocols being the difference in the two.

DEFINING A NEW PROTOCOL

The Winsock Proxy service enables you to define new protocols to fit your specific needs. In the following example, you will define a new protocol called Inbound Telnet. This protocol allows incoming Telnet access through the Winsock Proxy service for a specific user or group of users. The predefined protocol called Telnet allows outbound initiated connections only. The permissions can be set according to the procedures shown above once the new protocol is defined.

1. Right-click **Winsock Proxy** in the scope pane.

2. Select **Properties**.

3. Select the **Protocols** tab. Figure 7.6 shows the resulting screen.

4. Select the **Add** button.

5. Enter **Inbound Telnet** as the **Protocol name**.

6. Enter **23** as the **Initial connection** port number.

7. Select **TCP** as the protocol **Type**.

8. Select **Inbound** as the **Direction**.

9. Select **OK**.

The new protocol is added to the list of available protocols. Permissions can now be assigned for this protocol to a specific set of users, as shown in the previous section.

UNLIMITED ACCESS PROTOCOL

One of the predefined protocols in the Winsock Proxy service is the Unlimited Access protocol. This is a special protocol that gives a user or group of users complete access through the Winsock Proxy to all protocols and ports whether they are listed in the Protocols section or not. This gives the target user(s) permission to use the Winsock Proxy to its fullest extent, so take care when setting up users with this protocol.

FIGURE 7.6 The Protocols tab of the Winsock Proxy server node

Socks Proxy

Socks Proxy permissions are completely different from those shown in the previous two sections. A Socks Proxy service works on the principle of matching packets against a rule table. The rules are based on source and destination IP address/subnet mask combinations and port numbers.

The rule table used to define Socks permissions is ordered with an entry for source address, destination address, port number, and the action for a match (Permit or Deny). The minimum entry for a rule in this table is for a source and action for a match. The example below adds a sample rule to this table.

1. Right-click **Socks Proxy** in the scope pane.
2. Select **Properties**.
3. Select the **Permissions** tab. The rule table is blank by default.
4. Select **Add**. Figure 7.7 shows the resulting **Socks Permission** screen.
5. Select the **Action** that should be taken if a match occurs. The options are **Permit** and **Deny**.

6. Enter a meaningful comment for this rule.

7. Select a **Source** address. This can be an individual IP address and mask, all addresses, or a domain.

8. Enter a **Destination** if required. Again this can be an individual IP address and mask, all addresses, or a domain name. If none is supplied, then all addresses match the rule.

9. Enter the **Port** rules as described below.

10. Select **OK**.

The new rule is added to the Permissions table. Permissions can be ordered using the *Move Up* and *Move Down* buttons on the *Properties* screen. When a request arrives at the Socks Proxy service, it is checked against the rules table and action is taken according to the first rule in the list that matches the request. If the request does not match any rule in the list (or if the rule list is empty), the request is denied automatically.

PORT RULES

The rules for defining port matches contain six possible tests that can be applied to a port number or service name.

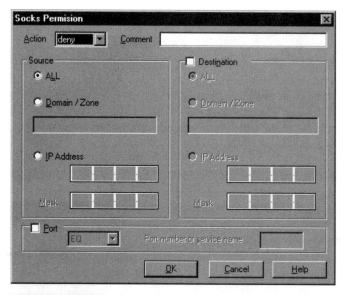

FIGURE 7.7   The Socks Permission dialog requires at least the Action and Source field entries

- **EQ.** This test returns a value of True if the port number in the request is equal to the port number in the rule.

- **NEQ.** This test returns a value of True if the port number in the request is NOT equal to the port number in the rule.

- **GT.** This test returns a value of True if the port number in the request is greater than the port number in the rule.

- **LT.** This test returns a value of True if the port number in the request is less than the port number in the rule.

- **GE.** This test returns a value of True if the port number in the request is greater than or equal to the port number in the rule.

- **LE.** This test returns a value of True if the port number in the request is less than or equal to the port number in the rule.

Packet Filtering

One of the best features of Microsoft Proxy Server is the ability to filter packets both inbound and outbound so as to provide a fine-grained level of control over the data passing through the Proxy Server.

Unlike the permissions on the Proxy services, which need to be configured individually, packet filtering is configured on a Proxy Server basis and applies to all three services equally.

Packet filtering is enabled on the external interfaces of a Proxy Server. Internal interfaces are not controlled by packet filtering. The Proxy Server must have at least one external interface enabled (or Auto-Dial set for a dial-out connection) before packet filtering can be enabled and configured.

Packet filtering works by intercepting inbound packets before they are passed on to a proxy service or the internal network. Packet filtering can use both static and dynamic filtering methods to determine which packets are directed to the internal service or network. This takes some of the onus away from the administrator, who may have had to unbind specific unused services from the external adapters to protect the internal network. Now the dynamic filtering takes care of this procedure by only opening specific ports when they are requested for use and by tearing down the connection and closing ports immediately after usage has finished.

It is important to understand that packet filtering works on a denial-first basis. Packet filtering is disabled by default. When it is enabled, it effectively blocks *all* packets except those in the exceptions list. If no exception exists for a particular port or protocol, then the port or protocol is disabled once packet filtering is enabled.

Enabling Packet Filtering

Packet filtering is disabled by default for all server services. It is enabled and configured for all three services at the same time. When a change is made to packet filtering for any one service, that change is automatically propagated to the other two services. Follow the instructions below to enable packet filtering for Winsock Proxy, Web Proxy, and Socks Proxy.

1. Start the **Proxy Server management console (IIS)** as described in the *Administering Proxy Server* section.

2. Right-click any of the **XXX Proxy** entries in the scope pane; **XXX** is **Socks**, **Web,** or **Winsock**.

3. Select the **Security** button in the **Shared services** box. Figure 7.8 shows the resulting Security dialog box.

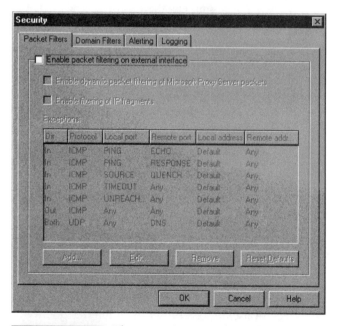

FIGURE 7.8   The same Security dialog box for all three proxy services

4. Place a check mark in the **Enable packet filtering on external interface** check box to allow the remainder of the screen to be accessed. Note that dynamic filtering is automatically selected when you do this.

5. Place a check mark in the **Enable filtering of IP fragments** check box.

The instructions outlined above enable packet filtering, with the default settings plus the filtering of IP fragments, for all three proxy services. Any one of the three services can be used to enable packet filtering and to make amendments to the settings described in this section. Packet filtering is part of the Shared Services setup facility supported by Proxy Server.

Packet filtering can only be enabled on external interfaces on the Proxy Server. There can be multiple external interfaces, and the packet filtering settings apply equally to all of them.

The *Enable filtering of IP fragments* setting allows you to filter packets that have been known to be used to facilitate spoof attacks and frag attacks on systems. This setting provides a formidable barrier against these types of attacks.

At this point, only packets and datagrams that match the filtering exceptions list will be allowed in or out of the Proxy Server. The next stage is to build up a list of exception entries that allow your users to get through the Proxy Server, using just the protocols and ports that are strictly necessary for the users to do so.

Adding a Predefined Exception Rule

The *Exceptions* list shown grayed-out in Figure 7.8 shows a list of predefined exceptions to the Deny All rule that have been enabled by default. These govern the actions of the packet filtering module of Proxy Server. An exception rule is made up of the following six entries.

- **Direction.** This can be set to In, Out, or Both. It refers to the direction of travel when arriving at the external interface.
- **Protocol.** The entry here refers to the transport protocol used by the packet or datagram.
- **Local Port.** This refers to the local service port used for communications for a particular transport protocol.
- **Remote Port.** This refers to the remote service port used for communications for a particular transport protocol.
- **Local Address.** This is usually set to Default referring to the Proxy Server itself. It can be set to an internal address if your design requires.
- **Remote Address.** This refers to the external Internet addresses that the Proxy Server can communicate with.

There are more predefined rules that are not enabled in this list. Follow the instructions below to add a predefined rule to the exceptions list to allow outbound HTTP and HTTPS access to all Internet destinations.

1. Enable packet filtering as shown in the *Enable Packet Filtering* section.
2. Select the **Add** button to display the Packet Filter Properties screen, shown in Figure 7.9.

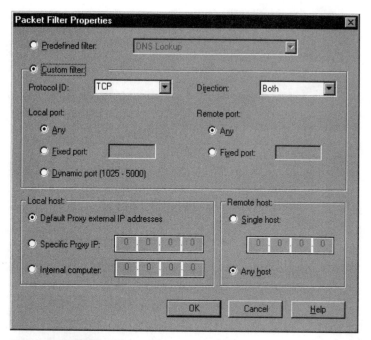

FIGURE 7.9   The same Packet Filter Properties screen for all three Proxy services

3. Select the **Predefined filter** radio button.

4. Scroll down the drop-down list of filters and select **HTTP Server (port 80).**

5. Leave the default setting for the **Local host** as **Default Proxy external IP addresses**.

6. Leave the default setting for the **Remote host** as **Any host**.

7. Select **OK**. The predefined filter has now been added to the exception list to enable *Inbound* HTTP protocol transport from any external address.

8. Repeat steps 2 through 7, choosing the **HTTPS Server (port 443)** from the drop-down filter list.

9. Select **OK**. The second predefined filter is added to the exceptions list. Figure 7.10 shows the exceptions list with the two predefined filters enabled.

The two additions to the exceptions table allow both HTTP and HTTPS communications inbound to the Proxy Server.

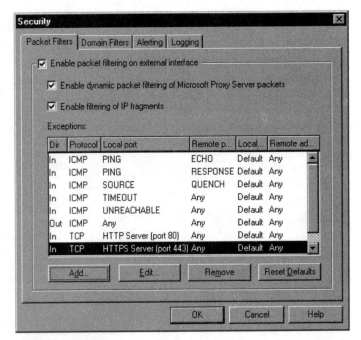

FIGURE 7.10   The predefined filters are now listed in the exceptions list allowing the Proxy Server to pass matching packets through

Creating a Custom Exception Rule

You can create custom exception rules to meet the needs of your particular environment. The many possible selections available for each section enable you to make extensive use of customized filter exceptions.

One reason to create a custom filter exception is if you have a cascaded Proxy Server design where packets are exchanged between Proxy Servers.

Remember that Proxy Servers can have many external interfaces. You may have one interface protecting your internal network from the Internet, while a second may be protecting your department from a more trusted business partner site. Different levels of filtering can be applied to the separate external interfaces (although filtering cannot be applied per user or group).

In the following example, we create a custom filter to enable all internal users to make any outgoing TCP transport requests on a specific external interface of the Proxy Server. This filter can be applied to the trusted external partner connection.

1. Enable packet filtering as described in the previous section.
2. Select the **Add** button. The Packet Filter Properties screen is displayed.

3. Select the **Custom filter** radio button.

4. In the **Protocol ID** box select **TCP**.

5. In the **Direction** box select **Out**.

6. Select the **Any** radio button for the **Local Port**.

7. Select the **Any** radio button for the **Remote port**.

8. Select the **Specific Proxy IP** radio button for the **Local Host**.

9. Enter the IP address of the external proxy interface connected to the trusted partner.

10. Select the **Any host** radio button for the **Remote host**.

11. Select **OK**. The new custom filter is added to the exceptions list.

Editing Existing Exception Rules

Custom filters and predefined filters can be edited once they are placed in the exceptions list. Predefined filters limit the editing options available, depending on the individual filter. Custom filters can have any setting changed.

To make changes to a filter in the exceptions list, simply highlight the required filter and select the **Edit** button. The same dialog box for adding filters is used for editing them.

Removing Exception Rules

You can remove filters from the exceptions list by simply highlighting the required filter and selecting the Remove button. No confirmation is requested for this action.

Reset Defaults

The Reset Defaults button situated below the Exceptions list resets the exceptions list entries to match those of the default installation. In most cases, the default packet filter settings, once you have enabled them in the Security dialog box shown in Figure 7.8, provide adequate protection for an internal network as long as there is only the one Proxy Server and no other communication-oriented applications are run on the Proxy Server machine.

Domain Filtering

Domain filters either grant access from your internal network to selected external sites or deny access from the internal network to selected external sites. The filters define the target site and can be set for single IP addresses, an IP subnet or a domain. The procedures for either denying access or granting access are similar for both Web and Winsock services.

Granting or denying access to external sites by using the Web and Winsock Proxy services is a matter of finding the correct direction to approach from.

If you have more sites that you wish to grant access to than deny, you should grant all access and then list the exception sites to which access will be denied.

If you have more sites that you wish to deny access to than grant access to, you should deny access to all sites and then enter a list of exceptions to which access is granted.

Once you have created an exception list, you can remove or change entries using the Remove and Edit buttons on the dialog screen.

Granting Access: Web and Winsock Services

When you first configure domain filtering, the exceptions list is empty and the Granted radio button is selected. This setting allows access to all external sites. Follow the instructions below to grant access to the Microsoft Web site for all users on your internal network and to deny access to all other destinations.

1. Start the **Proxy Server management console (IIS)** as described in the section *Administering Proxy Server*.

2. Right-click one of the **XXX Proxy** entries in the scope pane; **XXX** is either **Web** or **Winsock**. Note that the domain filters for the Socks service are defined in the Socks Permissions dialog screen. Instructions for this procedure can be found later in this section.

3. Select the **Security** button in the **Shared services** box.

4. Select the **Domain Filters** tab. Figure 7.11 shows the resulting screen.

5. Ensure that the **Enable filtering** check box is selected. The list of filters is empty by default.

6. Select the **Denied** radio button. With an empty exceptions list, this means that access to all external sites is now denied for all internal users.

7. Select **Add** to add an exception to the *All Denied* rule that you have just set.

8. Select the **Domain** radio button.

9. Enter the domain name www.microsoft.com. Figure 7.12 shows the resulting exceptions list.

10. Select **OK** to save the changes.

The other two available options for this entry are *Single computer* or *Group of computers*. These are defined by a single IP address or an IP address and Subnet Mask combination respectively.

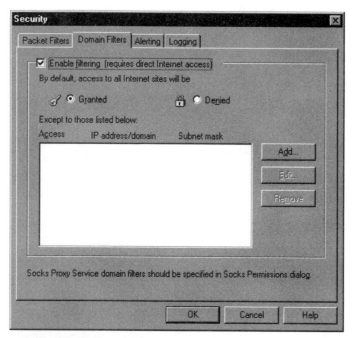

FIGURE 7.11 Domain filters set to either Grant or Deny access to external sites

When granting or denying access to Internet sites by using the Winsock Proxy service, you should create a filter for both the domain name of the site and the IP address of the site. The way in which Winsock Proxy converts domain names to IP addresses before attempting connections requires these two filters.

Denying Access: Web and Winsock Services

Denying access to sites is similar to granting access, as in the example above. When denying access, you first grant all access to sites, following the steps 1 through 5 in the example above. At step 6 you simply select the **Granted** radio button instead of the **Denied** button. Once access is granted to all sites, follow the remainder of the instructions shown above to create a list of exceptions to the *Grant All* rule.

Domain Filtering with Socks Proxy

The procedures for adding domain filters for a Socks Proxy service are the same as those covered in *Permissions* section earlier in this chapter. All Socks access is governed by the same rule table, so domain filtering can be achieved through the Permissions procedure.

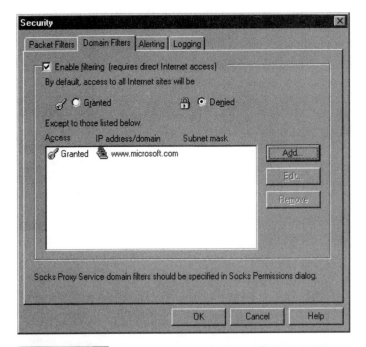

FIGURE 7.12 Adding exceptions to the Grant All or Deny All rule

Alerting

Certain types of events that may harm your system or prevent it from working correctly can be monitored, and alerts can be generated to warn you that these events are taking place. The alerts can be sent to a mail system or logged in the Windows NT Event log. You can switch off alerting for any or all of the alerting categories, but doing so could severely limit your view of what is going on with your Proxy Server and is not recommended.

Event alerting can only be set if packet filtering is first enabled and configured. Three categories of events can be tracked with this packet filtering.

- **Rejected Packets.** This alert is generated after the rejected packets count reaches a certain value and can be used to detect possible system attacks.

- **Protocol Violations.** This alert is used to watch the external interfaces for recognizable packets that could be potentially malicious.

- **Disk Full.** This is a simple alert for full disk systems.

Rejected Packets

Alerts are generated under this category when a threshold setting that tracks the number of rejected packets is passed. This can be a useful indicator for attempted attacks on your network. The rejected packet count includes all rejected packets regardless of which rule may have been applied to drop the packet. Follow the procedure set out below to enable alerting for rejected packets.

1. Start the **Proxy Server management console (IIS)** as described in the section *Administering Proxy Server*.
2. Right-click any of the **XXX Proxy** entries in the scope pane; **XXX** is **Web**, **Winsock**, or **Socks**. Alerting is set for all three proxy services at the same time.
3. Select the **Security** button in the **Shared services** box.
4. Select the **Alerting** tab. Figure 7.13 shows the resulting screen.
5. From the **Event** drop-down list, select **Rejected packets**.

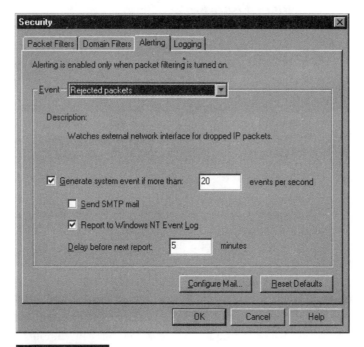

| **FIGURE 7.13** | The Alerting setup dialog box for packet rejection

6. Adjust the threshold setting from the default of 20 events per second to a figure that suits your environment. An event is logged when this threshold is reached. The default value is a good starting point for monitoring your network.

7. Place a check mark in the **Send SMTP mail** check box to send alerts by email. The configuration of this option is discussed below.

8. Place a check mark in the **Report to Windows NT Event Log** to place an alert message in the system log when the threshold is reached.

9. Adjust the figure, which is measured in minutes, in the box **Delay before next report** box to an appropriate value. Again, the default value is a good starting point. If you set this figure too low, then you may find that you have too many events trapped. Setting the figure too high may not record an accurate picture of an attempted attack.

10. Configure the email settings if required.

11. Select **OK**.

Protocol Violations

Alerts are generated here when the threshold for protocol violations, which is set by default at 1 event per second, is exceeded.

Microsoft Proxy Server can detect certain rejected packets as being potentially threatening. This setting allows you to generate an event whenever this very important threshold is exceeded. Follow the instructions below to enable alerting for this category.

1. Follow steps 1 through 4 in the *Rejected packets* section.

2. From the **Event** drop-down list, select **Protocol violations**. Figure 7.14 shows the resulting screen.

3. Adjust the threshold setting from the default of 1 event per second to a figure that suits your environment. An event is logged when this threshold is exceeded. Use the default value of 1 event per second unless you have a good operational reason to use another value.

4. Place a check mark in the **Send SMTP mail** check box to send alerts by email. The configuration of this option is discussed below.

5. Place a check mark in the **Report to Windows NT Event Log** to place an alert message in the system log when the threshold is reached.

6. Adjust the figure, which is measured in minutes, in the **Delay before next report** box to an appropriate value. Because this alerting category is often a direct warning about an attack on your network, do not exceed the default value of 1 minute between reports unless you have a good operational reason to do so.

7. Configure the email settings if required.

8. Select **OK**.

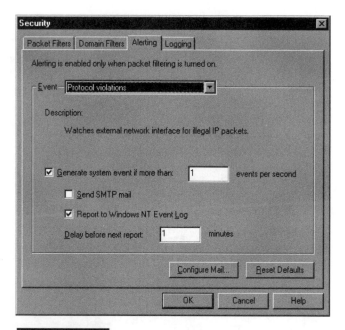

FIGURE 7.14 The Alerting setup dialog box for protocol violations

This category of alerts is an important early warning tool that should not be disabled unless it is completely unavoidable and you understand the ramifications completely.

Disk Full

As the name suggests, this category sends an alert when a failure is caused by a disk being full. Disk space should be monitored as an operational issue anyway, but this alerting category specifically tracks Proxy Server services and alerts when disk space affects a service. To enable this alerting category follow the steps outlined below.

1. Follow steps 1 through 4 in the *Rejected Packets* section.
2. From the **Event** drop-down list, select **Disk Full**. Figure 7.15 shows the resulting screen.
3. Retain the default setting of 1 event per second.
4. Place a check mark in the **Send SMTP mail** check box to send alerts by email. The configuration of this option is discussed below.
5. Place a check mark in the **Report to Windows NT Event Log** to place an alert message in the system log when the threshold is reached.
6. Adjust the figure, which is measured in minutes, in the **Delay before next report** box to an appropriate value for your network.

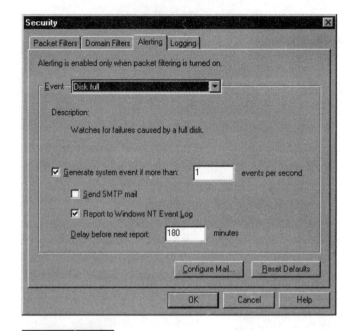

FIGURE 7.15 The Alerting setup dialog box for Disk Full errors

7. Configure the email settings if required.

8. Select **OK**.

Switching Off Alerting

Alerting can be turned off for any one of the three alerting categories. Microsoft Proxy Server is a security tool that protects your internal network against intrusion or attack from an external network. For this reason, alerting is a very important and integral part of the whole setup. Alerting should be enabled at all times when the external interfaces are connected to the Internet. For operational reasons or testing reasons, you may wish to disable alerting for one or more of the categories. Follow the instructions below to do this.

1. Start the **Proxy Server management console (IIS)** as described in the section *Administering Proxy Server*.

2. Right-click any of the **XXX Proxy** entries in the scope pane; **XXX** is **Web, Winsock**, or **Socks**. Alerting is set for all three proxy services at the same time.

3. Select the **Security** button in the **Shared services** box.

4. Select the **Alerting** tab.

5. From the **Event** drop-down list, select the category for which you wish to disable alerting.

6. Remove the check mark from the **Generate system event if more than** check box.

7. Select **OK**. Alerting for this one category is now disabled.

8. Repeat the steps above to disable either one or both of the remaining alerting categories.

Again it is worth stressing the importance of this feature, and if packet filtering is used, then alerting should be turned on whenever external interfaces are connected to the Internet.

Configuring Email

You can configure SMTP-compliant email as a means of notifying administrators or other staff members when an alert is generated. Note that email is only configurable for all alerting categories at the same time. Follow the instructions below to configure the email setting for alerting within Proxy Server.

1. Start the **Proxy Server management console (IIS)** as described in the section *Administering Proxy Server*.

2. Right-click any of the **XXX Proxy** entries in the scope pane; **XXX** is **Web, Winsock**, or **Socks**. Alerting is set for all three proxy services at the same time.

3. Select the **Security** button in the **Shared services** box.

4. Select the **Alerting** tab.

5. Ensure that the **Send SMTP mail** check box is selected.

6. Select **Configure Mail** to open the **Configure Mail Alerting** dialog box, as shown in Figure 7.16.

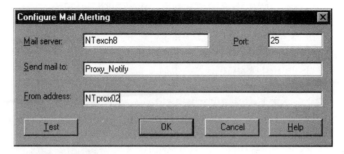

FIGURE 7.16 The Alerting configuration for the Configure Mail option

7. In the **Mail server** box, enter your mail server name.

8. In the **Port** box, enter a valid port number.

9. In the **Send mail to** box, enter a valid recipient address.

10. In the **From address** box, enter a valid address to be used by the Proxy Server for sending.

11. Select **OK**.

12. Select **OK** to confirm.

When configuring the email option for alerting, you should bear in mind that your own email system may have certain conditions that must be met before this option will work. For example, Microsoft Exchange will require the client to have a valid domain account before it can be used to send the alert emails. You should use your email client documentation in conjunction with the Proxy Server documentation to configure your email client properly.

When using the email interface ensure that you send the email to an internal address as opposed to an Internet address. Sending an alert on an external interface about a possible attack on that interface is not a very good idea.

Services Logging

Logging can be enabled on a services basis, which can track all access to your network using the three proxy services, or for packet filtering, which includes some of the alert information discussed in the previous section. Packet filter logging is discussed in the next section. Logging can be performed to a text file or ODBC-compliant database.

Logging is an integral part of the Proxy Server setup and should be enabled at all times. Logs should be reviewed regularly and discrepancies followed up. Disabling logging could mean that you leave yourself open to sustained attacks and provides an insecure defense. Think about using the *Stop service* functionality when a disk is full. This allows the services to be stopped when no more logging space is available. This is probably a better idea than to continue allowing the services to run with no logging facilities.

Services logging is available in *regular* mode or *verbose* mode. Regular mode can be used when disk space is at a premium and only the essential information can be stored. Verbose mode gives far more detail than regular mode and should be used if disk space is not a problem.

Windows NT Event Log

The Windows NT Event log is used to record events for the three system ser-vices: Winsock, Web, and Socks. The system Event log is used to record these events and can also be used to record packet filter events. The following list shows the source names recorded in the event log and which services the source name refers to.

- **MSProxyAdmin**—Refers to administrative events for the Proxy Server.
- **PacketFilterLog**—Refers to events generated by the packet filtering function of Proxy Server, as described in the *Alerting* section. This log source does not record packet filter events which are recorded in the individual proxy service log. Only packet filter alerts are recorded here.
- **SocksProxy**—Refers to events generated by the Socks Proxy service.
- **SocksProxyLog**—Refers to events generated by the logging actions of the Socks Proxy service.
- **WebProxyCache**—Refers to the caching events of the Web Proxy service.
- **WebProxyLog**—Refers to events generated by the logging actions of the Web Proxy service.
- **WebProxyServer**—Refers to events generated by the Web Proxy service.
- **WinsockProxy**—Refers to events generated by the Winsock Proxy service.
- **WinsockProxyLog**—Refers to events generated by the logging actions of the Winsock Proxy service.

Text File Logging

Text file logging is the default format used for all logging activities within Microsoft Proxy Server. This option allows logs to be automatically deleted after a set period of time by defining the number of old log files to keep.

Text file logs are kept in the `%Windir%\System32\Msplogs` directory by default and follow the format laid out below.

- **W3*filename*.log**—Used for the Web Proxy service.
- **WS*filename*.log**—Used for the Winsock Proxy service.
- **SP*filename*.log**—Used for the Socks Proxy service.

The *filename* portion of the name can vary depending on how the logging is set up. The following list shows the available options and when they are used.

- **yymmdd**—Used when the log file renewal is set to be daily. Year, month, and day settings are automatically entered.

- **Wyymmw**—Used when log file renewal is set to be weekly. The first character indicates that this is a weekly log. The **yy** refers to the year, the **mm** refers to the month, and the single **w** at the end holds a value between 1 and 5 inclusive to reference the week of the month.

- **Myymm**—Used when the log file renewal is set to be monthly. The first character indicates that this is a monthly log, and **yy** and **mm** refer to the year and month, respectively.

SETUP FOR TEXT FILE LOGGING

Logging is set up for each of the three proxy services individually. The procedures for configuring the logging parameters are the same for all three services. Follow the instructions below to configure logging for the Socks Proxy service.

1. Start the **Proxy Server management console (IIS)** as described in the section *Administering Proxy Server*.

2. Right-click the **Socks Proxy** entry in the scope pane.

3. Select the **Logging** tab.

4. Ensure that the **Enable logging using** check box is selected (default).

5. Select either **Regular** or **Verbose** from the **format** drop-down list.

6. In the **Log to file** section, select the new log file open frequency from the drop-down list. The available options are **daily**, **weekly**, and **monthly**.

7. If necessary, select the **Limit number of old log files to** check box and enter the appropriate number for the new log file frequency, for example, if the new log files are opened monthly, you may consider keeping 12 logs; if daily, you may decide to keep 360 logs.

8. Ensure that a check mark is placed in the **Stop services if disk full** check box.

9. Select a different log file directory if required.

10. Select **OK**.

The procedure for logging to text file for the other two proxy services is exactly the same (obviously apart from selecting the required service in step 2 above).

Database Logging

Microsoft Proxy Server can log to any ODBC-compliant database, including Microsoft Access and SQL Server. There is an extra overhead in system resources when logging to a database rather than to text files, although you do gain better control over querying and reporting.

One of the first steps to complete when you decide to log to a database is to install the database and the ODBC interface driver. Once the database is installed, you must create a Data Source Name (DSN) to be used to refer to the database and server on which it is installed. Appendix B contains a listing of the field entries in the database and a brief description of their contents.

Two sample database files are included with the Proxy Server installation. They are stored in the %Windir%\help\proxy\misc directory. One file, Msp.sql, is used as a template for the three proxy services. The other file, Pf.sql, is used as a template for the packet filtering database (the logging of which is discussed later in this section). These files can be used to create the databases, using the correct field definitions, before database logging can be started.

The procedures for installing the database product, creating the DSN, and building the database tables are beyond the scope of this book; consult the database product documentation for details on how to complete these tasks.

TABLE STRUCTURE

The same table is used for both regular and verbose logging for the three proxy services. The same table is also used regardless of whether the setting calls for regular or verbose logging. The only difference is in which fields are populated and which are not for regular logging. Table 7.1 lists the database fields and shows if they are used by regular, verbose, or both logging formats. The values in parentheses are the actual field names as defined in the database table.

SETUP FOR DATABASE LOGGING

The procedure for setting up logging to place data in a database is similar to that of text file logging. The instructions below describe the procedure for logging Web, Winsock, and Socks Proxy service events to a database. All Proxy Server service events are logged to the same table when using database logging, as opposed to the three services being split over separately configured text files when logging in this manner. Assumptions for this example are that you have already installed a database product and an ODBC driver and have built the necessary database table.

TABLE 7.1   ODBC database structure for services logging

Field Name (Literal Field Name)	Included in Regular Logging?	Included in Verbose Logging?
Authentication Status (ClientAuthenticate)		Yes
Bytes Received (BytesRecvd)		Yes
Bytes Sent (BytesSent)		Yes
Client Agent (ClientAgent)		Yes
Client Computer Name (ClientIP)	Yes	Yes
Client Platform (ClientPlatform)		Yes
Client User Name (ClientUserName)	Yes	Yes
Destination Address (DestHostIP)		Yes
Destination Name (DestHost)	Yes	Yes
Destination Port (DestHostPort)	Yes	Yes
Log Date (LogDate)	Yes	Yes
Log Time (LogTime)	Yes	Yes
Object MIME (MimeType)		Yes
Object Name (Uri)	Yes	Yes
Object Source (ObjectSource)	Yes	Yes
Operation (Operation)		Yes
Processing Time (ProcessingTime)		Yes
Protocol Name (Protocol)	Yes	Yes
Proxy Name (ServerName)		Yes
Referring Server Name (ReferredServer)		Yes
Result Code (ResultCode)	Yes	Yes
Service Name (Service)	Yes	Yes
Transport (Transport)		Yes

1. Start the **Proxy Server management console (IIS)** as described in the section *Administering Proxy Server*.
2. Right-click the **Socks Proxy** entry in the scope pane.
3. Select the **Logging** tab.
4. Ensure that the **Enable logging using** check box is selected (default).

5. Select either **Regular** or **Verbose** from the **format** drop-down list.

6. Select the **Log to SQL/ODBC database** radio button.

7. Enter the **DSN** name that you have already created.

8. Enter the **Table** name that has been defined for the Services logging.

9. Enter a valid **User name** and **Password** combination for the database. Figure 7.17 below shows the completed dialog box for database logging.

10. Select **OK**.

Packet Filter Logging

As discussed in the previous section, logging can be enabled on a services basis or for packet filtering. As with services logging, packet filter logging can be performed to a text file or ODBC-compliant database.

Packet filter logging is available in r*egular* mode or v*erbose* mode. Regular mode can be used when disk space is at a premium and only the essential information can be stored. Verbose mode gives far more detail than regular mode and should be used if disk space is not a problem.

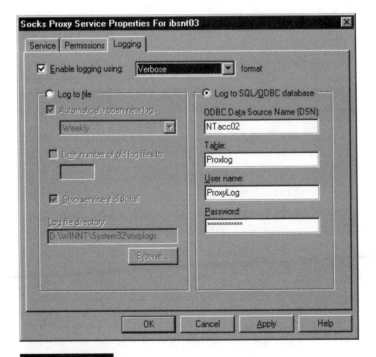

FIGURE 7.17   Database logging for all three proxy services

Text File Logging

Text file logging is the default format used for all logging activities within Microsoft Proxy Server. This option allows logs to be automatically deleted after a set period of time by defining the number of old log files to keep.

Text file logs are kept in the %Windir%\System32\Msplogs directory along with the Services log files; the file name format is similar. The file PF*filename*.log is used for the Packet Filter alerts.

The *filename* portion of the name can vary depending on how the logging is set up. The following list shows the available options and when they are used.

- **yymmdd**—Used when the log file renewal is set to be daily. Year, month, and day settings are automatically entered.

- **Wyymmw**—Used when log file renewal is set to be weekly. The first character indicates that this is a weekly log. The **yy** refers to the year, the **mm** refers to the month, and the single **w** at the end holds a value between 1 and 5 inclusive to reference the week of the month.

- **Myymm**—Used when the log file renewal is set to be monthly. The first character indicates that this is a monthly log, and **yy** and **mm** refer to the year and month, respectively.

SETUP FOR PACKET FILTER LOGGING (TEXT FILES)

When you configure text file logging for packet filtering the configuration is applied to all three services at the same time. You can use any one of the services to configure the settings. The procedure below used the Socks Proxy service to configure text file logging for packet filtering.

1. Start the **Proxy Server management console (IIS)** as described in the section *Administering Proxy Server*.
2. Right-click the **Socks Proxy** entry in the scope pane.
3. Select the **Security** button.
4. Select the **Logging** tab.
5. Ensure that the **Enable logging using** check box is selected (default).
6. Select either **Regular** or **Verbose** from the **format** drop-down list.
7. In the **Log to file** section, select the **new log file open frequency** from the drop-down list. The available options are **daily**, **weekly**, and **monthly**.
8. If necessary, select the **Limit number of old log files to** check box and enter the appropriate number for the new log file frequency.

9. Ensure that a check mark is placed in the **Stop services if disk full** check box.

10. Select a different log file directory if required.

11. Select **OK**.

This setting now controls the packet filter logging for all three proxy services.

Database Logging

Before proceeding with this section be sure that you have read the previous section on database logging for proxy services, which defines the requirements for the ODBC database. Appendix B contains a listing of the field entries in the database and a brief description of their contents.

TABLE STRUCTURE

The table structure for packet filter logging is shown in Table 7.2.

TABLE 7.2	ODBC database structure for packet filter logging
Literal Field Name	**Included in Regular Logging?**	**Included in Verbose Logging?**
DestinationAddress	Yes	Yes
DestinationPort	Yes	Yes
FilterRule	Yes	Yes
Interface	Yes	Yes
IPHeader		Yes
Payload		Yes
PFlogTime	Yes	Yes
Protocol	Yes	Yes
SourceAddress	Yes	Yes
SourcePort	Yes	Yes
TcpFlags		Yes

SETUP FOR PACKET FILTER LOGGING (DATABASE)

The following procedure enables packet filter logging to a database. Assumptions made for this example are that you have already installed a database product and an ODBC driver and have built the necessary database table.

1. Start the **Proxy Server management console (IIS)** as described in the section *Administering Proxy Server*.

2. Right-click the **Socks Proxy** entry in the scope pane.

3. Select the **Logging** tab.

4. Ensure that the **Enable logging using** check box is selected (default).

5. Select either **Regular** or **Verbose** from the **format** drop-down list.

6. Select the **Log to SQL/ODBC database** radio button.

7. Enter the **DSN** name that you have already created.

8. Enter the **Table** name that has been defined for the Services logging.

9. Enter a valid **User name** and **Password** combination for the database.

10. Select **OK**.

General Proxy Server Guidelines

The following are guidelines to securing your external interfaces with Microsoft Proxy Server. Not all of the recommended settings will fit every network design or external connectivity design, but you should think carefully before using Proxy Server without implementing all of the guidelines.

- **Retain dynamic packet filtering.** This feature is enabled by default when you enable packet filtering and should remain enabled. It protects your internal network by opening and closing ports only when needed, thus reducing the number of available opportunities for attack.

- **Censor the LAT table.** The Local Address Table should not contain any entries that refer to external interfaces. The addresses in the LAT are used to determine if the packets should be sent through the Proxy Server or directly to the address. Including an external address in the LAT could result in the Proxy Server being bypassed.

- **Remove client DNS settings.** DNS settings at the client can be used in conjunction with gateway settings to bypass the Proxy Server when accessing an external network. These settings should be removed on client installations and from DHCP servers so that they cannot be used for this purpose.

- **Disable IP forwarding.** IP forwarding should be disabled on your Proxy Server so that it cannot be used to relay packets between internal and external interfaces, bypassing the proxy services. IP forwarding is disabled from the TCP/IP Properties page on the Protocols tab in the Network applet of Control Panel. This setting can be enabled when installing certain packages including the routing and remote access service (R & RAS). If you install the service after Proxy Server is installed then you must manually disable IP forwarding again.

- **Restrain powerful accounts.** Limit the use of administrative accounts and other user accounts that could allow an attacker to gain a higher level of access than ordinary users. Powerful accounts should be actively blocked from gaining outside connectivity because of the risk of downloading malicious code which could operate in an administrative context on the internal network.

- **Disable unused system services.** Any system services that are not required should be disabled.

- **Unbind system services from external adapters.** System services such as the Server service can be unbound from the external adapters on the Proxy Server by means of the Networks applet in Control Panel. The fewer services interfacing with the external world the less chances of an attacker using one to gain access to the internal system.

- **Set minimum share permissions.** Share permissions should be set to the minimum needed (read-only recommended) if you require them to be available to external users.

- **Set access control.** Access control must be set in order for authentication levels to be set for the services.

- **Isolate the Proxy Server application.** The Proxy Server should only be used for this one purpose if at all possible. No other services or applications should be loaded on the same machine except for those required for this installation.

- **Deny unlimited access to Winsock Proxy.** Do not use this permissions setting for the Winsock Proxy service unless you absolutely have to and are certain that other restrictive controls (password length and complexity limits) are used.

- **Set Challenge and Response authentication for IIS.** If using IIS for hosting purposes, ensure that the authentication level is set to Challenge and Response to provide security when passing passwords over the Internet. You will need to use a browser that directly supports this form of authentication.

- **Disable RPC listening on external interfaces.** RPC listening uses ports 1024-1029 and should be disabled for external interfaces so that only the internal network can use the services.

The guidelines above were developed with the understanding that all other security-related recommendations that are not specific to Proxy Server are being adhered to. This includes strong password policies, good account policies enforcing password restrictions and account lockouts, user permissions only as needed, periodic reviews of security settings, and an audit policy with regular audit log checks.

Registry

In this chapter, step-by-step guides address the security concerns surrounding the Windows NT system registry. For both file system security and internal registry access, methods to customize protection to meet the needs of your environment are provided.

The system registry is a complicated set of database files that interact to perform many essential tasks on a Windows NT computer. Inadvertent changes in the registry can lead to serious system problems. The step-through guides in this chapter should be tested on nonproduction machines to make sure that your system configurations can benefit from them without harm.

People unfamiliar with the system registry should take steps to familiarize themselves with the structure and workings of this database before making any changes. This chapter focuses on security issues and presumes a high level of system familiarity on the part of the reader.

Introduction

The system registry is simply a collection of files that store information about system hardware, system software, registered applications, and users. The registry was designed as a replacement for older ways of tracking this information, such as with .INI files.

The registry lies at the heart of a Windows NT system. If hackers can get free access to the registry, then they have access to the system. If the registry is attacked successfully, then it may require a system installation to recover.

Securing the registry from both malicious attacks and from accidental damage must be a priority in the overall security of a Windows NT network.

Registry Structure

Files

The registry database files are stored by default in the `\Winnt\System32\Config` directory. Additional registry files exist for each user in the `\Winnt\Profiles` directory or on domain controllers for users with roaming profiles. The files that combine to make up the registry are listed below.

- `Default`
- `Sam`
- `Security`
- `Software`
- `System`
- `Userdiff`
- `NTuser.dat`

The only one of these files that you may decide to actively load into the registry editor and manipulate is the `NTuser.dat` file. The remainder of the files are loaded by the registry editor as needed and should not be interfered with individually.

NTFS FILE PERMISSIONS

The NTFS file permissions are set automatically on the `\Winnt\System32\Config` directory and its contents, as shown in Table 8.1 below.

It is important to make sure that the security does not vary from this setting. Unauthorized access to these files could lead to their being interfered with by use of third-party tools.

TABLE 8.1	Registry directory NTFS permissions
User/Group	**Permission**
Administrators	Full Control (All)(All)
Everyone	Read and Execute (RX)(RX)
System	Full Control (All)(All)

You might consider changing the Everyone group to the Users group to add an extra element of security. If you choose to do this, you must ensure that all users who wish to use the machine are included in the Users group.

Handle Keys

Handle keys are logical groupings of registry settings that are used to gather together keys in a manner that reflects functionality. These groupings do not reflect similar groupings in the registry files. Registry manipulation is accomplished with the handle key groupings, as opposed to the physical file structures discussed earlier. Five handle keys are available for Windows NT 4.0:

- HKEY_USERS
- HKEY_CLASSES_ROOT
- HKEY_CURRENT_USER
- HKEY_CURRENT_CONFIG
- HKEY_LOCAL_MACHINE

Although there are five available handle keys, only the first and last listed above are actually stored permanently on the NT machine.

HKEY_LOCAL_MACHINE

This handle key stores information pertinent to the machine on which it resides. Hardware configurations, software configurations, network shares, security settings, and logon validation information are all examples of the type of settings stored in this registry handle.

When the machine is started up, the HKEY_CLASSES_ROOT and the HKEY_CURRENT_CONFIG handle keys are created from information stored in the HKEY_LOCAL_MACHINE handle key. When the machine is shut down, the information in these handles is copied back into the master handle and they then cease to exist until they are created at the next reboot.

HKEY_USERS

This handle stores all relevant user information for the current authenticated user and the settings for the default user. Control Panel options, fonts and colors, desktop icons, and Start menu options are examples of the settings contained in this handle key.

The HKEY_CURRENT_USER handle is supplied by the information in this handle. HKEY_CURRENT_USER does not hold the default user information.

Subkeys

Handle keys contain several layers of subkeys. These subkeys are arranged in a hierarchical structure for ease of navigation.

Values

Keys can contain subkeys, values, or both. Values are the last child object in the hierarchy and contain the actual information needed to run the systems. There are many different types of values, which are intended to hold different types of data (e.g., REG_SZ is a text string value and REG_DWORD is a 32-bit hex, decimal, or binary value).

Registry Tree Permissions

The registry tree is protected by ACL permissions in the same way as the NTFS. The available permissions are slightly different from those of NTFS, however. Table 8.2 shows the available special access permissions along with a description of the effect this setting has on a registry key.

TABLE 8.2 Registry ACL special access permissions	
Identifier	**Meaning**
Query Value	Allows the user to read the values contained in a key.
Set Value	Allows the user to write a value to a key.
Create Subkeys	Allows the user to create a subkey.
Enumerate Subkeys	Allows the user to identify subkeys.
Notify	Allows the user to audit notification events from a key.
Create Link	Allows the user to create a symbolic link in a particular key.
Delete	Allows the user to delete a key.
Write DAC	Allows the user to write a Discretionary ACL to a key.
Write Owner	Allows the user to take ownership of a key.
Read Control	Allows the user to read a key's ACL.

The special access permissions shown in Table 8.2 above are grouped together in permission sets for convenience of use. These preconfigured sets are shown in Table 8.3.

Registry Editing Tools

There are two direct editing tools that can be used on a Windows NT 4.0 system.

Regedit.exe

This tool is well known as the registry editor for Windows 95/98. It is included in the Windows NT software because it has some extra features not included in the main NT registry editor, for example, more advanced search functionality and a keyname copy function.

TABLE 8.3	Registry ACL permission sets	
Name	**Permission Contents**	**User has this access**
Read	Query Value/Enumerate Subkeys/Notify/Read Control	The combined Special Access permissions of (QENR) give the user the ability to read the registry but not to make any changes at all.
Full Control	All Permissions	The combination of all permissions gives the user total control over the registry and all subkeys.
Special Access	-	The Special Access permission is made up of one or more of the selections from the previous table.

Regedit.exe does not allow security changes to be made to the registry on an NT machine and so is of little use in the context of this chapter.

Remember that the only compatibility between Windows NT registry and Windows 95/98 registries is the Regedit.exe tool. The format of the registries themselves is different and completely incompatible.

Regedt32.exe

The native NT registry editor is a much more powerful beast than the previously mentioned version. All registry security can be manipulated from here as well as changes to all allowable registry hives (which excludes the SAM and security hives that are edited through tools such as User Manager).

Regedt32.exe does lack some advanced functionality such as context menus and the ability to search data and values.

Care needs to be taken when using this tool, which can be set to commit changes instantly with no warning. Read-only mode is a must when using this tool.

Setting and Viewing Registry Permissions Directly

Registry permissions are set directly with the Regedt32.exe tool. "Directly" means that you can use the tool to apply permissions to different keys in the registry for users as you need to. This use is as opposed to the use of indirect editing tools such as the System Policy Editor or User Manager.

The following example shows you how to apply permissions to a registry key for a defined user. The first stage in the process is to add a dummy key to work with.

1. Select **Run** from the **Start** menu.

2. Enter **Regedt32.exe** and select **OK**.

3. Choose the required handle key from the Window menu. For this example, we are using HKEY_LOCAL_MACHINE.

4. Select the **SOFTWARE** key.

5. Select **Add Key** from the **Edit** menu. Figure 8.1 shows the Add Key dialog box.

6. Enter the keyname **TestSoft** and select **OK**.

| **FIGURE 8.1** | Adding a registry key with Regedt32.exe |

The new key has now been added to the registry as a subkey to SOFT-WARE. The next step is to change the permissions on the key. It does not matter that the key has no values or subkeys. The procedures are the same in all cases.

1. Select the **TestSoft** key.

2. Select **Permissions** from the **Security** menu.

3. Use the ACL editor to set permissions in the usual manner.

4. Select **OK**. Changes are committed instantly.

Setting and viewing permissions on the registry keys uses the same ACL editor that Explorer uses for NTFS permissions unless you have installed the Security Configuration Manager for NT 4.0, which replaces the NTFS ACL editor.

Auditing Activity on a Registry Key

Activity can be audited on registry keys as long as File and Object Access audit is turned on by the User Manager tool. See Chapter Nine, *NT Audit*, for more details on this procedure.

Follow these instructions to switch on auditing for the TestSoft registry key that was created in the earlier example.

1. Select the **TestSoft** key.

2. Select **Auditing** from the **Security** menu. The current values have been inherited from the parent key.

3. Select **Add** to add a user or group.

4. Select the user to audit and choose **Add**. In this case, the **Network** group is selected.

5. Select **OK**. Figure 8.2 shows the Registry Key Auditing dialog box with the new group added.

6. Select the events that you wish to audit and choose **OK** to confirm.

You use the *Audit Permission on Existing Subkeys* check box to propagate any changes made here down through subkeys of the current location. The audit events are recorded in the security Event log and can be viewed with event viewer. See Chapter Nine for more details on viewing audit events. Table 8.4 lists the available registry audit options and describes their usage.

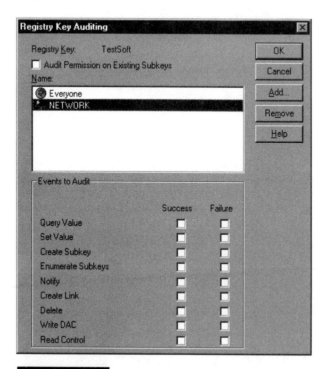

| **FIGURE 8.2** | Registry Key Auditing dialog box |

TABLE 8.4	Registry audit options
Identifier	**Usage**
Query Value	Audits activity that attempts to read a value entry from a registry key.
Set Value	Audits system activity that attempts to set value entries for a registry key.
Create Subkeys	Audits system activity that attempts to create a subkey from the audited key.
Enumerate Subkeys	Audits system activity that attempts to identify a subkey.
Notify	Audits notification events for the selected key.
Create Link	Audits system activity that attempts to create a symbolic link from the key.
Delete	Audits system activity that attempts to delete a key.
Write DAC	Audits system activity that attempts to write a discretionary ACL on a key.
Read Control	Audits system activity that attempts to read the ACL of a key.

Taking Ownership of a Registry Key

As with files and directories, the permissions setup of registry keys allows you to deny access to all users (either on purpose or by accident). You may find yourself in the situation where a registry key or set of subkeys is inaccessible. The only option left for you as an administrator is to take ownership of the keys so that you can then reset permissions.

For the following example, the TestSoft registry key has had permissions set so that the Administrator account has no rights to the key. The only user with permissions set on the key is TempUser1. Figure 8.3 shows the registry key grayed out for the current user (Administrator).

The registry key is only accessible by the one user. Permissions are stored as ACEs in the ACL of the registry key, and they represent the permitted user (TempUser1) as a SID entry.

Then, the user TempUser1 is deleted. Now there is no valid user with permissions to the registry key. Even a new user called TempUser1 is created, that user has a different SID and it is the SID that is stored as an entry in the ACL to grant permissions.

The way to recover the access permissions to this directory is to use the Owner selection in the Security menu of the Regedt32.exe program.

1. Log on as Administrator.

2. Start the **Regedt32.exe** program.

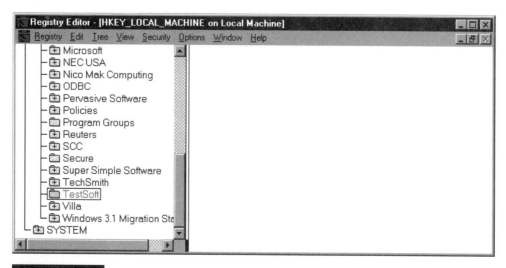

FIGURE 8.3   Registry key grayed out when access is denied

3. Select the **TestSoft** registry key.

4. Select the **Security** menu.

5. Select **Owner**. This step would show you the ownership of the registry key if you had permissions. A warning appears as shown in Figure 8.4 because you do not have permission to view ownership.

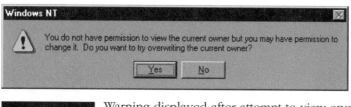

FIGURE 8.4   Warning displayed after attempt to view ownership without the correct permissions

6. Select **Yes**. You are offered the chance to take ownership of the directory. Figure 8.5 shows the Take Ownership dialog box.

7. Select **Take Ownership**.

The Administrator user is now the owner of the TestSoft registry key and can grant access as required.

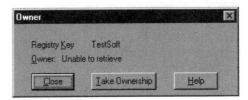

FIGURE 8.5 The Take Ownership dialog (to recover access to registry keys)

Security-Related Registry Settings

Whenever you decide to change permissions on registry keys or subtrees, be very careful. You must decide for yourself after considering the needs of your environment whether the suggested registry settings in this section will affect your systems adversely.

This section describes some of the more sensitive areas of the system registry along with default values, suggested amendments to these, and an explanation of each amendment.

Legal Notice at Logon

A notice at logon, which notifies both unauthorized and authorized users of company policy or warns about the consequences of misuse, may be part of your corporate policy or a way to dissuade "browsing" users from trying to enter a system that they shouldn't use. To set up this notice alter the two registry values shown below.

```
HKEY_LOCAL_MACHINE\Software\Microsoft\Windows NT\Current-
Version\Winlogon
```
       Value: `LegalNoticeCaption`
       Data Type: `REG_SZ`
       Setting: A caption to appear at the head of the notice

```
HKEY_LOCAL_MACHINE\Software\Microsoft\Windows NT\Current-
Version\Winlogon
```
       Value: `LegalNoticeText`
       Data Type: `REG_SZ`
       Setting: The text of the notice goes here

Event Log Access by Unauthenticated Users

The system and application Event logs are accessible by default by Guest and any unauthenticated users for Read. To prevent this access, add the two registry values shown below.

```
HKEY_LOCAL_MACHINE\System\CurrentControlSet\Services
\EventLog\System
      Value:        RestrictGuestAccess
      Data Type:    REG_DWORD
      Setting:      1


HKEY_LOCAL_MACHINE\System\CurrentControlSet\Services
\EventLog\Application
      Value:        RestrictGuestAccess
      Data Type:    REG_DWORD
      Setting:      1
```

The security Event log is not accessible by Guest or unauthenticated users by default.

Disable Registry Editors

The disabling of registry editors will only prevent the curious from running tools that you would rather they didn't. Many other tools exist to edit registry entries that are not blocked by this setting. However, protection from the curious is just as important as protection from malicious users. Set the key and value shown below to prevent the usual registry editing tools from running.

```
HKEY_CURRENT_USER\Software\Microsoft\Windows\CurrentVersion
\Policies\System
      Value:        DisableRegistryTools
      Data Type:    REG_DWORD
      Setting:      1
```

Remote Registry Editing

Windows NT allows the registry to be edited by means of the editor tools on a remote machine. The remote access is governed by standard NT security rules, including secondary logon authentication and ACL restrictions placed on the registry keys themselves. A local registry setting that denies access to the local registry editing tools could be circumvented by using remote access or by using a simple program that is not recognized by NT as a registry editor.

To restrict anonymous remote registry access (fixed as part of Service Pack 3), set the registry key as shown below.

```
HKEY_LOCAL_MACHINE\SYSTEM\CurrentControlSet\Control\LSA
     Value:        RestrictAnonymous
     Data Type:    REG_DWORD
     Setting:      1
```

To secure your machine from authenticated yet unwanted remote access, set the ACL on the key shown below to restrict the users that can use remote access entry to the registry. The ACL is used along with the ACL set for the registry keys that are accessed to determine if a user has permission.

```
HKEY_LOCAL_MACHINE\SYSTEM\CurrentControlSet\Control
\SecurPipesServers\Winreg
     Key ACL:      Administrators—Full Control
```

Prevent Print Driver Installations

Print drivers are used to move data on your network. A maliciously written print driver could be used to copy data or divert the prints. To prevent all users except administrators, print operators, and power users from installing new print drivers, set the registry key and value as shown below.

```
HKEY_LOCAL_MACHINE\System\CurrentControlSet\Control\Print
\Providers\LanMan Print Services\Services
     Value:        AddPrintDrivers
     Data Type:    REG_DWORD
     Setting:      1
```

Password Restrictions

By default, Windows NT does not place any password restrictions on your system. Account policies can be used to tighten security surrounding the logon process, but the choice of content for the password is ultimately left uncontrolled. Windows NT 4.0 ships with a `.DLL` file, called `Passfilt.dll`, which should reside in the `\Winnt\System32` directory and be read-only for all nonadministrative users. This password filter `.DLL` enforces certain restrictions to be placed on the password when it is changed by the user. These restrictions mean that the password must contain at least three out of the following four character sets.

- At least one uppercase letter
- At least one lowercase letter
- At least one digit
- At least one nonalphanumeric character

This `.DLL` file can be supported by or replaced by another `.DLL` file that enforces different rules. The `.DLL` files read the password as it is entered and so must come from a trusted source and must be protected within the system directory from interference. Set the registry key and value as shown below to enforce this option.

```
HKEY_LOCAL_MACHINE\System\CurrentControlSet\Control\Lsa
```
Value: Notification Packages
Data Type: REG_MULTI_SZ
Setting: PASSFILT

The registry value is a multiple-string data type that may already contain entries, so the PASSFILT file name should be placed on its own line in the multiple-contents list.

Windows NT can pass a password through to another operating system when a user is setting a password, so that the passwords can be synchronized on all systems. This is accomplished by means of the registry key shown above. A common example would be the Microsoft CSNW software using the FPNWCLNT.DLL file to interface with Novell NetWare. Again, the files listed in this registry key need to be trusted and protected: the very functionality supported here means that as passwords are entered, they are passed to this .DLL file so that they can be used on a NetWare system.

Removing POSIX and OS/2 Subsystems

POSIX and OS/2 subsystems are included in Windows NT for compatibility. If you do not use these subsystems, remove them from the system. The security risk is difficult to identify, but the removal of the subsystems is included in the C2 configuration program, so removing them is worthwhile. To remove the subsystems, delete the corresponding entries from the multiple-string registry value shown below.

```
HKEY_LOCAL_MACHINE\System\CurrentControlSet\Control
\Session Manager\Subsystems
```
Value: Optional
Data Type: REG_MULTI_SZ
Setting: Remove Os2 and Posix from list

Restrict Access to Floppies and CD-ROMs

You can limit access to both floppy drives and CD-ROM drives to the currently logged-on user so that the drives cannot be used remotely by third parties. To do this, set the two registry values shown below.

HKEY_LOCAL_MACHINE\Software\Microsoft\Windows NT\Current-
Version\Winlogon
    Value: AllocateCDroms
    Data Type: REG_SZ
    Setting: 1

HKEY_LOCAL_MACHINE\Software\Microsoft\Windows NT\Current-
Version\Winlogon
    Value: AllocateFloppies
    Data Type: REG_SZ
    Setting: 1

Last Logged-on Username Display

When a user logs on to a Windows NT machine, the default display settings reveal the name of the last logged-on user. This feature can give a potential hacker a helping hand by giving him the username half of the authentication combination. In most cases, this possibility is not considered to be a big risk because username transmission on the network is not encrypted and user names are not considered to be secret by most users. If you wish to implement this setting, set the registry key and value as shown below.

HKEY_LOCAL_MACHINE\Software\Microsoft\Windows NT\Current-
Version\Winlogon
    Value: DontDisplayLastUsername
    Data Type: REG_DWORD
    Setting: 1

NTuser.dat Registry File

The NTuser.dat (or NTuser.man on mandatory profiles) file holds registry entries for user profiles. All user profiles contain this file; it holds information that can be set through user profiles, which are normally stored in the system registry.

    This file can be loaded into the registry and the settings changed in the same way as the local registry files are amended. The procedures for editing these files are discussed in Chapter Four, *User Profiles*.

NT Audit

This chapter discusses the concepts involved in implementing a thorough and sustainable audit policy for NT networks.

The chapter takes you through processes from initial design of an audit policy, through implementation, to managing the defined policy and monitoring the captured audit events.

Introduction

An audit policy and a means of implementing and tracking the policy is a prerequisite of any networked operating system today. Client/server network systems have historically been lacking in their implementation of audit policies.

The first Microsoft operating system to contain a securable audit system was Windows NT 3.x. Since this first version of Windows NT the audit capabilities of networked operating systems have become more and more important.

Windows NT 4.0 contains audit features that give the administrator the opportunity to track systemwide events. Audit capabilities can be extended by means of an ODBC-compliant query language that can be used to provide reporting functionality.

Windows NT Audit Basics

Audit functionality can be divided into four main areas.

1. Audit policy design
2. Audit policy setup
3. Audit event capture setup
4. Event monitoring

Before looking at the various parts of audit setup and analysis, you should understand the extent of the auditing functionality on your system. What your chosen operating system can audit influences your overall audit design. The Microsoft Windows 4.0 event logging system is capable of tracking many security-related events. The audit functionality of Windows NT is made up of three distinct areas.

System Audit

System audit tracks system-related events. Examples of system audit events are a system service failing to start at boot time or a network adapter failing to bind with a protocol. These events affect the way in which your system operates, and the tracking of these events is done by the system itself. For instance, you cannot turn event logging off so that system services failing to start do not get logged. Although the events tracked by this log can be critical to the well-being of your system, they are not considered to be security settings and are not covered in detail here.

Application Audit

Application audit tracks events relevant to running applications. When programmers write applications to run on Windows NT, they should set their error traps to write information to the application Event log. This log provides a central repository for application event information. Examples of an entry in the application Event log are the following: an application tries unsuccessfully to access a memory space; a particularly complicated startup routine for an application logs the results of each startup phase so that failures can be tracked through the successful startup modules directly to the failure point. Application events are not covered in detail here.

Security Audit

Security audit is what we concentrate on in this chapter. Unlike the previous two audit event types, the security audit is configurable by the user. Security audit tracks security-related events throughout the system. Examples of security-related events are user logon/logoff, system startup/shutdown, object access, and use of privileges.

Windows NT Security Audit Capabilities

Microsoft Windows NT 4.0 can audit many security-related events. Table 9.1 outlines the types of events that can be tracked. There are two possible outcomes to all of the events that are logged: success and failure. You can choose to track either one or both of these possible outcomes for the events whose security you want to audit.

TABLE 9.1	Events tracked in the security Event log
Event Type	**Description**
Logon and Logoff	Tracks all user logon and logoff functions for the local system.
File and Object Access	Tracks access to files folders or printers set for auditing.
Use of User Rights	Tracks use of rights except those for logon and logoff.
User and Group Management	Tracks user and group management including creating, amending, and deleting.
Security Policy Changes	Tracks changes to the user rights policy or the audit policy.
Restart, Shutdown, and System	Tracks restart and shutdown of the computer. Also tracks changes to the security log.
Process Tracking	Tracks process creation through program activation.

Audit Policy Design

When you understand the capabilities of the security audit system, you can begin to design the audit policy that you wish to put in place. You can start the design by answering the questions below with regard to your own installation.

What to Audit

How many events you wish to audit is a very subjective question. The answer depends on what you need to keep trails for and why you need to keep them. The scenario outlined below shows various reasons for applying audit trails; that scenario will be used later in the chapter to enforce the audit policy design.

Whom to Audit

Certain sections of security auditing can be applied to individual users or groups of users, whereas other sections can only be turned on or off for everybody. An example of the latter would be logon and logoff auditing. The settings for this option are applied to all users of the machine, as opposed to file and object access audit, which is applied to individual users or groups.

People to whom you should apply audit tracking depends largely on your own circumstances and the type of audit tracking you are implementing. However, certain users should always be high up on the list of targets. Users with superior privileges, such as administrators or account operators should be selected so you can keep track of the use of these privileges.

When to Audit

When to audit can be an important part of the audit policy design. You may wish to track logon events during the night when few people should be logging on and not track the events during the day when thousands of users log on. Windows NT does not have a timing mechanism for allowing audit tracking like this. The nearest way to achieve the desired results is to track the events all of the time and then filter them when viewing or reporting on them.

When to Clear the Audit Log

Event logs can hold massive amounts of data if you choose to track many types of events. You must decide how long the information needs to be kept in the Event log and when to archive to event files.

Example Audit Scenario

- User logons need to be tracked. Your enterprise has no wish to know when individuals log on successfully but wishes to track failure to log on in case this is an indication of a potential hacker trying to break passwords.

- Application access. Your enterprise runs a particularly sensitive application that initiates cash payments. It is a requirement to track each occurrence of the application being started successfully as well as any failed attempts.

- Color printer usage. You wish to track use of an expensive color printer system to which everybody has access.

- Audit policy changes. It is always wise to track security policy changes so that any interference with security policy is also logged.

- Machine restarts and shutdowns. You wish to track system restarts and shutdowns on your server. You also wish to track attempted shutdowns even if they are not accomplished.

- User account manipulation. You wish to track all account management changes such as password changes, group membership, etc.

- The security audit logs must be cleared every 14 days and must be set to hold all tracked events generated in that time period. Every 14 days the security audit log must be archived.

- The system audit logs must be cleared every 14 days and must be set to hold all tracked events generated in that time period. Every 14 days the system audit log must be archived.

- The application audit logs do not need to be saved and can run continuously even if old events are overwritten.

Event Viewer

The event viewer program is used as the default means of tracking event information on a Windows NT computer. It is used to access the three Event logs (system, application, and security). The Event logs are stored in the `%System-Root%\system32\config` folder as `AppEvent.evt`, `SysEvent.evt`, and `SecEvent.evt`.

By default the security is set on the event viewer so that the application and system logs can be viewed by anybody, including anybody logged on with Guest access. The security log is only accessible by administrators or system by default. Anybody can be given access to the security log by using the *Manage Audit Logs* right in User Manager (for Domains).

To tighten up security on the event viewer, follow the steps outlined below.

Restrict Guest Access

1. Log on as an administrator equivalent.
2. Select **Start > Run**.
3. Enter **Regedt32** and **OK** to run the registry editor. Make certain that you understand the dangers of editing the registry before proceeding. See Chapter Eight, *Registry*, for more details.
4. Select the **HKEY_LOCAL_MACHINE** hive.
5. Select the key **\System\CurrentControlSet\Services\EventLog\Application**.
6. Select **Add Value** from the **Edit** menu. Figure 9.1 shows the dialog screen for adding the new value.

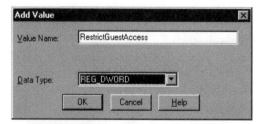

FIGURE 9.1   Adding the RestrictGuestAccess value in the registry to deny guest access to the Event logs

7. In the **Value Name** box, type **RestrictGuestAccess**.

8. In the **Data Type** box, select **REG_DWORD**.

9. Select **OK**. The DWORD editor is invoked.

10. Enter the value **0**. Select **OK**. The new value is added in the results pane for the key.

11. Select the **key \System\CurrentControlSet\Services\EventLog\ System**.

12. Repeat steps 6 through 10 above.

13. Exit the registry editor. Changes will take effect after the system is rebooted.

Check Registry Security

As with any change in registry keys to add security, you must restrict access to the registry key itself so that the security setting cannot be removed. Security on this registry key defaults to Full Control access for Administrators, Owners (Administrators), and System. The group Everyone has Read access. To check the security applied to these registry keys, follow these steps.

1. Start the **registry editor**.

2. Select the **HKEY_LOCAL_MACHINE** hive.

3. Select the key **\System\CurrentControlSet\Services\EventLog\Application**.

4. Select **Permissions** from the **Security** menu. The active permissions are shown. Ensure that they match the permissions shown above. Use the *Add* and *Remove* buttons to alter permissions to match the default if necessary. Be careful not to alter permissions for Administrators, System, and Owner.

5. Confirm any necessary changes and exit the registry editor.

Audit Policy Setup

Audit policies must be implemented on a per-machine basis. Every Windows NT computer has its own Event log and audit policy settings. Audit policies must be set on the target machine that needs to be tracked. For example, if you wish to track network logons on a domain, you would need to set the policy on *all* of the authentication servers. If you wish to track the use of an application, you must set the policy on the machine on which the application resides.

Auditing is switched off by default in Windows NT. There can be a large overhead in disk space if auditing is enabled unnecessarily. You must decide which parts of the system usage you need to keep track of and enable auditing only for that particular area.

One point worth mentioning now concerns file and folder audit tracking. Audit functionality is part of the Windows NT security subsystem. When you install your Windows NT system, file and folder security can only be applied to NTFS volumes. Any volumes formatted with the FAT file system cannot be secured with file and folder security measures (unless you convert them to NTFS first). This applies to audit as well. You cannot audit file and folder access on non-NTFS volumes.

In this next section, we implement the audit policy designed previously.

Event Log Settings

All audit events are written to the security Event log. To view the events logged, follow these steps.

1. Select **Programs** from the **Start** menu.

2. Select **Administrative Tools**.

3. Select **Event Viewer**.

4. Select **Security** from the **Log** menu. Figure 9.2 shows a sample security Event log.

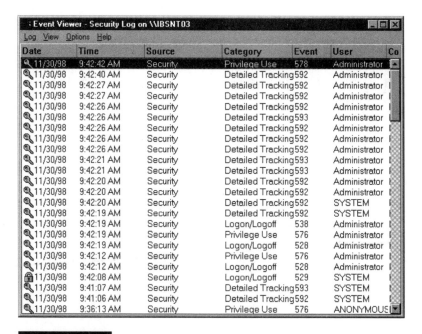

Date	Time	Source	Category	Event	User	Co
11/30/98	9:42:42 AM	Security	Privilege Use	578	Administrator	
11/30/98	9:42:40 AM	Security	Detailed Tracking	592	Administrator	
11/30/98	9:42:27 AM	Security	Detailed Tracking	592	Administrator	
11/30/98	9:42:27 AM	Security	Detailed Tracking	592	Administrator	
11/30/98	9:42:26 AM	Security	Detailed Tracking	592	Administrator	
11/30/98	9:42:26 AM	Security	Detailed Tracking	593	Administrator	
11/30/98	9:42:26 AM	Security	Detailed Tracking	592	Administrator	
11/30/98	9:42:26 AM	Security	Detailed Tracking	592	Administrator	
11/30/98	9:42:21 AM	Security	Detailed Tracking	593	Administrator	
11/30/98	9:42:21 AM	Security	Detailed Tracking	593	Administrator	
11/30/98	9:42:20 AM	Security	Detailed Tracking	592	Administrator	
11/30/98	9:42:20 AM	Security	Detailed Tracking	592	Administrator	
11/30/98	9:42:20 AM	Security	Detailed Tracking	592	SYSTEM	
11/30/98	9:42:19 AM	Security	Detailed Tracking	592	SYSTEM	
11/30/98	9:42:19 AM	Security	Logon/Logoff	538	Administrator	
11/30/98	9:42:19 AM	Security	Privilege Use	576	Administrator	
11/30/98	9:42:19 AM	Security	Logon/Logoff	528	Administrator	
11/30/98	9:42:12 AM	Security	Privilege Use	576	Administrator	
11/30/98	9:42:12 AM	Security	Logon/Logoff	528	Administrator	
11/30/98	9:42:08 AM	Security	Logon/Logoff	529	SYSTEM	
11/30/98	9:41:07 AM	Security	Detailed Tracking	593	SYSTEM	
11/30/98	9:41:06 AM	Security	Detailed Tracking	592	SYSTEM	
11/30/98	9:36:13 AM	Security	Privilege Use	576	ANONYMOUS	

FIGURE 9.2   Event viewer security log

There are three log files viewed through this program corresponding to the three distinct areas of audit functionality described above.

- The *System log* is written to by the NT system itself and reports facts about the status of the operating environment. If a service fails to start up at system boot time, then the error will be recorded in this log.

- The *Application log* file records messages from applications. A program may record an initialization error in this log file.

- The *Security log* file captures security-related events. Any audit events that you enable in User Manager will be recorded here.

Event Log Distribution

An Event log exists on every NT machine (both workstation and server). You must be careful when implementing an audit strategy to configure the policies in the correct place. If you wish to audit a file access on a local workstation, then set the policy on that machine. The ensuing events will be recorded in the Event log on that machine.

If you wish to audit logon times for individual users in a domain environment, you must remember that users can be authenticated to different domain controllers depending on the prevailing situation. The logon event will only be recorded in the Event log of the domain controller that carried out the authentication.

 Event logs can become full very quickly. If you decide to audit successful file access on a heavily used directory, then a huge number of events will be logged. Choose your audit strategy carefully. Are you really interested in successful logons or only in failures (possible attempts at a break-in)?

Enabling Audit Policies

Audit policies are enabled in at least two phases. In the first step, you switch the audit policy on. In the second step, you choose the individual items to be tracked. Depending on the type of policy, there is usually a third step: select the system objects and users to whom you would like to apply the policy. Step one and step two can be carried out for multiple audit scenarios. All of the audit items that you wish to track can be selected at the same time during this setup. For the purposes of the step-through guides, we will only activate one of the audit features at a time to demonstrate the effect of the choice.

To turn on the audit policy, follow these instructions.

1. Select **Programs** from the **Start** menu on the target machine.

2. Select **Administration Tools**.

3. Select **User Manager for Domains** (domain controller) or **User Manager** (workstation).

4. Select the **Policies** menu.

5. Select **Audit**. Figure 9.3 shows the Audit Policy screen in User Manager for Domains. All audit events are turned off by default.

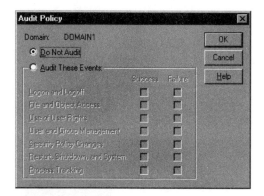

| **FIGURE 9.3** | Audit policy

6. Select **Audit These Events** radio button. This completes the first step of enabling audit events. No events are actually tracked yet because all of the *Success* and *Failure* boxes are still blank and the OK button needs to be chosen to confirm settings.

Note that the audit criteria can be set to *Success*, *Failure*, or both.

LOGON AND LOGOFF TRACKING

Now we can start to apply the audit policy design discussed in the previous section. First we set the audit events for tracking user logon and logoff.

1. Make sure that the **Audit These Events** radio button was selected at the end of the last step-through exercise. The event types listed in Table 9.1 in the *Windows NT Security Audit Capabilities* section are shown. This was the first step in enabling any audit activity.

2. Select the **Failure** radio button next to logon and logoff. The audit policy scenario only requires failures to be tracked, so leave the Success button blank.

At this point only the logon and logoff failures are being tracked. If this was the extent of your policy design, then no more need be done. Before continuing with the remainder of the audit policy, we can check to make sure these events are being logged properly.

1. Choose **OK**. This confirms your choice to track logon and logoff failures.

2. Log off from the computer on which you have set the audit policy.

3. Use the Secure Attention Sequence (<CTRL><ALT><DEL>) to initiate the logon process.

4. Enter the *wrong* password for your user name. You will receive an error message.

5. Log on to the machine correctly.

6. Select **Programs** from the **Start** menu on the domain controller.

7. Select **Administration Tools**.

8. Select **Event Viewer**.

9. Select the **Log** menu and choose **Security** to set the security log file as the focus of the operation.

10. Look for the **Logon/Logoff** entry under the **Category** column at the top of the security log.

11. Double-click the event to look at the details. Figure 9.4 shows the detailed log entry for a bad logon attempt.

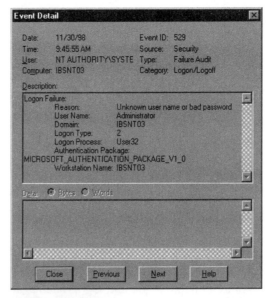

FIGURE 9.4   Detailed view of a bad logon attempt tracked in the Event log

The description of the event message tells you that an attempt to log on was unsuccessful due to either a bad username or mismatched password. The information displayed in the log helps you track the event. It is important to track the following information when looking at logon failure events.

- **Date and Time.** Look for a pattern to see if your system is the target of a systematic attack or if the attempt was made when the user was away.
- **Reason.** This field will always contain "Unknown user or bad password" for this type of event.
- **User Name.** This field contains the user name entered at the logon prompt.
- **Workstation Name.** This field contains the machine name from which the bad logon attempt originated.

The event viewer that is used to view the audit event information is an integral part of the audit policy process in Windows NT, discussed in the *Event Viewer* section of this chapter.

Now that we have seen that auditing is switched on and is logging events to the security log, we can set the audit policy to track all of the events previously discussed in the audit scenario.

APPLICATION ACCESS

The audit scenario calls for the use of a particular application to be tracked. The following example uses the `Wordpad.exe` program as the target of the audit tracking. The actual applications you wish to track will vary according to your own circumstances.

1. Select **Programs** from the **Start** menu on the target machine.
2. Select **Administration Tools**.
3. Select **User Manager for Domains** (domain controller) or **User Manager** (workstation).
4. Select the **Policies** menu. The policy should still be set to track user logon and logoff failures.
5. Select **Audit**. The policy should still be set to track user logon and logoff failures.
6. Select the **Success** and **Failure** radio buttons for **File and Object Access**.
7. Select **OK** to confirm the choice.

This selection in the audit policy is different from all others in that it requires a third step to be implemented. It does not take effect until you assign a target for the operation. To assign the target of the operation, you must select the files, folders, or other object you wish to track.

1. Select **Programs** from the **Start** menu on the machine that holds the application and that has had the audit policy set as above.

2. Select **Windows NT Explorer**.

3. Drill down the menu structure until you find your application file. For our scenario, select **C:\Program Files\Windows NT\Accessories\wordpad.exe**. Amend the choice as necessary if you have installed Windows NT on another drive.

4. Right-click the **Wordpad.exe** file and select **Properties**.

5. Select the **Security** tab. If the Security tab does not exist, most likely the file resides on a non-NTFS volume and so security and audit functions cannot be applied at the file or folder level.

6. Select **Auditing**. Figure 9.5 shows the file auditing setup screen.

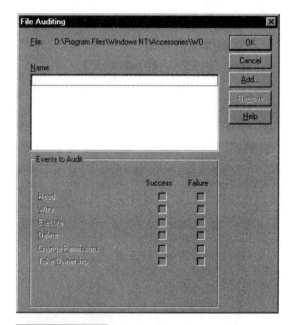

FIGURE 9.5 File auditing setup screen

The file auditing setup screen is blank by default. Before you can choose the events to audit, you must choose the users or groups to be tracked.

7. Select **Add** to begin choosing users to track. A list of all groups known on the local system is displayed. To see a list of users as well as groups, you would select the Show Users button. For our practice scenario, we will select a group of users to track.

8. Scroll down the list and select the **Domain Admins** group (or any other group that you belong to). If you are not using a domain structure, select the **Administrators** group.

9. Select **Add**.

10. Select **OK**. The Events to Audit radio buttons are now available for selection. Table 9.2 shows the available options and what they track.

11. Select the **Success** and **Failure** radio buttons for **Execute**.

12. Select **OK**.

13. Select **OK** again. You have set the auditing attribute for the Wordpad.exe file so that an event will be logged every time the application is run.

TABLE 9.2   File auditing: Available events

Event Type	Description
Read	Audits the display of file data, attributes and permissions, and owner.
Write	Audits changes to the file data or attributes. Also tracks display of attributes and owner.
Execute	Audits running of program files. Also tracks display of attributes and owner.
Delete	Audits file deletion.
Change Permissions	Audits changes to file permissions.
Take Ownership	Audits changes to file ownership.

Although the practice scenario does not call for directory auditing, we show the applicable directory auditing events in Table 9.3.

TABLE 9.3   Directory auditing: Available events

Event Type	Description
Read	Audits the display of file NAMES, attributes and permissions, and owner.
Write	Audits creation of subdirectories and files, changes to attributes, and the display of permissions and ownership.
Execute	Audits display of attributes, permissions, and ownership. Also tracks changes to subdirectories.
Delete	Audits directory deletion.
Change Permissions	Audits changes to directory permissions.
Take Ownership	Audits changes to directory ownership.

Now that all of the necessary steps have been completed to enable file auditing on the `Wordpad.exe` program, we can test the result.

1. Select **Programs** from the **Start** menu.

2. Select **Accessories** > **Wordpad**.

3. Select **Programs** from the **Start** menu.

4. Select **Administrative Tools** > **Event Viewer**.

5. Select **Security** from the **Log** menu. An event with a category of Object Access and the event number of 560 should have been entered into the Event log.

6. Double-click event number 560.

The detail of the event message tells you that a successful attempt to run the `Wordpad.exe` application was made. The information displayed in the log helps you to track the event. The most important fields are:

- **Date and Time.** Showing when the attempt was made.
- **Type.** Showing in this case that the attempt was successful.
- **Primary User Name.** Showing the user who made the attempt.
- **Accesses.** Showing the type of access used. In this case, it is either Read or Execute/Traverse.

COLOR PRINTER USAGE

The audit procedure for tracking the use of a color printer is similar to that of file and directory auditing. The first step is to enable File and Object Access tracking in the audit policy. If you have followed the step-through guides in this chapter, you have already done this step. See the *Application Access* section. When the File and Object Access tracking is enabled, you must assign the printer as the target for audit tracking.

1. Select **Settings** from the **Start** menu.

2. Select **Printers**.

3. Right-click the printer you wish to track. Note that this must be done on the machine that acts as the print server or on the machine with the printer defined locally. Choose any installed printer for the purposes of this exercise.

4. Select the **Security** tab.

5. Select **Auditing**. A screen similar to the one for File Auditing is displayed.

6. Select **Add**. Choose the user or group to audit. For this exercise, choose the Domain Users group.

7. Select **Add**.

8. Select **OK** to confirm. The options for print tracking are now available to choose from. Table 9.4 shows the available options and their usage.

9. Select the **Success** radio button for the print audit option.

10. Select **OK** to confirm the change.

TABLE 9.4	Print auditing: Available events
Event Type	**Description**
Print	Tracks all print jobs to the device.
Full Control	Tracks the use of Full Control rights.
Delete	Tracks the use of Delete right.
Change Permissions	Tracks permission changes to the printer object.
Take Ownership	Tracks the use of the Take Ownership right.

Auditing is now set for the printer of your choice. An entry will be made in the security Event log for every successful print job on this device by a member of the Domain Users group.

This exercise demonstrates what can be audited and how auditing is achieved. As noted earlier, you must be careful to audit only the events that you need to. Too many audited events may mean that the Event logs are not checked very thoroughly and that something of importance slips through.

AUDIT POLICY CHANGES

Audit and security policy changes are among the most important events to track if you decide to use audit policies in your enterprise. If these events are not tracked, then auditing could be switched off and back on again with no clue in the Event logs. The next exercise sets up audit policy change-tracking.

1. Select **Programs** from the **Start** menu on the target machine.

2. Select **Administration Tools**.

3. Select **User Manager for Domains** (domain controller) or **User Manager** (workstation).

4. Select the **Policies** menu. The policy should still be set to track user logon and logoff failures.

5. Select **Audit**. The policy should still be set to track user logon and logoff failures.

6. Select the **Success** and **Failure** radio buttons for **Security Policy Changes**.

7. Select **OK** to confirm the choice.

Security policy changes are tracked from now on. No more configuration is necessary. The remainder of the audit policy scenarios can be set up and then the security Event log can be checked to make certain that the changes to the security policy have been tracked.

MACHINE RESTARTS AND SHUTDOWNS

1. To activate the tracking of these events, follow the same instructions as those above to enter the audit **Policies** menu.

2. Then, select the **Success** and **Failure** radio buttons for **Restart, Shutdown**, and **System**.

It is worth noting again that this audit policy must be implemented on the machine you wish to track.

USER ACCOUNT MANIPULATION

1. Follow the same instructions as those above to enter the audit **Policies** menu.

2. Select the **Success** and **Failure** radio buttons for **User and Group Management.**

Figure 9.6 shows the Audit Policy screen when all of the audit tracking items set out in the practice scenario have been enabled.

AUDIT LOG CONFIGURATION

Now, complete the remaining audit policy work by using the event viewer program to configure the Event logs. Follow these instructions to configure the Event logs to match the requirements of the practice scenario.

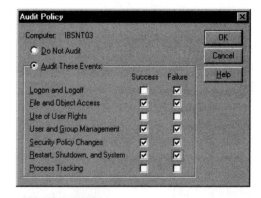

FIGURE 9.6 Completed audit policy scenario

1. Select **Programs** from the **Start** menu.

2. Select **Administrative Tools**.

3. Select **Event Viewer**.

4. Select **Log**.

5. Select **Log Settings**. Use the **Change Settings for** selection box to choose the log file you wish to configure.

6. Select the **Security** audit log.

7. Set the **Maximum Log Size** to 4096 Kilobytes. This size may be insufficient to hold all of the events that you wish to track; you should monitor it over time to see if the size needs to be changed.

8. Select the **Do Not Overwrite Events (Clear Log Manually)** radio button. This will mean that you do not accidentally lose events from the end of your log. It also means that new events are not logged if the maximum log size if reached. Figure 9.7 shows the security log file settings screen.

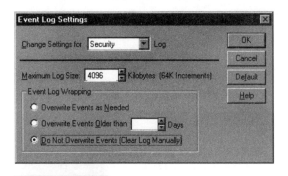

FIGURE 9.7   Security Event log settings

9. Next, select the **System** log file.

10. Select the **Do Not Overwrite Events (Clear Log Manually)** radio button.

11. Next, select the **Application** log file.

12. Look at the default settings but do not change them. Events in this log file can be overwritten when necessary.

13. Select **OK** to confirm the settings.

The settings for the security and system log files ensure that events are not dropped off the end of the log file to make way for newer events. This does mean that you must keep track of the size of log files and amend the sizes according to your needs.

SAVING LOG FILES

The final part of the practice audit scenario requires the security and system audit logs to be saved and cleared every 14 days. To save these log files follow these steps.

1. Start the **Event Viewer**.

2. Switch to the Event log you wish to save. First, select the **Security** log.

3. Select **Log > Save As**. This will prompt you for a file name and location for your saved log files.

4. Enter a file name and select **Save**. When choosing a file name, indicate the time period covered by the log file and which of the three log files is included.

5. Select the **System** log file.

6. Repeat the steps above, saving this log to a file name that indicates the contents. The scenario does not require the application log file to be saved. If you require this at your site, then it is saved in the same manner as the others.

CLEARING LOG FILES

Log files can be cleared with the event viewer.

1. Start the **Event Viewer**.

2. Select the Event log you wish to clear.

3. Select **Log > Clear All Events**. You are prompted to save the log before clearing. You may choose to save your log at this point.

4. Answer **Yes** or **No**. If you answer Yes, enter the file name for the log. After either answer (Yes or No), you are reminded that the Event log clearance is irreversible.

5. Select **Yes** to continue. The chosen Event log is cleared. Repeat as necessary for the other two Event logs.

If you chose to clear the security Event log, an entry is made after the log is cleared to show that a user has cleared the Event log. This means that a user with privilege enough to make system changes that appear in the Event log, and with enough rights to clear the Event log to hide the traces of these changes, is still tracked and shows up as having cleared the Event log.

Viewing Event Data

The only native means of viewing event data tracked by the audit policy is with the event viewer. This is not a very good solution if you have large amounts of events to track.

The data tracked by the audit policy is stored in an ODBC format suitable for extracting or querying with a third-party product. Many third-party products can be used for this purpose, and it is beyond the scope of this book to recommend any one in particular.

Summary

Auditing computer systems is rarely an IT function within large organizations. The information shown in this chapter should give non-IT staff an insight into what the Windows NT system is capable of tracking and how it can be implemented.

While it would be wrong to suggest that the implementation of system audit features should be carried out by non-IT staff, somebody should always be in a position to monitor the system administrators. Audit policy design is usually a matter for security or compliance officers.

Microsoft Management Console

This chapter introduces one of the newer features of NT 4.0, a feature that will be at the center of the management and administration of Windows 2000 in the future. Microsoft Management Console (MMC) will be used as the management tool for all aspects of the Windows 2000 network.

This chapter includes some step-by-step instructions for setting up your own security management console and will accustom you to the look and feel of the MMC. To take full advantage of the step-through examples included in this chapter, you must have access to a machine on which Windows 2000 is installed and you must have Administrator rights. The Windows NT 4.0 MMC requires Service Pack 4 support for the Security Configuration Manager (see Chapter Eleven).

Because MMC is new to Windows NT 4.0, with only a small amount of functionality, and because of its extensive use throughout Windows 2000, this chapter discusses features available for NT 4.0 SP4 and Windows 2000 and points out any differences in the two formats.

Introduction

Microsoft Management Console (MMC) is an ISV-extensible, common console framework for management applications. English translation: management applications can be brought together to run on top of one common platform (the MMC), which can accommodate third-party management applications as well as those developed by Microsoft.

The MMC is supplied in Windows NT 4.0 with Service Pack 4 as an optional installation (i.e., it is not installed automatically). Windows 2000 contains the MMC as a native product.

The MMC acts as a platform for running management tools within a Windows NT 4.0 or 2000 system. The MMC is only a host platform and does not provide any management activity on its own. Instead it relies on *snap-in* tools written to run on top of the MMC to provide the utilities required for server and workstation management. Snap-in tools perform the required management function while conforming to the format required to present a uniform MMC interface. A snap-in tool can be made up of more than one snap-in extension tool. Microsoft has designed the MMC architecture in such a way as to allow ISVs to write their own snap-in programs.

The MMC interface is concerned only with the way in which information is presented to the user. The underlying architecture of the different programs using the interface has no relevance to the MMC. The overriding purpose of the MMC is to provide a convenient, easy-to-understand, uniform look to the management consoles for the different products. MMC streamlines the system management process by unifying system tasks under the one host application. Microsoft is promoting the MMC interface as *the* way of managing Windows systems for the future.

MMC Panes

The MMC console screen is usually divided into two panes.

- **Scope Pane.** The left hand pane is known as the scope pane. This pane shows that node information and items within this pane can be expanded or reduced by a single-click on the + or − sign next to the node. The absence of a sign means that there are no more child items in the list.
- **Results Pane.** The right-hand pane is known as the results pane. Any node manipulation completed in the scope pane will show the results in this pane.

Throughout the following discussions and the remaining chapters, the scope pane and the results pane are mentioned frequently.

Consoles

MMC is simply a host application for management tools. The format and layout of these tools can be saved in views known as *consoles*. MMC allows different console looks to be saved so that administrators can open a particular console when they need to complete a particular task. These consoles can be emailed or otherwise transmitted so that uniform administration tool looks can be used by others.

A major benefit of the console files is that an administrator can build a custom console to delegate certain system tasks to users, groups, or computers. The saved file (in .MSC format) can be transmitted to or shared with users, and access can be controlled by policy settings for the domain or by computer.

Note that it is only the console that is saved and not the underlying snap-in tool. If you receive a console from another administrator, you need to have the snap-in tools referenced by the console available locally.

Microsoft Management Console is a huge step forward in system management for Microsoft. The scope of this book does not allow for an extended description of MMC. This introduction to MMC is relevant here in the context of the security applications that will run on top of it in the Windows NT 4.0 SP4 and Windows 2000 environments.

Creating Your Own Consoles

With the version of the MMC delivered in Windows NT 4.0 and the limited amount of snap-in tools available, your ability to build a custom console is fairly limited. The console creations discussed below cover both versions of the MMC but concentrate on the Windows 2000 version, which has more functionality and many more available snap-in tools to look at.

Creating your own console can help you to bring together all of the tools that may be necessary to complete a business process. For example, when a new person starts work in a business, many different tasks need to be completed before the person is able to use the computer equipment provided. You will need to set up the new user account. Maybe the new user needs a digital certificate. Access restrictions need to be defined. Object access (printers, disk volumes, etc.) needs to be defined. With Windows 2000 MMC, the management tools needed to complete these tasks and any of the others necessary for new starters can be grouped in a single console so that you can use the group whenever a new person joins your company.

Some of the snap-in tools used in this console can be used (along with others) in a console designed for a different purpose altogether. Any of the tools can be used in different combinations and saved as a console, so in theory you could build a console for every set of management tasks.

It is important to understand how the MMC looks and feels. Follow the example outlined below to configure and save a sample MMC console in Windows NT 4.0 for the Security Configuration Manager and in Windows 2000 for local system management purposes. To complete the latter steps, you must be logged on to a Windows 2000 computer as Administrator or equivalent.

Windows NT 4.0 SP4

1. Ensure the Security Configuration Manager is installed according to the instructions in the Readme.txt document included with the software. The software can be downloaded from the Microsoft FTP site at FTP://ftp.microsoft.com/bussys/winnt/winnt-public/ tools/SCM. The SCM for NT 4.0 and its installation are covered in detail in Chapter Eleven.

2. Select **Run** from the **Start** menu.

3. Enter **MMC** and select **OK** to start the Microsoft Management Console.

4. Select the **Console** menu.

5. Select **Add/Remove Snap-in** to display the Add/Remove Snap-in dialog box.

6. Select **Add**. Figure 10.1 shows the Add Standalone Snap-in dialog box for Windows NT 4.0. This is the default dialog box that displays most snap-in additions.

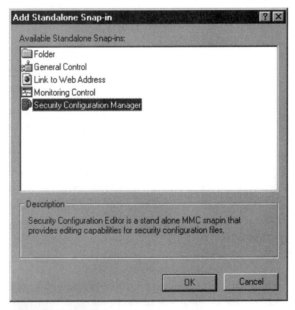

FIGURE 10.1   Dialog box showing the available standalone snap-ins for Windows NT 4.0

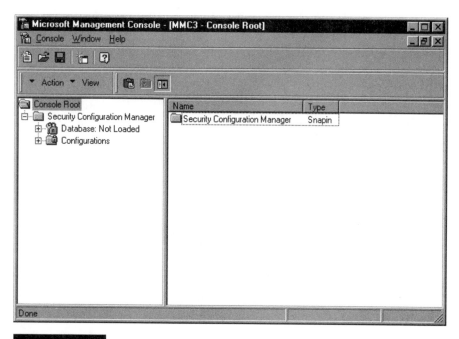

FIGURE 10.2 A sample MMC console screen for NT 4.0

7. Select **Security Configuration Manager**.

8. Select **OK**.

9. Select **OK** to confirm. Figure 10.2 shows the resulting console screen.

The console can now be saved. Follow the instructions in the *Saving Your Consoles* section to do this.

Windows 2000

1. Select **Run** from the **Start** menu.

2. Enter **MMC** and select **OK** to start the Microsoft Management Console.

3. Select the **Console** menu.

4. Select **Add/Remove Snap-in** to display the Add/Remove Snap-in dialog box.

5. Select **Add**. Figure 10.3 shows the Add Standalone Snap-in dialog box. This is the default dialog box that displays most snap-in additions.

Add Standalone Snap-in   [?] [X]

Available Standalone Snap-ins:

Snap-in	Vendor
Active Directory Manager	Microsoft Corporation
Active Directory Schema Manager	Microsoft Corporation
Active Directory Sites and Services ...	Microsoft Corporation
Active Directory Tree Manager	Microsoft Corporation
Admission Control Services Manager	Microsoft Coporation
Certificate Manager	Microsoft Corporation
Computer Management	Microsoft Corporation
Device Manager	Microsoft Corporation
Disk Defragmenter	
Disk Management	VERITAS Software Cor...

Description

Active Directory Manager allows management of users, groups, organizational units, and all other Active Directory objects.

[Add]   [Close]

FIGURE 10.3   Dialog box showing some of the available standalone snap-ins for Windows 2000

6. Scroll through the list of available snap-ins and highlight **Event Viewer**.

7. Select **Add**. The resulting screen asks you to choose the local computer or to browse for another computer.

8. Select **Local Computer** (default) and choose **Finish**. The Event Viewer (Local) snap-in is added to the Add/Remove Snap-in dialog box.

9. Next, highlight **File Service Management** and select **Add**. The resulting dialog box contains contextual selections in addition to the default choice of computer.

10. Select **Local Computer** and **All** in the View box (both default options).

11. Select **Finish** to add File Service Management to the Add/Remove Snap-in dialog box.

12. Select **Close**.

13. Select the **Extensions** tab. The resulting list contains all snap-ins that have extensions available (File Service Management, in this case). By default the **Add all extensions** box is checked. Unless you have a reason to disable a particular extension, then leave this box checked to gain all functionality.

14. Select **OK**. Figure 10.4 shows the resulting console screen.

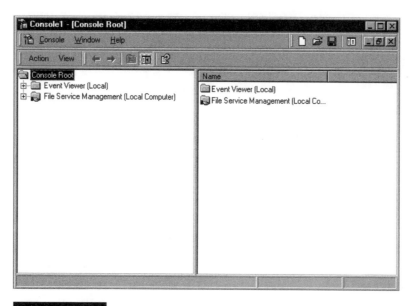

FIGURE 10.4   A sample MMC console screen for Windows 2000

Console Layout

When you have loaded all of the snap-ins that you wish to use, you can customize the layout of the console to suit your own needs. The following example changes the layout of the sample console created in the steps above. This functionality is really only useful in Windows 2000 because of the large number of potential snap-ins that you could load.

1. Right-click **Event Viewer (Local)** in the scope pane.
2. Select **New window from here** to open a second window in the console with the Event Viewer as the root of this window.
3. Switch back to the window named **Console Root**.
4. Right-click **File Service Management (Local Computer)** in the scope pane.
5. Select **New window from here** to open a third window in the console with the File Service Management as the root of this window.
6. Switch back to the window named **Console Root**.
7. Right-click on the top left-hand corner of the **Console Root** window and choose **Close**. You are now left with the two new windows.
8. Select the **Window** menu and choose **Tile Horizontally**. Figure 10.5 shows the resulting console layout.

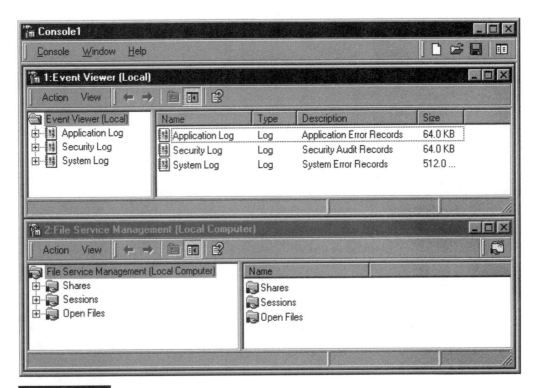

FIGURE 10.5   Console layout customized to best fit requirements

Saving Your Consoles

MMC consoles can be created and saved so that tasks needed to accomplish repetitive or ongoing objectives (system monitoring or new-user creation) can be grouped together and then be available easily in the future. Follow the steps outlined below to save the console you have just created in Windows NT and Windows 2000.

1. Select **Save** from the **Console** menu.

2. Enter a name for the console you are creating. Normally, the name would be meaningful and relevant to the tasks being covered. In the case of both the Windows NT 4.0 and Windows 2000 versions, name the console **My Management Console**.

3. Select **Save**.

The resulting console file can then be sent via email or file transfer to colleagues who can open the same view and use the file as their own.

Accessing Saved Consoles

If a console has been transmitted to you, then save it in a convenient location first. To open a saved console, follow the steps outlined below.

1. Select **Run** from the **Start** menu.
2. Enter **MMC** and select **OK** to start the Microsoft Management Console.
3. Select **Open** from the Console menu.
4. Browse the directory structure to locate the console that you wish to open. By default, the saved files are stored in the path `%System-Root%\profiles\%Username%\Start Menu\Programs\My Administrative Tools` with a file extension of **.MSC**.
5. Select the console file and choose **OK**.

Console Security Settings

There will be times when you wish to create a console for others to use and you want to protect the console from changes by those other users. With the MMC version released for Windows NT, this is not an option because there is a limited amount of functionality that could be protected. The MMC in Windows 2000 is designed so that consoles can be opened in four different modes.

- **Author Mode.** This is the default mode that the sample console would have been opened in and would continue to be opened in. It is the default mode for all new consoles. It allows full access to anybody with the correct file access permissions to make changes, amendments, or deletions. Snap-in programs can be added or removed and the console resaved.

- **User Mode—Full Access.** This mode provides some security for your saved consoles. Any users with the correct file access permissions can open and run the console with the full functionality allowed by their user profile (e.g., domain administration tasks could not be carried out by normal users just because they have access to a console file with the snap-in enabled). Users cannot add or remove snap-ins. Users can, however, change the layout of the windows, including closing any windows. This mode combines full functionality with some console security.

- **User Mode—Delegated Access, Multiple Window.** This mode is more restrictive than the previous two. It allows full functionality of the snap-ins, as described above, but does not allow changes to be saved in the layout. Multiple windows can be used as long as they existed when the console was saved. Full functionality of the snap-ins is only available if the required views were open when the console was saved. This mode provides good functionality (as long as the console is designed well, showing all views necessary for the required tasks) and prevents any tampering with the console contents or style.

- **User Mode—Delegated Access, Single Window.** This mode is similar to the delegated access mode above, except only one window is available to the user. If you try to save a console containing multiple windows while using this mode you are warned that only the current active window will be available when it is reopened.

For all newly created consoles, the default security option is set to Author mode. Some of the predefined administrative tools shipped with Windows 2000 are saved in Delegated mode under either single or multiple windows structure.

To change the security options for the console created above, follow these instructions.

1. Select the **Console Menu** and choose **Options**.
2. Select the **Console** tab. The available console modes are shown in the drop-down box, and a context-sensitive description is available as each one is selected.
3. Select **User Mode, Delegated Access, Multiple Window**. These options gives the greatest security with all the functionality that is generally needed.
4. Select **OK**.
5. Select **Save** from the **Console** menu.

The options take effect the next time the console is opened in a new MMC instance.

Summary

The Microsoft Management Console has only recently been introduced into Windows NT 4.0. The limited functionality is not a poor reflection on the MMC. Instead, it represents the first step toward clustering into a single platform host the management techniques necessary for a large enterprise network. The host will interpret between the underlying program functionality, which implements and manages systems, and the user interface, which receives a standard look and feel that leads to intuitive use of new products and services.

Take a moment to review Figures 10.1 and 10.3. Even if you do not have a Windows 2000 system to use for these practice sessions, look at the number of available snap-in programs for Windows 2000 compared to Windows NT 4.0. Remember that this is a static view; the scroll bar in Figure 10.3 indicates that a large number of snap-ins remain unseen on the list. This difference in the numbers of available snap-in programs shows how committed Microsoft is to bringing together the management features of their systems under the umbrella of this one, easy-to-use management host application. If you intend to be supporting Windows NT and Windows 2000 networks in the future, then consider this area a must for further investigation.

Security Configuration Manager for NT 4.0

This chapter introduces the Security Configuration Manager for Windows NT 4.0. The SCM is a snap-in tool for the Microsoft Management Console, which is the new host tool designed for managing Microsoft systems.

The Security Configuration Manager for NT 4.0 coupled with the MMC moves the management of Windows NT 4.0 networks in the same direction Microsoft has taken in its design of Windows 2000.

Introduction

The Security Configuration Manager for NT 4.0 (SCM-NT) is a Microsoft Management Console (MMC) snap-in tool that makes the task of securing a Windows NT 4.0 system much more simple, thus reducing the cost of ownership.

An MMC snap-in tool is a program or suite of programs written to run on top of the MMC host platform described in Chapter Ten. This particular MMC snap-in program brings together these capabilities: to apply security models to your system, to save benchmark settings to databases, and to analyze your system periodically against these benchmark settings to find any differences.

While Windows NT 4.0 has many beneficial security features and has a robust, scalable security subsystem that can cope with the requirements of large installations, the security management features have been spread throughout many graphical tools, and administrators must use some or all of these tools to keep on top of the security installation on an NT network. This new centralized security management tool will allow administrators to make better use of their time. While time spent on security administration is rarely wasted, a more streamlined approach can save time and money as well as making the entire effort much simpler. The simpler the task, the less likely it is to be done incorrectly or not at all.

Security analysis is another area of Windows NT 4.0 that can be improved. The focal point of security analysis at the moment is the event viewer. While this viewer can be used successfully to monitor security, it is not user friendly and lacks the real power needed to analyze a security implementation. The analysis functionality incorporated in the SCM-NT establishes a central point where a security policy can be designed, configured, and monitored.

The SCM-NT does not replace all existing security-related tools. Certain functionality does exist in this tool and also in some of the previous tools and procedures discussed in this book. The design goal is that all these tools eventually will be run under the umbrella of the MMC, which will be the management focal point of the Windows NT/2000 network.

The SCM-NT has a large amount of built-in functionality. When looking at the question of security within your systems, you have many different areas to consider: file and directory permissions, registry security, user account security, group membership, system resources and services, etc. There are many areas to look at, and it is only after you build a complete picture of the relevant settings in all of these areas and adjust the settings to take care of any problems that you can say "Yes, the system is secure."

The amount of time spent answering the question Is my system secure? can be immense. One of the design goals of the SCM-NT was to make this security much easier to accomplish. Bringing several of the security-related tasks into the one tool can make the administrator's life much easier.

The question to ask one week after asking it previously is, "Is my system secure?" This question should be asked over and over on a regular basis. What is secure one day is not necessarily secure another day, especially in a fast-paced environment where changes are made all the time. New servers being added might not have all of the required security settings applied. New workstations come on line as fast as they can be built. Not enough administrative resources are available to allow someone to be dedicated to security alone. These are all familiar features of IT life. The lack of a good analysis tool can mean that you go over the same things time and again simply because you have to be sure of your security status. The SCM-NT brings together a functionality set that can alleviate the strains caused by the events outlined above.

The Dangers of the SCM

SCM-NT carries with it the same responsibility as the use of all the separate security management tools in Windows NT 4.0. This tool brings together the ability to affect almost all of the NT system and delivers it in an easy-to-use interface. The danger here is the same as the benefit: it is very easy to apply a security template and make changes throughout your system. When using the SCM-NT, make sure that you test all settings thoroughly. Ensure that all of the examples and step-through exercises in this chapter are carried out on a machine that you can afford to lose in a worst case. *Never test templates on a production machine.*

These warnings are all standard and apply as much to any new piece of software. This tool, however, is a powerful means to protect your systems. The idea behind it is that you can dramatically limit unauthorized and unnecessary access. If used incorrectly or if settings are applied by mistake, this tool could cause you to lose access and be restricted.

Make sure that you read all of this chapter before attempting to use the SCM-NT on a system that you cannot afford to lose. Do not even install the product on a production system until you are completely familiar with the product and any changes it makes to your systems upon installation.

The last thing to remember here is that even if you only want to change one setting, everything contained in the database will be applied when you configure the system. For that reason, other security-related tools are not being replaced by the SCM-NT. If you only want to set permissions on a directory structure, use the Window NT Explorer context menu. If you want to set the minimum password length in the account policies, use User Manager (for Domains). SCM-NT is intended for initial security installations and then for analyzing the security settings on an ongoing basis.

Installation and Configuration

The SCM-NT is included as an optional extra in the Service Pack 4 for NT 4.0, and so it is not installed by default. Follow these instructions to install the SCM-NT.

1. Install **Internet Explorer** 3.02 or higher. You can download it from the Microsoft Web site, or you can install Internet Explorer 4.01 from the Service Pack 4 CD.

2. Install the **Windows NT Service Pack 4**. Instructions are contained on the Service Pack 4 CD.

3. Locate your copy of the SCM-NT. You can find it on the Service Pack 4 CD under the \MSSCE\I386 folder or download it from FTP: //ftp.microsoft.com/bussys/winnt/winnt-public/tools/SCM.

4. Run the program **MSSCE.EXE**.

5. Choose **Yes** to the **Full Install** prompt.

6. Choose **Yes** to install **Microsoft Management Console**.

7. Select **OK** to acknowledge the reboot warning message.

8. Accept the License Agreement. Files are now decompressed and copied to the destination folders. You may be prompted to reboot the system after the successful MMC install finishes. If so, restart this procedure from step 4 above and select **No** to skip the second MMC install to complete the installation.

The Security Configuration Manager for Windows NT 4.0 SP4 is now installed. The MMC console now has to be configured to enable the use of the SCM-NT. We covered this procedure in Chapter Ten, so if the console is already saved, you can skip this section.

1. Select **Run** from the **Start** menu.

2. Enter **MMC** and select **OK** to start the Microsoft Management Console.

3. Select the **Console** menu.

4. Select **Add/Remove Snap-in** to display the Add/Remove Snap-in dialog box.

5. Select **Security Configuration Manager**.

6. Select **OK**.

7. Select **OK** to confirm. The console can now be saved.

8. Select **Console > Save**. Enter the name **My Management Console**.

9. Select **Save**.

The console is now created and saved. During the exercises that follow in this chapter, do not save the console when exiting the Microsoft Management Console unless the instructions expressly tell you to do so.

SCM-NT Functionality Overview

There are three main areas of functionality covered by the SCM-NT snap-in tool.

Template File Definition

Security configuration files are flat text files that store settings for all of the different available parameters in each security area. Ten files are installed by default with the SCM-NT. Table 11.1 lists these files and describes their use.

TABLE 11.1 Standard security configuration template files	
File Name	**Description**
Basicdc4.inf	Contains sample configuration for a basic security level NT 4.0 domain controller.
Basicsv4.inf	Contains sample configuration for a basic security level NT 4.0 server (nondomain controller).
Basicwk4.inf	Contains sample configuration for a basic security level NT 4.0 workstation.
Compdc4.inf	Contains sample configuration for a basic-to-medium security level NT 4.0 domain controller.
Compws4.inf	Contains sample configuration for a basic-to-medium security level NT 4.0 workstation.
Hisecdc4.inf	Contains sample configuration for a high security level NT 4.0 domain controller.
Hisecws4.inf	Contains sample configuration for a high security level NT 4.0 workstation.
Off97sr1.inf	Contains sample configuration for file and directory security settings pertinent to the default installation of Office 97 SR1.
Securdc4.inf	Contains sample configuration for a medium-to-high security level NT 4.0 domain controller.
Securws4.inf	Contains sample configuration for a medium-to-high security level NT 4.0 workstation.

All of the security areas are looked at in detail later in the chapter.

The configuration files are stored by default in the `%SystemRoot%\security\templates` directory and have the extension `.INF`. The files can be opened for viewing with a text editor such as Notepad, but changes should only be made through the SCM-NT interface so that the file structure is correct.

The template files can be used in their shipped state to provide various levels of security to your systems. Each template file contains exactly the same number of security areas and the same number of subsections containing parameters relevant to the security area as the others.

The difference between the various template files is the value that is stored for each of the available settings. For example, a basic-security template may set the *Minimum Password Length* variable in the *Account Policies* area to be 0, which means anything from no password upward is acceptable. The high-security templates may set this value to six so that only six characters and above are acceptable.

The example used above highlights an important fact about these security templates. One person's definition of "high security" and another person's can be quite different. A 6-character minimum password length is too short (in my opinion) for an administrative account on a high-security domain controller. Other settings in the template files also differ from my view of high security, medium security, and basic security. The point I am making is that they differ from *my* opinion, which in part is influenced by the clients that I provide services to. Your own opinion and the opinion of your colleagues and management of your organization will influence your decision on what settings are suitable and under which circumstances. I would never recommend blindly taking one of the template files and implementing the raw settings that are provided within it. You must investigate the needs of your own organization and the settings provided by each of the templates before you can move forward with any implementations.

Security Configuration

System security configuration is taken care of through the same GUI interface used for all other operations discussed in this chapter. The template files discussed above are used as input files to a database where the system configuration is performed.

The default security database file used in this version of the SCM is Sce-setup.sdb, residing in the directory %SystemRoot%\security\database. This database file is fed from the *Import Configuration* SCM menu command and can be used to output to a template file (.INF) with the *Export Configuration* menu command. Both of these menu options are discussed later in this chapter.

You can create many more database files and load any one of them to perform system analysis or to use for system configuration. When a new database is created, it is associated with a particular template file. This association can be changed at any time by the *Import Configuration* menu command.

Security Analysis

System security analysis is performed by comparing the setting in one of the template files with the settings in your system and looking at the highlighted differences. You can use one of the standard template files, or you can define your own and use it as the benchmark to analyze against.

When you run an analysis, the currently configured system settings and the benchmark settings are displayed with differences highlighted. You can implement the benchmark settings after looking carefully at the differences, or you can amend your benchmark settings to meet your current configuration and then save the settings back to the template file.

Security Configuration Areas

When designing the SCM-NT, Microsoft looked at the different types of security-related tasks that were carried out on an NT system. The design for the SCM-NT incorporates seven standard *security areas*. These security areas are really a grouping of related options that affect the security of the systems. Table 11.2 shows the seven standard security areas configured by default in the SCM-NT.

TABLE 11.2	Security configuration areas
Area Name	**Area Contents**
Account Policies	Password policy.
	Account lockout policy.
Local Policies	Audit policy.
	User rights assignment.
	Security options for the local machine. Many of these options are specific
	registry entries on the local machine.
Event Log	Settings for Event logs.
Restricted Group	This area is used to set policies for membership to groups that are deemed to
	be sensitive by the administrator. These could include the Domain Admins
	group and the Account Operators group as well as any other groups necessary.
	This area also allows group nesting on domain controllers (one group residing
	within another) for policy application.
System Services	Settings for service startup mode and security.
	Access control for system services.
Registry	Registry access control.
File System	This area is used to grant rights and permissions for users in the domain or
	from trusted domains to files and directories.

The seven security areas shown above are the ones supported by the SCM-NT at the moment. This list can be added to in the future, and indeed a similar list shown in the *Security Configuration Tool Set* section of Chapter Twelve shows the extended security area list for the Windows 2000 version of the tool.

SECEDIT Command-Line Utility

A comprehensive command-line tool provided with the SCM-NT installation can be used to perform all tasks that the GUI interface is capable of performing. Figure 11.1 shows the initial command-line screen for the SECEDIT.EXE program.

The only shortfall in the command-line tool is that you cannot visually analyze the output of an analysis operation in the way that you can with the GUI interface. The GUI interface uses colors and icons to represent differences to investigate.

The command-line utility is simple to use and a faster way to accomplish certain tasks. One task in particular is extremely useful in the command-line version. If you decide to edit a template file by using a text editor such as Notepad, then you need to make sure that the resulting file has all of the correct syntax in place. To do this, you can use the Validate option in SECEDIT.EXE.

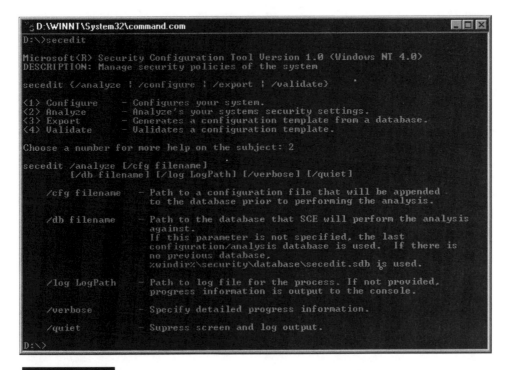

FIGURE 11.1   `SECEDIT.EXE` command-line utility showing the analyze options

1. Open a **Command Prompt**.

2. Type **Secedit /validate %SystemRoot%\security\templates\
   filename.inf**, where *filename* is the name of the template you
   wish to validate. Change the path if you have stored the template
   in a different location.

3. When the file is validated, the system returns to the prompt and displays
   the message **Template %SystemRoot%\security\templates\
   filename.inf is validated**.

You can use the command-line utility if you think it is of benefit in
your particular circumstances. To receive help on the command-line syntax,
enter the `SECEDIT` command with no parameters. The remainder of the
chapter looks at the GUI interface because it offers all of the functionality
contained within the SCM-NT.

Unconfigured System Analysis

The SCM-NT can analyze security settings in all of the security areas shown in Table 11.1 in the section *SCM-NT Functionality Overview*. The procedures for analyzing security settings can be divided into two methods, one of which is Unconfigured System analysis. The other method, Configured System analysis, is covered later in the chapter.

Unconfigured system analysis is generally performed before your security configurations are set with the SCM-NT. An Unconfigured System analysis is performed on a system that has not been configured with any of the configuration template files. You can use this analysis information to show the differences between suggested settings in a template file and your current settings. You can also look at the potential impact of a configuration template on your systems. Follow the instructions below to perform an Unconfigured System analysis on a Windows NT 4.0 standalone server. If you do not have a standalone server, then a workstation will suffice. The analysis compares the Hisecws4.inf template file, which contains configuration settings for a high-security workstation or standalone server, with the current settings.

1. Ensure that the Security Configuration Manager, including the MMC interface, is installed on the target machine and the My Management Console file has been created, as described in *Installation and Configuration*.
2. Run **MMC.EXE** to start the MMC program.
3. Select **Open** from the **Console** menu.
4. Enter **My Management Console** and select **Open**. Figure 11.2 shows the SCM-NT console the first time it is started.

The console shown in Figure 11.2 has a message stating the database (Secedit.sdb) does not exist. The database can be populated by means of the Import Configuration. The next step is to import the settings from the Hisecws4.inf template file that will be used as the benchmark against which we will analyze the system.

1. In the scope pane, right-click **Database:*Databasename*** and select **Import Configuration**.
2. Select the **%SystemRoot%\security\templates\Hisecws4.inf** file.
3. Select **Open**. Figure 11.3 shows the import dialog box.
4. Select the check box labeled **Overwrite existing configuration in database**. This is not selected by default and should look as it does in Figure 11.3.
5. Select **Open**. The database is ready to be populated now.

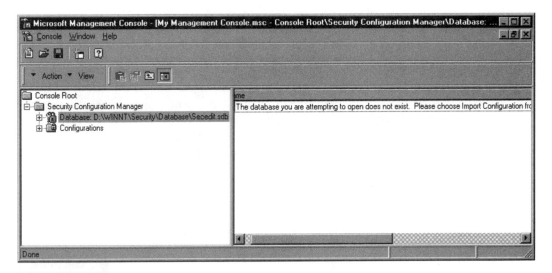

FIGURE 11.2 The SCM-NT console started for the first time

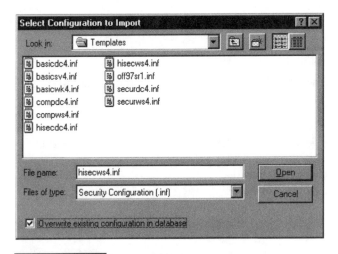

FIGURE 11.3 Import configuration dialog box for the SCM-NT

If you find that you have selected the wrong template file at this stage, you can go back and change the selection. Following the instructions above to do this will bring up a warning message, as shown in Figure 11.4. Answer OK to this message, and continue with the remainder of the steps.

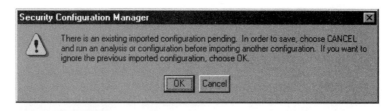

FIGURE 11.4 Selecting another import file from the warning dialog box

Now we are ready to analyze the system. The database file will be created when the analysis is complete.

1. Right-click **Database:***Databasename* in the scope pane to reveal the context menu, shown in Figure 11.5.
2. Select **Analyze System Now**.
3. Accept the default path for the log file or enter your own preference.
4. Select **OK**. Figure 11.6 shows the analysis in progress. The analysis can take some minutes, depending on the size and speed of your system.

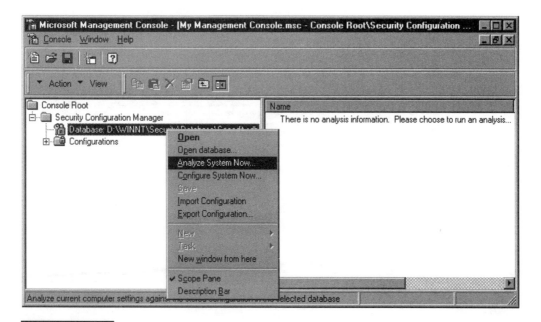

FIGURE 11.5 The context menu for the database

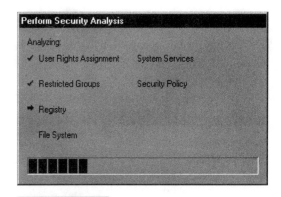

FIGURE 11.6   The indicator in the analysis function

The database file is now populated and the analysis is complete. Use the analysis information to compare your current settings with those recommended in the template file. Figure 11.7 shows the password policy settings within the Account Polices area.

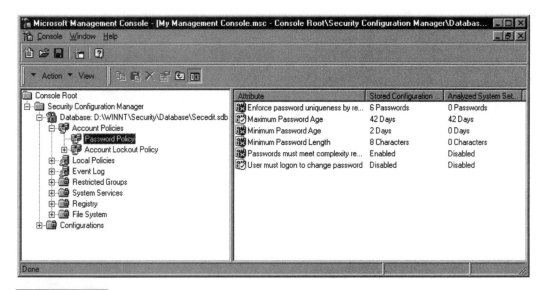

FIGURE 11.7   Comparing settings between benchmark template file and live system

Comparing Analysis Results

Now that a system analysis has been completed, you can look at the analysis results and compare the existing system settings with the configuration file settings.

The analysis results in Figure 11.7 show the differences between the settings for the *Stored Configuration* (the template file) and the *Analyzed System Settings* (current system).

Three different results can be represented on the left-hand side of the results pane by three different icons.

- **Blue icon with a red cross mark.** This icon represents a difference between the two settings. This difference can be a stronger setting or a weaker setting. It simply means that the two settings are different and you should investigate.

- **Blue icon with a white tick mark.** This icon represents a match between the two settings.

- **Plain blue icon.** This icon represents the Not Configured state of the template file setting. You can exclude a setting so that it is not configured at all in the template file. This is not the same as setting a value to 0, but is a conscious decision to exclude the setting from being checked in the analysis or configurations.

When you run the analysis of your systems and start to look at the differences highlighted by the process, you will find that some of the suggested settings in the template file will make sense and that some of the current settings on your system make more sense. This perception is influenced by your own environment and needs to be considered carefully. The analysis function of the SCM-NT allows you to compare your current system settings with those stored in any one of the template files mentioned above or in any custom template file you wish to create.

Applying a Standard Security Configuration File

After you have run the unconfigured system analysis and have compared the results, you are ready to apply security to your own system. Everything that has been done up to this point has not affected your live system settings.

If you have installed a new system and you wish to accept the suggested settings contained in one of the template files after you have run the analyses and compared the results, you can use the SCM-NT to implement the settings. In the example below, the file `Hisecdc4.inf` is used as a template to apply security to a primary domain controller of a new domain. You can use the same principles to apply one of the other template files to a non-DC machine if you do not have one that can be used for testing. First, you need to run the Unconfigured System analysis.

1. Run an Unconfigured System analysis as shown above on the domain controller. The SCM-NT software must be installed locally. Use `Hisecdc4.inf` as the template file.

2. When the analysis has ended, compare the results that show the differences between the two systems. The new domain should have a very low level of security applied.

Now that the analysis is completed, the database holds the settings of the current system and the suggested settings from the template file. Follow these instructions to implement the suggested settings.

3. Right-click **Database:***Databasename* in the scope pane.

4. Select **Configure System Now**.

5. Accept the default log file name and path.

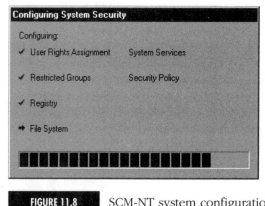

FIGURE 11.8 SCM-NT system configuration indicator

6. Select **OK**. Figure 11.8 shows the configuration status screen.

The current live settings have now been changed to match those of the template file. When you look at the settings shown in the results pane, all configurations either match between the two settings or they are in a Not Configured state.

Saving the New Configuration

Whenever you use the SCM-NT to apply security to any of your systems, you should save the same settings to a template file so that the file can be used as the input the next time you run an analysis. This analysis could be carried out on a weekly basis so that any changes in the system security are noted and fixed as appropriate.

Follow these instructions to save the settings that have just been applied to the live system in the section above.

1. Right-click **Database:***Databasename* in the scope pane.

2. Select **Export Configuration**.

3. Enter a meaningful file name such as System/Domain name and the date. In this case, I used **Domain1-091998.inf**.

4. Select **Save**.

The system configuration is now stored in the new template file. Figure 11.9 shows the new configuration file that now appears in the list of template files. This file can be loaded into a database at any time in the future so that a Configured System analysis can be run and security configuration changes can be found. If these changes are not authorized or you have another reason to reset the security, then you can use this configuration to reset security.

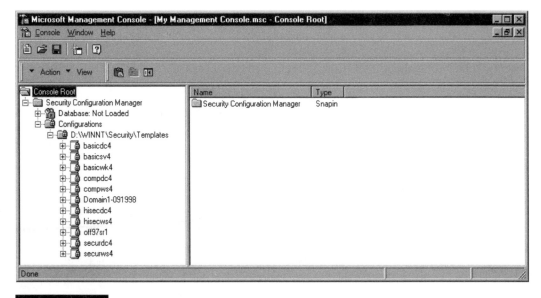

FIGURE 11.9   List of the newly saved template files when the console is reopened

Template Files

The template files shown in Figure 11.9 are all located by default in the `%SystemRoot%\security\templates` directory. Any time you save a template file, the default location is this same directory. You can change settings contained within the security areas of the template file by following the instructions in the relevant security area description discussed in the *Security Areas* section later in the chapter.

Custom Template File Location

Template files are read and loaded at the time that the SCM-NT snap-in program is initialized. Any files that exist in this directory are opened and loaded by default. If you save files on a regular basis here, you may find that the program takes longer and longer to open. Saving custom template files to another location will solve this problem. To do this, simply change the location when you perform the save outlined in the section above. You can also move files with NT Explorer after they have been saved.

You can add more template locations to the available list if you wish. You may decide to store your custom template files in an archive directory when they are superseded, and you can add this directory to the available list at any time so that the archive files can be loaded and accessed. Follow these instructions to add a second directory to the Configurations list.

1. Start the **SCM-NT**.
2. Expand the **Configurations** section in the scope pane. There should be one configurations directory listed, which by default is `%System-Root%\security\templates`.
3. Right-click **Configurations** in the scope pane.
4. Select **New configuration search path**.
5. Use the browser to select the destination directory.
6. Select **OK**.

Creating a Blank Template

A blank template file is one that has all values set to Not Configured in the security areas that are defined as containing *static definitions*, (see *Security Areas* later in the chapter) and that has no entries in the security areas that are defined as containing *dynamic definitions*, (see *Security Areas*). The only exception to this is the System Services security area, which will always contain a list of valid system services.

Follow these steps to create a blank template file.

1. Start the **SCM-NT** and expand the **Configurations** node in the scope pane.

2. In the scope pane, right-click the directory location where you wish the template file to be created. This location must already exist or be created according to the instructions above.

3. Select **New Configuration**.

4. Enter the new configuration name and description.

5. Select **OK**. The new template file is created in the defined location.

6. Right-click the new template in the scope pane and select **Save**.

The new template file contains only the following four lines of code.

```
[Version]
signature="$CHICAGO$"
[Profile Description]
Description=This is an example new configuration file
```

Whenever you select an item in a security area and remove the *Exclude this item* check mark, then amendments are made to this file. The file builds up to contain all of the settings that you wish to configure or analyze with this template file.

Creating Custom Templates

You create custom template files by using any of the default template files as the input or you can create them from scratch. You can then adjust the settings that you wish to change and save the file for later use. To create a custom template from an existing file, follow these steps.

1. Start the **SCM-NT**.

2. Expand the **Configurations** section in the scope pane.

3. Expand the template file directory.

4. Expand the template you wish to base your new configuration file on.

5. Make the changes to the security settings.

6. Right-click the template file in the scope pane.

7. Select **Save As**.

8. Select the destination directory and file name.

9. Select **Save**.

The new template file is automatically loaded and displayed in the available template list. If you chose a destination directory that was not already defined as a configuration file path, then it is added automatically to the Configurations node in the scope pane.

Template Descriptions

Template files can be given a description that can help to keep track of the contents of the particular file. Such a description is helpful if you have a lot of templates. Follow these instructions to change the description of the template file saved early in this chapter.

1. Start the **SCM-NT**.
2. Expand the **Configurations** section in the scope pane.
3. Expand the template file directory.
4. Right-click the **Domain1-091998** template.
5. Select **Set Description**.
6. Enter a descriptive text for the file.
7. Select **OK**.

The description is now set. Select the template directory in the scope pane to list the templates in the results pane. Figure 11.10 shows the results pane with the template file and description highlighted.

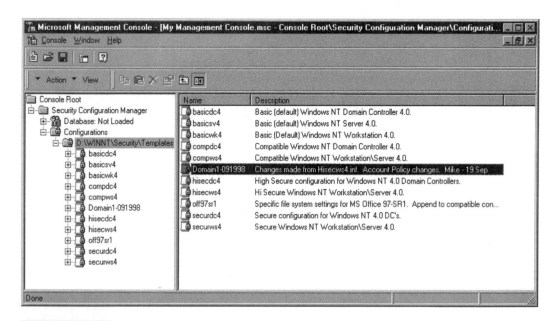

FIGURE 11.10 Text for tracking the content of template configuration files

Configured System Analysis

A Configured System analysis is performed on a system that has already been configured by means of a configuration template file. The template file is then used as the benchmark against which the analysis of the current settings takes place. Differences in the security settings between the two configurations will show up any amendments that have been made since the last time the template was applied. You must have applied a configuration template to your system so that you can compare your system to the benchmark template. For this exercise to be useful, a few changes need to be made to the system security so that discrepancies will show up in the analysis. Follow the procedure below to make some minor security changes on your domain controller (or the substitute machine you are using for testing).

1. Run **User Manager for Domains**.
2. Select **Policies > Account**.
3. Set the **Maximum Password Age** to **60**.
4. Set the **Minimum Password Length** to **5**.
5. Select **OK**.
6. Close **User Manager for Domains**.

Now that the security settings have changed on your system, you can run an analysis to see the differences. Follow the procedures below to perform a Configured System analysis. First the correct template must be loaded.

1. Run **MMC.EXE** to start the MMC program.
2. Select **Open** from the **Console** menu.
3. Enter **My Management Console** and select **Open**.
4. In the scope pane, right-click **Database:*Databasename*** and select **Import Configuration**.
5. Select the **%SystemRoot%\security\templates*Template.inf*** file where *Template.inf* was the template file saved after you configured your system. See the *Saving the New Configuration* section for details. In this case, the file is **Domain1-091998.inf**.
6. Select **Open**.
7. Ensure the check box labeled **Overwrite existing configuration in database** is selected.
8. Select **Open**.

When the template is finished loading we can analyze the system.

1. Right-click **Database**:*Databasename* in the scope pane.

2. Select **Analyze System Now**.

3. Accept the default path for the log file or enter your own preference.

4. Select **OK**. Figure 11.11 shows the differences noted for investigation in the password policy section.

The database file is now populated and the analysis is complete. You can use the analysis information to compare your current settings with those previously stored in the saved template file. If you find discrepancies between the two groups of security settings displayed in the results pane, you must investigate these to make sure that they can be accounted for. When they are accounted for, you may decide that the discrepancies are caused by known changes to the system and you wish to keep these settings.

The SCM-NT gives you the opportunity to change the template settings that you have placed in the database to reflect your current system settings. Changes can only be made to individual settings. Follow the instructions below to change the template file settings for the password policy shown in Figure 11.11 so that the settings replace those stored in the template file.

1. Expand the **Password Policy** node in the scope pane, as shown in Figure 11.11.

2. Right-click the **Maximum Password Age** in the results pane.

3. Select **Security**. Figure 11.12 shows the resulting dialog box.

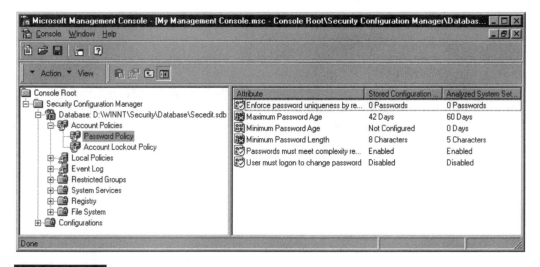

FIGURE 11.11 Security changes in Account Policies, show in the analysis

FIGURE 11.12 Dialog box for changing database setting to reflect system setting

4. In the **Change configuration setting in database to** box, change the setting to **60** days to change the database file setting to reflect the live system setting.

5. Select **OK**. The icon on the left-hand side of the results pane changes to show that the two settings (database and current system) now match.

6. Right-click on **Minimum Password Length**.

7. Select **Security**. Figure 11.13 shows the resulting dialog box.

FIGURE 11.13 Dialog box for storing database changes

8. Set the value to **5** characters to match the current system settings.

9. Select **OK**. Figure 11.14 shows the results pane after the settings are synchronized.

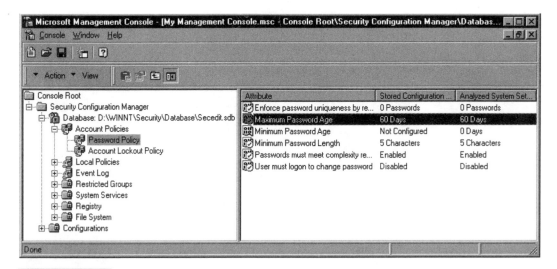

FIGURE 11.14   Changing settings and saving to a template file

You have two choices when saving the new settings to a template file. You can overwrite the template file that you used as input to the database for analysis, or you can create a new template file reflecting the fact that you have made changes (recommended for audit trail purposes). Follow these steps to accomplish either one of these choices.

1. Right-click **Database:***Databasename* in the scope pane.
2. Select **Save** to commit the changes you have made to the database file.
3. Right-click **Database:***Databasename* in the scope pane.
4. Select **Export Configuration**.
5. Choose the file that you opened as input to the database, or enter a new file name.
6. Select **Save**.

This file is now the latest version of your system settings. For safety and audit trail purposes, consider choosing a new file name every time you make and save changes to the system. You then have a trail of changes and can step back to a previous system setting if you need to.

Security Areas

The seven security areas covered by the SCM-NT product include all of the major security settings that you might be concerned with as a system administrator or security professional. The following sections discuss the security areas and their contents. The link between the security area and the "traditional" tool set used for implementing the specified settings is explored. The seven security areas can be loosely grouped into two sections.

- Those containing **static definitions.** This first group is static and cannot be added to. All of the settings within the three security areas in this group exist in all templates and configuration databases (although they may have different values). This group includes the three security areas that are configured with separate tools within Windows NT 4.0, such as User Manager and the System Policy Editor.

- Those containing **dynamic definitions.** This second group of security areas includes contents that can be added to or removed. These contents include security settings for files and directories, registry hives, user groups, and system services. If a relevant item does not already exist within these security areas, then it can be added and secured. For example, if you have an important application directory that is not part of the Windows NT system file installation. You can add this directory to the File System security area and then apply security as needed. You may also decide to apply security to the directory using other means (context menus in NT Explorer) and use this function to analyze security at a later date to ensure that it is still in place.

Static Definitions

The next three sections discuss the security areas contained in the static definitions group.

Account Policies

The Account Policies security area contains settings for user account policies as set in the *User Manager for Domains > Policies > Account* menu (for domain controllers) or the *User Manager > Policies > Accounts* menu (all other machines). Two subcategories in this area control the settings available to you in the User Manager tool set under Account Policies: password policy and account lockout policy

The available options under this security area are shown in Figures 11.15 and 11.16.

To make changes to the setting in this security area, follow this generic procedure and adjust it to fit the setting that you wish to amend.

1. Start the **SCM-NT** and expand the **Configurations** node in the scope pane.

2. Expand the template file that you wish to amend.

3. Expand the **Account Policies** security area and either of the two subcategories.

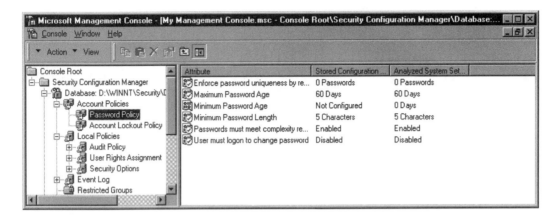

FIGURE 11.15   Available options for account policies: Password policy

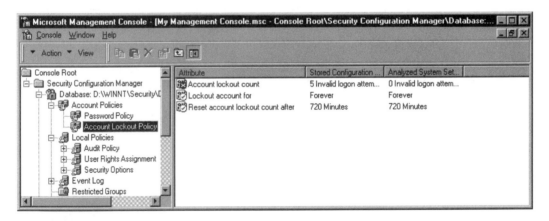

FIGURE 11.16   Available options for account policies: Account Lockout policy

4. Right-click one of the items in the results pane. For this example, use the **Lockout account for** in the **Account Lockout Policy** section.

5. Select **Security**. Figure 11.17 shows the resulting dialog box.

6. Enter the amount of time to lock out the account or select the **Exclude this setting** box. The **Exclude this setting** option means that no value will be stored here, and if this template is used to configure a system or analyze one, this setting will not be included in the process.

7. Select **OK**. The setting is now changed.

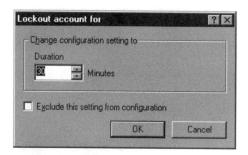

FIGURE 11.17 Setting in the Account Policies security area

Local Policies

The Local Policies security area contains settings that can be applied with the *User Manager* (for domains) tool and also settings that are generally applied directly in the registry or by using the Policy Editor tool. There are three subcategories in the security area.

- Audit policy
- User rights assignments
- Security options

The three available options under this security area are shown in Figures 11.18, 11.19, and 11.20.

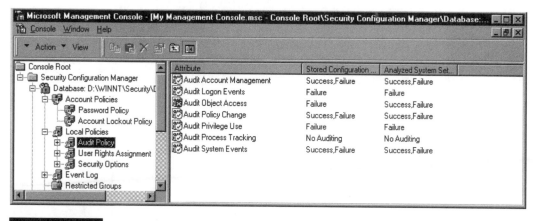

FIGURE 11.18 Available options for local policies: Audit policy

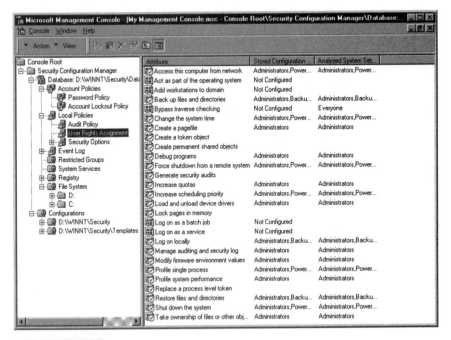

FIGURE 11.19   Available options for local policies: User Rights Assignments

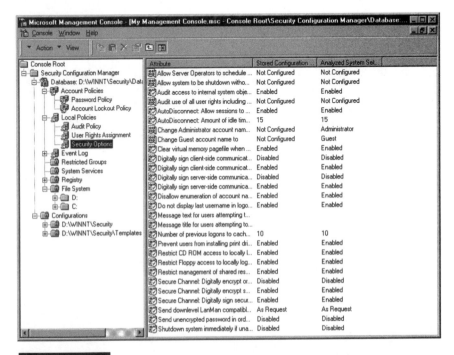

FIGURE 11.20   Available options for local policies: Security Options

To make changes to the setting in this security area, follow this generic procedure and adjust it to fit the setting that you wish to amend.

1. Start the **SCM-NT** and expand the **Configurations** node in the scope pane.

2. Expand the template file that you wish to amend.

3. Expand the **Local Policies** security area and the **User Rights Assignment** subcategory. This category controls settings available in **User Manager for Domains > Policies > User Rights**.

4. Right-click the **Log on locally** setting.

5. Select **Security**. Figure 11.21 shows the resulting dialog box. Note that the **Exclude from future configurations and analyses** check box is selected.

6. Deselect the **Exclude from future configurations and analyses** check box.

7. Select **Add**.

8. Select the Domain Admins group and choose **OK**.

9. Select **OK**. The Domain Admins group is now included in the **Stored Configuration Setting** column.

FIGURE 11.21   Assigning User Rights though the SCM-NT

When the value for an option is set as *Exclude* from future configurations and analyses, it does not mean that the value is set to disabled. It means that when a configuration is performed using this template file, whatever value the option has on the live system remains unchanged. When the analysis is run, the value is not tested against the live system value. This is different from the value being set to disabled. Many of the available security settings have a valid *Disabled* option, which, when chosen, actively sets a registry value to turn an option off. See the example in *Event Log* below.

Event Log

The Event Log security area contains only one subcategory, which configures the parameters concerned with Event Log access and configuration, and which can also be set with the Event Viewer application. Figure 11.22 shows the available parameters for this option.

To make changes to the setting in this security area, follow this generic procedure and adjust it to fit the setting that you wish to amend.

1. Start the **SCM-NT** and expand the **Configurations** node in the scope pane.
2. Expand the template file that you wish to amend.
3. Expand the **Event Log** security area and the **Settings for Event Log** subcategory. This category controls settings available in the **event viewer**.
4. Right-click **Restrict Guest access to System log**. Figure 11.23 shows the resulting dialog box. The *Disabled* option and the *Exclude* option have two very distinct functions, as described in the previous section. These options should not be confused with each other.
5. Choose your preference and select **OK**.

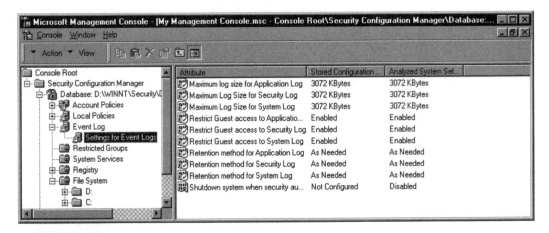

FIGURE 11.22   Available options for Event Log: Settings for Event Log

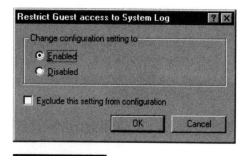

FIGURE 11.23   Guest access dialog box

Dynamic Definitions

The next four sections discuss the security areas that can be added to and deleted from to suit the needs of your installation. The content of these security areas varies according to the template file used.

Restricted Groups

The Restricted Groups security area is blank by default in all of the configuration templates supplied with the product. The Restricted Groups security area in the database node, however, contains six preconfigured groups:

- Administrators
- Backup operators
- Guests
- Power users
- Replicator
- Users

The groups listed here can be added to if you wish to monitor the membership of other sensitive groups.

The Restricted Groups area is used to define user groups whose membership is restricted. You can use this security area to keep track of sensitive groups such as Administrators or Domain Admins and to define who is allowed to belong to these groups. When an analysis is run, the exception reporting will show up any variances from the defined group membership rules. Follow the steps outlined below to define a restricted groups rule, configure the system with the rule, break the rule, analyze the results, and investigate discrepancies.

First, we need to set the rule and select the restricted group and members. For this example, the local Administrator should be the only member of the Administrators group.

1. Start the **SCM-NT** and expand the **Configurations** node in the scope pane.

2. Expand the template file that you wish to use to configure the system. This example uses **Hisecws4.inf**.

3. Right-click **Restricted Groups** in the scope pane.

4. Select **Add Group**.

5. Select the local **Administrators** group and choose **Add > OK**. The Administrators group is displayed in the results pane.

6. Right-click the **Administrators** group in the scope pane.

7. Select **Security**.

8. Select **Add** in the **Members of Administrators** dialog box.

9. Select the local **Administrator** and choose **Add > OK**.

10. Select **OK** to confirm. The local Administrator is now shown in the results pane alongside the Administrators group.

11. Right-click **Hisecws4** under the **Configurations** node in the scope pane.

12. Select **Save As**. Enter the new template name **Template1.inf**. The configuration to be applied and tested in this section is now stored in the Template1.inf file.

This restricted group rule defines the local Administrators group as the target for the rule and the local administrator as the only allowed member of that group. Now, we need to apply the settings to the system. In doing so, we also apply all other settings contained in the template file. Make certain that this is a test system that you can afford to break before proceeding. The next step is to apply the configuration to the system.

1. Right-click **Database:***Databasename* in the scope pane.

2. Select **Open Database**.

3. Enter the name of a new database file for this test. This example uses **Newconf.sdb**.

4. Select **Open**. You are now prompted to associate a template file with the new database file, as shown in Figure 11.24.

5. Ensure that the **Overwrite** check box is selected and choose the Template1.inf file.

6. Select **Open**.

7. Accept the default setting for the log file. An analysis is performed automatically because this database file is new.

Figure 11.25 shows the resulting analysis screen.

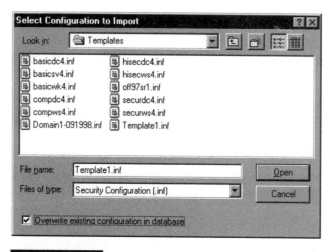

FIGURE 11.24 Template file as associated with every database file

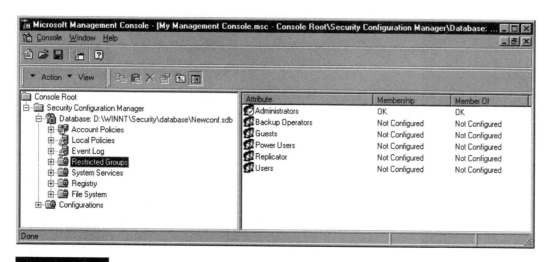

FIGURE 11.25 Analysis results showing Restricted Groups setting

The analysis that runs automatically shows that the restricted groups rule is being adhered to because the local administrator is the only member of the group. Note also the other five groups are part of the Restricted Groups database settings by default. These are all set to the Not Configured state by default. The next step in the demonstration is to break the restricted groups rule for the Administrators group and run the analysis again.

1. In **User Manager**, add the **Guest** account to the **Administrators** local group. This breaks the rule set previously for group membership of Administrators.

2. In the SCM-NT, right-click **Database:***Databasename* in the scope pane.

3. Select **Analyze System Now**.

4. Accept the defaults for the log file.

5. Select **OK**. The analysis starts to run. Figure 11.26 shows the SCM-NT after the latest analysis has completed.

Any changes made in the restricted groups rules are indicated with the usual icon in the results pane and also by the word Investigate in the column that contains the discrepancy. Follow these instructions to investigate the problem.

1. Right-click on the **Administrators** group in the results pane.

2. Select **Security**.

3. Select the **Members** tab. Figure 11.27 shows the resulting screen.

The screen displayed in Figure 11.27 shows that in the configured settings (those contained in the database file), the only allowed member of the Administrators group is the Administrator user. In the analyzed settings (those found to be in place on the live system), the actual members are both Guest and Administrator.

You are not allowed to make changes to the *Analyzed Settings* check boxes because it presents the current settings and can only be adjusted by changing the current settings and performing an analysis again.

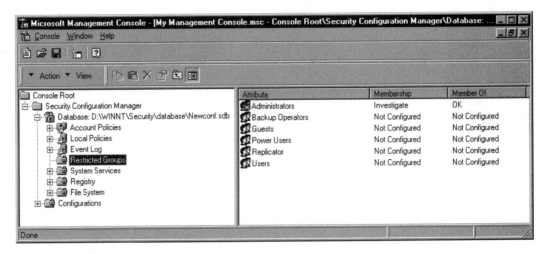

FIGURE 11.26 Restricted Groups entry that needs investigation

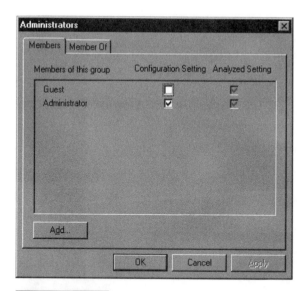

FIGURE 11.27 Culprit for the investigation warning

You can, however, change the *Configuration Setting* section if you find that the investigated settings are acceptable. To accept that Guest should be a member of the Administrators group and to change your database file setting, follow this procedure. Note that this is done as an example and that the Guest account is not recommended to be a member of the Administrators group.

1. In the **Members** tab of the Administrators Restricted Groups page, place a check mark in the **Guest > Configured Setting** box.
2. Select **OK**. Note that the Investigate notice has now been removed from the Administrators group.
3. Right-click **Database:***Databasename* in the scope pane.
4. Select **Save** to place the new setting in the database file.
5. Right-click **Database**:*Databasename* in the scope pane once more.
6. Select **Export Configuration**.
7. Select the **Template1** template file.
8. Select **Save**. The setting is now placed in the `Template1.inf` file for use in future configurations.

System Services

The System Services security area enables control of certain general aspects of the system services on a Windows NT machine. These general aspects include the startup mode for the service (Automatic, Manual, or Disabled) as well as the access that users have to the service.

This security area is extendable by an ISV. The ISV must provide a DLL file defining the available settings for the new system service. The general settings shown above should still be controlled by the SCM-NT.

By default, all settings for every system service are excluded from configuration and analysis runs, effectively disabling the whole of the System Services security area. The following instructions take you through the steps necessary to configure the startup option for the *Alerter* system service using the SCM-NT. In the first steps, we create a new template file and make the change to the system setting in that file. Remember, if you use a template file that has many different settings to your current system, then all of these settings will be changed on your system when you apply the template.

1. Start the **SCM-NT** and expand the **Configurations** node in the scope pane.
2. Expand the template file in which you wish to make the changes.
3. Select the **System Services** security area within the template file in the scope pane.
4. Double-click the **Alerter** service in the results pane. Figure 11.28 shows the resulting dialog box.

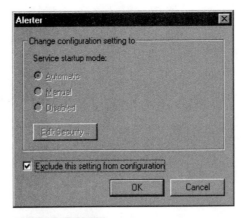

FIGURE 11.28   Default exclusion of system services from configurations

5. Remove the check mark from the **Exclude this setting from configuration** check box.
6. Select the **Service startup mode** radio button of your choice. Make sure that you understand the ramifications of changing this setting and that you are using a test machine.

7. Select **OK**.

8. Right-click on the template file in the scope pane and select **Save**.

The *Edit Security* button shown in Figure 11.28 invokes the new ACL Editor, which is part of the SCM-NT product. This ACL Editor is used to apply security directly to a system object and is discussed in more detail in the section *ACL Editor* later in this chapter.

The next step in the process is to load the template file and apply the configuration.

1. Right-click **Database:***Databasename* in the scope pane.

2. Select **Open Database**.

3. Enter a new database name to associate with this template file.

4. Select **Open.**

5. Select the template in which you have just made the changes.

6. Select **Open**.

7. Accept the default log file path and select **OK**. The analysis will run automatically. Check to make sure the analysis results are as expected.

8. Right-click **Database:***Databasename* in the scope pane.

9. Select **Configure System Now**. The configuration will start immediately.

The steps outlined above show one possible way to change the settings on a system service. The easiest way to make this change on a system is to use the *Control Panel > Services* applet. The SCM-NT is useful when you need to make several changes to the system or to analyze the current system settings against a baseline template file. The SCM-NT does not replace the tools used every day to maintain your security; rather, it works together with these tools to fill any gaps in the security implementation that may have existed previously.

Registry

The Registry security area can be used to apply ACL security to the different registry hives and their keys. This functionality already exists in the `Regedt32.exe` program, which is still the best interface to use for setting security on individual registry keys. The more useful functionality of this security area is exposed when you use it to analyze your system against saved baseline settings.

The registry on an NT system can be very large, and only those few keys that are interesting in the context of system security should be tracked. If you add too many keys to be tracked, then you could lose track of the important items because discrepancies are hidden among the many irrelevant keys shown in an analysis.

The SCM-NT security areas displayed in the Database:*Databasename* node of the scope pane and in the Configurations nodes in the scope pane display the security information in different ways.

DATABASE NODE DISPLAY

Registry key information is displayed in the Database:*Databasename* node gathered into the five relevant registry hive subsections for an NT 4.0 system, as shown in Figure 11.29.

The database is not populated until you run your first system analysis. At this point, the settings contained in the template file that was used to feed the database are compared with your current system settings.

CONFIGURATION FILE NODE DISPLAY

To add registry keys to the list of configured and analyzed keys, you must make the changes in the relevant configuration template file. The following procedure takes you through the steps necessary to add a registry key to a configuration file for analysis.

1. Expand the configuration file that you wish to use in the scope pane.

2. Expand the **Registry** node within the configuration file. The results pane shows the keys that are already defined within this template file.

3. Right-click the **Registry** node and select **Add Key**. Note that you only have a choice of the three main registry hives. CURRENT_* registry hives are made up from settings taken from these main hives and locally applied settings.

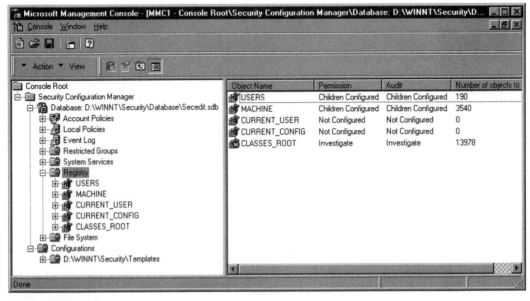

FIGURE 11.29   The five registry hives displayed in the Database:Databasename node of the SCM-NT

4. Navigate to the registry key that you wish to add.

5. Use the **ACL Editor** to set the required security.

6. Select **OK**.

7. Right-click the configuration file in the scope pane and select **Save**.

The registry key is now included in the configuration file. The configuration file must be applied to the system before the changes become active.

1. Right-click **Database**:*Databasename* in the scope pane.

2. Select **Import Configuration**.

3. Select the template file that you wish to import.

4. Select **Open**.

5. Right-click **Database**:*Databasename* in the scope pane.

6. Select **Configure System Now**.

7. Accept the default log file name and path.

8. Select **OK**. The system configuration will run automatically and may take some time.

The instructions outlined here can also be used in the next section, *File System*, to apply the configuration discussed there.

Changes in registry security are best made with the Regedt32.exe program. Reserve the use of the SCM-NT tool to analysis functionality where the registry is concerned.

File System

The File System security area is similar to the Registry security area in that it uses the ACL Editor to apply security to files and directories and can be used to analyze current system settings against a preconfigured template file.

As with the Registry security area, the File System security area is used to track security on files and directories that are important to system security or to your own specific security needs (perhaps the security on an important database system could be tracked). Be careful not to add too many files and directories to the list for analysis—you may lose sight of important discrepancies that may occur. The following instructions add security to a folder and look for any changes in this security through the analysis function. First, the security setup.

1. In the scope pane expand the configuration file through which you will apply the File System security.

2. Right-click **File System** and select **Add Folder**.

3. Navigate to the required folder.

4. Select **OK**. The security configuration dialog box appears.

5. Use the ACL Editor to configure the required security.

6. Select **OK**. The resulting dialog box is shown in Figure 11.30.

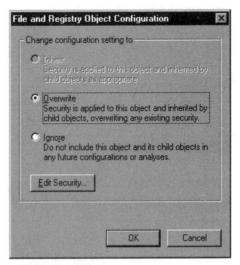

FIGURE 11.30   Choosing the Overwrite radio button to apply changes to child objects

7. Select **OK**, leaving the options at their default setting.

8. Right-click the template file and choose **Save**.

The *Inherit* option grayed out in Figure 11.30 is a Windows 2000 option and is not used for NT 4.0, as described in *Protection of Child Objects* in the next section.

The next step is to apply the configuration. Follow the instructions outlined above in *Registry* to apply the configuration.

Once the system has been configured, you can change the security that you have just set for the directory in question and run an analysis to look at the results. This procedure is covered in the section *Configured System Analysis*. Run the analysis and look at the results. You should have an Investigate notice on the directory for which you have change permissions.

Changes to file system security are best made using the context menus in Windows NT Explorer. Reserve the use of the SCM-NT to analysis functionality where file system security is concerned.

ACL Editor

The ACL Editor provides a new interface for amending security on system objects such as files, directories, system services, and registry keys. The new ACL Editor interface replaces the previous interface available when setting security with NT Explorer. The ACL Editor, with as seen in the context-sensitive menus contained in NT Explorer, is shown in Figure 11.31.

Protection of Child Objects

The new ACL Editor interface was designed originally for inclusion with Windows 2000 but was released earlier in a form compatible with Windows NT 4.0. The ACL security model available for Windows 2000 allows inheritance of security to be blocked by a child object. The ACL Editor accomplishes this by using the *Allow inheritable permissions from parent to propagate to this object* check box. When this check box is cleared, the object is *Protected*, and changes made to the parent object do not affect the child.

The ACL Editor used within the SCM-NT allows this protected status to be overridden from the parent directory by means of the *Overwrite* radio button in the Security Editor as shown in Figure 11.30.

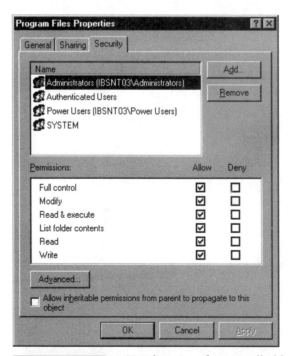

FIGURE 11.31   ACL Editor interface installed by Security Configuration Manager setup

The *Inherit* radio button is permanently grayed out, as shown in Figure 11.30, in the version of the SCM for NT 4.0. Windows NT does not allow for protection of child objects, so the default and only available setting here is for settings made at the parent to be propagated in full to all child objects. You may want to use the SCM-NT to set ACL permissions for objects and not to have these changes propagated to the child objects. If so, include the child objects by name in the configuration file and select the *Ignore* radio button so they are not included in the configuration run.

Inheritable Permissions

When you create a new folder, the default permissions for that folder are assigned automatically by the system and the permissions from the parent directory are used. The *Allow inheritable permissions from parent to propagate to this object* check box is selected by default, so the parent permissions are inherited. Figure 11.32 shows the inherited permissions on a new folder.

Compare figures 11.31 and 11.32. Figure 11.31 shows permissions that have been set directly on a folder. Figure 11.32 shows inherited permissions. Inherited permissions cannot be amended in any way other than complete removal. This is signified by the grayed-out boxes. Amendments to these permissions can only be made at the parent level where they have been explicitly applied.

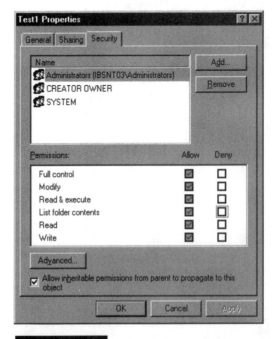

FIGURE 11.32   Inherited permissions cannot be amended at child level

To remove the inherited permissions, you must remove the check mark from the *Allow inheritable permissions from parent to propagate to this object* check box. Figure 11.33 shows the resulting warning message which presents options for replacing these permissions.

You are given a choice of two positive actions at this point. You can copy the parent permissions to the child object so that the child object has explicit permissions set, or you can remove the parent permissions and leave any explicit permissions. A new folder will not have any explicit permissions set, so these must be set before any user can access the new folder.

Advanced Attributes

The ACL Editor contains an *Advanced Attributes* page, which allows a fine-grained approach to securing objects within your system. Remember that this feature was originally destined for Windows 2000 only, so some descriptions and wording may seem a little strange at first or may not apply to NT 4.0 at all. Figure 11.34 shows the ACL Editor advanced attributes screen.

The advanced attributes screen allows you to apply a finer-grained security level to your system objects. The advanced attributes are split into three sections.

PERMISSIONS

The *Permissions* tab is used to control access permissions to the object. Figure 11.34 shows the permissions assigned to users and groups for the directory being looked at. By selecting the *View/Edit* button, you are presented with the screen shown in Figure 11.35, which is the key to applying finer-grained security access levels with the ACL Editor.

All of the permissions listed can be set to either *Allow* access or *Deny* access. Standard NT rules apply for deciding which setting takes precedence if permissions are set for a user in more than one way. See Chapter Three for more information.

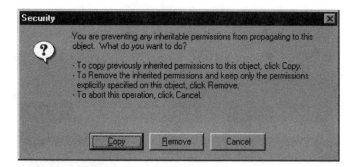

FIGURE 11.33 Replacing permissions when denying inheritance

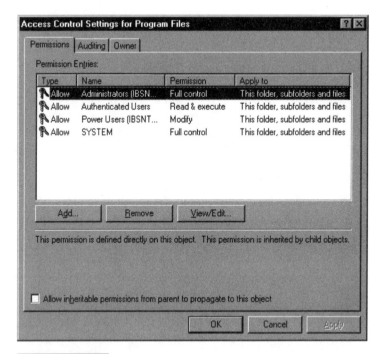

FIGURE 11.34 Advanced attributes in the ACL Editor

Some of the permissions listed have no effect in an NT 4.0 environment and are available here because the interface was originally intended for release with Windows 2000. The permissions that are most useful in this version of the ACL Editor are listed below.

- List folder / Read data
- Create files / Write data
- Create folders / Append Data
- Delete subfolders and files
- Delete
- Read permissions
- Change permissions
- Take ownership

In Figure 11.35, all of the check boxes in the Allow column are marked and have a white background. This white background signifies the ability to change the setting. If you do not have permission to change settings because they are inherited (see *Inheritable Permissions* above) then the background will be gray.

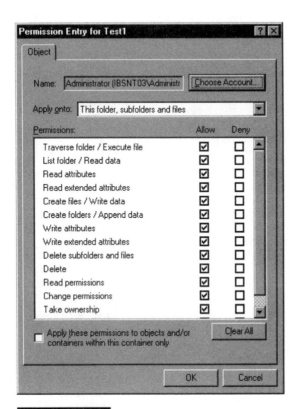

FIGURE 11.35   Finer-grained permissions possible with the ACL Editor

The *Clear All* button removes any setting that you have permissions to remove on the currently displayed user.

The *Apply onto* drop-down list governs the extent to which the permissions are applied. Figure 11.36 shows the available options on this list.

The *Choose Account* button allows you to select another valid user/group to apply the displayed settings to. This selection replaces the existing user. To add a user and keep all existing configured users, use the *Add* button on the advanced *Access Control Settings* screen.

AUDITING

The *Auditing* tab is used to audit the access to a file or folder. For any auditing to function on an NT machine the *Audit Policy* in *User Manager (for Domains)* must be enabled to track *File and Object Access*. See Chapter Nine, *NT Audit*, for more details.

Once the audit policy is set, you can use the ACL Editor to start auditing particular files or directories.

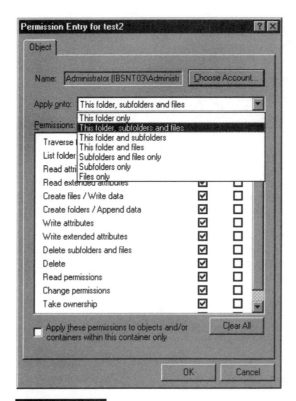

FIGURE 11.36   Controlling the scope of permissions

1. Select the **Auditing** tab.
2. Select **Add**.
3. Select the user or group you wish to track and select **Add**.
4. Select **OK**.
5. Select the access you wish to audit.
6. Select **OK**.
7. Select **OK** to confirm.

OWNER

The *Owner* tab allows you to view the owner of a file or directory or to take ownership if you have the correct permissions. The *Replace owner on subcontainers and objects* check box can be used to propagate the ownership change down the directory tree.

Updating the Baseline Template

When you make system changes by using the SCM-NT interface, it is important to carefully plan the way in which you intend to apply changes in the future. In any dynamic environment system, changes are made frequently, including changes to system security. The examples contained in this chapter have illustrated the procedures for applying a baseline security model to your systems as well as for making individual changes to many security areas.

It is important to remember that the analysis functionality within this product relies on a baseline against which it can measure the current settings. From the very beginning, when you first use the product to apply a security template to your system, you must bear this fact in mind. Every time you make a security-related change to your system, the system moves out of line with your baseline template (unless you use the template and associated database to apply *all* security changes, which could be quite cumbersome). When you run an analysis, you may find discrepancies between the baseline and the current settings. At such a time, you can use the procedures outlined in *Configured System Analysis* for updating your template file to match your current system. If you save the template file with a new (meaningful) name, you can keep an audit trail of changes and also use the previous version to revert to if there are any problems.

Summary

The Security Configuration Manager for NT 4.0 was originally destined for release with NT 5.0 (Windows 2000). The product brings together all of the available security features that exist in the many various tools such as User Manager (for Domains), `Regedt32.exe`, and event viewer. Although the tool should not be used as a replacement for all of the existing security tools, it is useful when applying large-scale security changes to your systems, and it is a vast improvement over event viewer for analyzing, viewing, and tracking security-related system changes.

When using the SMC-NT for analysis, make sure that all security changes that vary from the configured baseline template and that are made using tools other than the SCM-NT are reflected in your baseline configuration file; either enter the changes manually or run periodic analysis and accept each discrepancy as it is uncovered.

Looking Forward to Windows 2000

Chapter Twelve introduces some of the new features in Microsoft Windows 2000 operating system. Prominent in this list of features is the Microsoft Management Console.

Chapter Thirteen introduces the Microsoft 2000 Active Directory. This new directory service structure does not replace the domain structure familiar to anybody who has worked with Windows NT systems but enhances that familiar structure by applying an extra level to the domain hierarchy. The extra level in the hierarchy makes Windows 2000 networks almost infinitely scalable while making administration even simpler. Some of the more important features of the AD are discussed in this chapter and directory terminology is introduced. Step-through examples of some the newer administrative techniques demonstrate the added flexibility attained with Windows 2000.

Chapter Fourteen discusses the Microsoft Security Configuration Tool Set. This set of administrative tools forms the backbone of the security implementation and analysis functions in Windows 2000. The tool set and the implementation of the individual tools and services are discussed in detail in this chapter. Follow the step-through guides to configuring system security in this chapter to derive the greatest benefit from them.

Chapter Fifteen discusses group policies in Windows 2000 and how they help to apply not only security settings but all other computer and user-related settings throughout the Active Directory.

Chapter Sixteen introduces the file system security features of Windows 2000. The first part of the chapter discusses the new features that enhance the scalability of the Windows operating system, such as the Distributed File System, and the security issues surrounding their implementation. The second part of the chapter covers the new Windows 2000 Encrypting File System in some detail.

Windows 2000 Overview

This chapter introduces some of the new features in Microsoft Windows 2000 operating system.

Prominent in this list of features is the Microsoft Management Console. This chapter contains some step-by-step instructions on the creation of an MMC console; these steps can serve as an introduction to this new management feature.

Introduction to the Windows 2000 Infrastructure

When was the first time you heard that mainframes were dying out and that client/server was the way forward for computing? Mainframes were expensive pieces of equipment to buy and maintain, and client/server technology was heralded as the inexpensive alternative. Mainframes needed specialist support and acted as a single point of failure. Distributed server technology was set to overcome these drawbacks by providing a low-maintenance, inexpensive alternative.

The Reality of Client/Server Technology

As client/server technology took hold, it became apparent that the technology brought with it unexpected expense and maintenance issues. Client/server was rolled out in the same fashion as mainframes. Where one large mainframe supported an enterprise, smaller servers were rolled out to support individual business units. These servers were not used collectively to address business needs, but rather they were deployed separately and maintained as individual entities.

The reality of the early client/server technology boom was that much of the benefit gained from the lowering of initial investment and upgrade costs was lost in the extra overhead of distributed administration. The core operating systems did not contain integrated services to provide easy access to data (users needed to know the server name on which the data existed), and this meant that extra overhead was added to the already strained management system.

Client/server obviously brought benefits as well as a downside. Distributed systems meant that loads were placed on the individual PCs rather than on a central mainframe processor, thus freeing processing power for the larger centralized applications. The single point of failure (the central mainframe) was removed from the equation. Now, if a server went down, a much smaller business unit would be affected. Only the resources contained within that server would be unavailable.

Client/Server Moves On

With the design of Windows 2000, Microsoft has made huge strides toward the ultimate goal of a distributed computer system combining the benefits of lower cost of ownership, centralized management, and scalability.

Features

Windows 2000 is a feature-rich, scalable network operating system designed with management and security features built in as core components. For those of you who worked with NT version 3.51 or below and were stunned at the advances with the introduction of NT 4.0, I suggest you prepare yourself well before installing Windows 2000. Some of the new and improved features are outlined below.

MICROSOFT MANAGEMENT CONSOLE

A new approach to management with Windows 2000 sees the introduction of the Microsoft Management Console, first debuted as an add-on feature to Windows NT 4.0, as the management interface for all system-related tasks. MMC acts as a central host platform for management applications, gathering all of the important tasks in one easy-to-manage area. Microsoft Management Console is discussed in detail in Chapter Ten.

FILE SYSTEMS

An improved file system service introduces encryption to the file and directory structure. One of the qualities of a secure system is the ability to encrypt files and directories so that even if physical access is gained to the disk, data is still safe. The Windows NT operating system, while it improved data security with the introduction of NTFS, provides little protection against malicious data access if the physical disk becomes accessible. The Encrypting File System goes some way toward addressing this problem.

Distributed file system support allows files to exist on many different host server types and still be available transparently within the Active Directory.

File systems are discussed in Chapter Sixteen.

SECURITY CONFIGURATION TOOL SET

The tool set consists of the main tools used within the MMC console to apply security settings and to enable their easy review. The security database produced within the Security Configuration Editor can be analyzed; settings such as system policies, user permissions, and directory tree security can be controlled and implemented by the Security Configuration Manager. The Security Configuration Tool Set is discussed in Chapter Fourteen.

DISTRIBUTED SECURITY SERVICES

The distributed security services for Windows 2000 are a collection of security features and approaches to the management of the security model developed for the Windows 2000 operation system.

Security professionals today face far greater security-related challenges than did their predecessors. External partner connections, E-commerce, Internet access, intranet access, and globe spanning networks are all realities of today's business requirements. All of these new business opportunities bring with them more and more risks to the safety of the network. The more accessible we try to make a network, the more risk there is that somebody will try to penetrate the security.

The Windows 2000 network operating system security structure has changed significantly from that of Windows NT versions to meet the needs of existing challenges and prepare for future challenges. The new features of the Windows 2000 security model extend to all parts of the operating system architecture.

Where the Windows NT operating system utilizes a flat name-space to define the domain structure, Windows 2000 implements a hierarchical name-space design of multiple domains. This hierarchy is organized into a directory tree structure with users, files, printers, servers, and all other parts of the overall NT system being represented as objects within the tree. With the gathering together of all of the different system objects under one hierarchy, Microsoft has redefined the security model to reflect the new relationships between objects.

The use of *inheritance* to make the security definitions simpler and *delegation* to allow the security management to be distributed are both ways of lowering the total cost of ownership for the new systems by lowering the management overhead. These concepts are discussed in Chapter Thirteen, *Active Directory*.

The security layers connecting these objects have also been changed radically. Newer technologies, such as digital certificates, and existing protocols, such as SSL and Kerberos, will be used to create secure access and secure channels between parties.

SECURITY PROTOCOLS

All versions of the NT operating system were built around the goal of strong security. The design of Windows 2000 will increase the comfort factor tremendously by employing industry-standard encryption and secure channel techniques to safeguard against intrusion and eavesdropping.

The new Active Directory brings together all of the various aspects of NT security under one hierarchical structure for ease of management and tighter control of the enterprise network.

Microsoft has put a huge amount of time and effort into securing the transmission of data over the local and wide area networks as well as over the Internet. Many of the protocols supported by Windows 2000 seem to provide the same service as others. Microsoft has provided support for many different network and security protocols with this version of the network operating system. The reasons for this support are backward compatibility with Windows NT and other client operating systems, compatibility with networks comprising many different systems (the Internet, for one), and provision of the strongest possible security protocols when they can be utilized.

Chapter Six, *Cryptography*, discusses the different protocols in use in Windows NT today and also looks at the protocols used in Windows 2000, including when and where they are implemented.

SECURITY SUPPORT PROVIDER INTERFACE (SSPI)

Recall that the SSPI is an abstraction layer between the security providers of the NT distributed security services and the application-level communications mechanisms, such as RPC-enabled programs or Internet Explorer, which may need to use the secure communications methods.

Instead of the applications programmer having to write interfaces to each of the available security protocols, the SSPI sits in between and provides the programmer with a standard interface to write to. The transport layer applications use a mechanism to make a call to any one of the several security providers and receive an authenticated connection without knowledge of the involved security protocols (Kerberos, SSL, etc.).

An SSP (Security Support Provider) is a library that manages a particular cryptographic scheme. Together, the libraries make up the SSPI. The four supported SSPs in Windows 2000 are for the following security protocols:

- NTLM
- Kerberos
- SSL/PCT/TLS
- DPA

Figure 12.1 shows a simple model of application, SSPI, and security protocol interaction.

The security protocols listed above are discussed in Chapter Six, *Cryptography*.

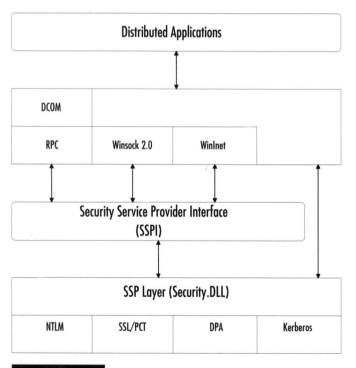

FIGURE 12.1   Windows 2000 security model

CRYPTOAPI

The CryptoAPI is a core component of the Microsoft NT security subsystem and will continue to be so in Windows 2000. The CryptoAPI is a set of 32-bit APIs that provide various cryptographic functions to the security subsystem. CryptoAPI is modular in design and allows different components to be replaced to suit the needs of the security environment and the applications that are written to use it. The replaceable modules (Cryptographic Service Providers, or CSPs) perform all of the actual cryptographic work, making the system independent of any one application or encryption method. Applications can be written for the CryptoAPI; then, different encryption algorithm modules can be slotted in to meet the needs of the users environment.

The CryptoAPI also includes the storage mechanisms for the secret key technologies in either software or hardware. Smartcards are the up-and-coming technology best placed to take advantage of CryptoAPI technology. Smartcards are made to be tamper proof and so provide the ideal portable storage mechanism for public key information.

Introduction of the Active Directory

The introduction of the Active Directory in Windows 2000 is probably the single biggest change between this version of the Microsoft operating system and all previous versions. In all previous versions of the operating system, Microsoft used a flat namespace approach when gathering computers, users, printers, and all other objects together to interact with one another. This technique has worked well up to now, but as computer networks continue to grow in size and complexity, this flat namespace becomes increasingly difficult to manage. In Windows NT versions of the operating system the highest point at which computers could be linked together and managed is the domain. While Microsoft has continued to use the domain as an important method of grouping computers, users, and resources together, they have introduced a higher level of management connectivity in the form of the Active Directory.

Hierarchical Namespace

The Active Directory is a hierarchical structure that allows a greater number of resources to be gathered together while providing a single point of administration. The introduction of this hierarchical namespace means that domains are now gathered in groups within the directory and that the boundaries for management no longer have to stop at the domain edge. The domains in turn can now be subdivided into units called organizational units or OUs. The namespace exists to allow objects to be named (and so found) within the directory.

Object Organization

Objects (users, printers, machines) can be organized logically within the domain tree to fit in with the actual organization of the company. Departments and other organizational structures within the company can be mapped directly to a corresponding OU, a feature that makes management tasks that much easier.

Restructures within the company can be reflected easily in the domain tree by renaming or moving objects and OUs accordingly.

Replicating the Active Directory

The Active Directory is made up of one or more domains. The corresponding portion of the active directory (user accounts, group profiles, etc.) are held on the domain controllers within the domain. Unlike the Windows NT operating system, which needs to differentiate between primary and backup domain controllers, Windows 2000 supports one single type of domain controller. Multiple master copies of the directory information can coexist within the domain tree. Now, changes to account information can be made on any domain controller within a domain, and these changes are replicated to all of the other domains. Multiple changes of the same information are accommodated by version mechanisms maintained within the domain.

Scalability

Scalability was one of the design goals prioritized early in the development process of Windows 2000; as a result, the Active Directory can begin life with just a single domain containing a few objects and scale almost effortlessly to over 10 million objects per domain, with multiple domains existing in the same directory tree.

A Complete Directory Solution?

Technology such as the Distributed File System support, the use of DNS as the main object location method, the use of industry-standard protocols, integration with the Internet, and the ability to use granular administrative approaches combine to provide a real step forward in the search for a complete global directory solution. The Active Directory is discussed in detail in Chapter Thirteen.

Do You Use Administrator Account Too Much?

The Administrator account will still be used in Windows 2000 in much the same way as it is now. It is still the all-encompassing security officer account for the domain.

One of the main security problems faced in Windows NT at the moment is the frequent use of the Administrator account to perform tasks that do not require this level of permission. It is much easier for a network administrator to use the one account for all work rather than multiple accounts with just the right amount of privilege for each task. This security exposure could lead to serious intrusion problems. For example, perhaps the person using the Administrator account (and so administrative security context within the system) visits a WWW site outside of her control. If malicious code was to be downloaded under the Administrative security context, then that code could operate freely on the system and cause major damage.

Microsoft has addressed this worrying issue by removing the need for a direct Administrator account logon to perform system-related tasks. The process is known as secondary logon and is likely to become a common way of operating highly sensitive accounts in a controlled fashion. Secondary logon is discussed in Chapter Thirteen, *Active Directory*.

Active Directory

This chapter introduces the Microsoft 2000 Active Directory. This new directory service structure does not replace the domain structure familiar to anybody who has worked with Windows NT systems but enhances that familiar structure by applying an extra level to the domain hierarchy. The extra level in the hierarchy makes Windows 2000 networks almost infinitely scalable while making administration even simpler.

Some of the more important features of the AD are discussed in this chapter and directory terminology is introduced. Step-through examples of some the newer administrative techniques demonstrate the added flexibility attained with Windows 2000.

What Is a Directory Service?

An enterprise network today can be a vast entity made up of large numbers of servers, each with large numbers of users, volumes, printers, print servers, and workstations. In a network environment this large, how can you be sure where anything is? How can you find a particular volume or a group of users? The answer to these questions is the Directory Services.

Directory Services provide the means to organize the objects within your enterprise, such as users and printers, in a manageable fashion. Directory Services provide the means to build a hierarchical view of your enterprise network and to locate objects easily.

A good Directory Service allows management functionality to be centralized or distributed as a matter of choice. It can help to bring disparate network systems together under the same administrative context, using common administrative tools.

Directory Terminology

The structure of a Windows 2000 enterprise network can be very different from that of Windows NT networks. The terms and phrases used when discussing these networks has evolved and changed dramatically as well. You will benefit from understanding the meaning of the following terms before looking at Windows 2000 and the Active Directory.

CONTAINER

A type of object. It gathers together other objects in the Active Directory.

DISTINGUISHED NAME (DN)

A name derived from starting at the top of the tree and adding every container name that is navigated to find the object. Every object in the directory has a unique DN. An example of a distinguished name is o=ibs.ou=london.ou=sales.cn=user1, where o=ibs is the Organization name, ou=london is the name of the next organizational unit container under ibs, ou=sales is the next organizational unit under london, and cn=user1 is the common name of the object. See Relative Distinguished Name (RDN).

DOMAIN TREE

Linked domains sharing the same schema and a contiguous namespace. An Active Directory is a domain tree.

FOREST

A set of one or more trees that do not share a contiguous namespace but do share the same schema.

GLOBAL CATALOG

The Active Directory can be made up of many partitions, as described above. The distinguished name of an object gives enough information to locate the partition holding the object, but if you don't have the distinguished name, you may need another way of finding the object. This is where the Global Catalog comes in. The Global Catalog contains information about all of the objects within the AD. It is built automatically by the AD installation but can be modified to suit the needs of the enterprise. Object attributes commonly used in search operations are listed in the Global Catalog. This might be first names and last names for the user objects. The catalog is extensible, so if your enterprise identifies people by employee ID, then this attribute can be attached to the user object and then gathered in the Global Catalog. The catalog holds a very small subset of attributes for the objects it describes and searches work faster if this subset is not increased too much.

LEAF OBJECT

Object in a container that cannot contain other objects. A leaf object is at the bottom of the tree structure.

NAMESPACE

An area within which a name can be resolved. This area could be a file system within which the name of a file can be resolved (found), the file itself, or an address book within which an address can be resolved to a location.

NETWORK DOMAIN

The building blocks of the Active Directory. An Active Directory is made up from one or more network domains. A network domain also represents a security boundary within which security settings are localized. Unless otherwise stated, the references to domains in this text refer to network domains.

OBJECT

An entry in the Active Directory representing any tangible "thing," including users, printers, print servers, and machines. It is actually the gathering together of the information representing the user, printer, etc.

ORGANIZATION

A container in a directory tree. An Organization represents the top level of containers in a tree. This is also a container because it holds other objects.

ORGANIZATIONAL UNIT (OU)

A type of container that groups together objects. Can contain other OUs, which in turn can contain objects (or more OUs).

RELATIVE DISTINGUISHED NAME (RDN)

The common name (referred to in the example in Distinguished Name: cn=user1). Every object has an RDN. The RDN is also known as the *Common Name* (CN=user1).

SCHEMA

The directory schema defines the attributes that make up each unique type of object. The schema also defines where each class of object can exist in the directory structure. The schema is extensible, and tools allow the administrator to amend the schema so that the restrictions on the class of objects that can be stored in certain areas are changeable.

SCOPE

The area covered by the Active Directory. Because of its scalability, can be a single domain, multiple domains, a WAN, or even multiple WANs.

SITE

Usually, one physical network that contains Active Directory servers. It is defined by a single TCP/IP subnet. A site is used to split the Active directory into physical locations for directory replication, among other things. Sites enable local users to find AD servers locally because they are on the same subnet. Authentication and other tasks are speeded up because local servers are contacted first.

STANDALONE DOMAIN

A single standalone machine. Standalone domains do not participate in the Active Directory.

TREE

A hierarchy of objects. A tree usually contains several levels of containers and subcontainers. The bottom-most point of a tree is the leaf object.

VIRTUAL CONTAINER

The exposure point in an Active Directory of another directory service. A foreign directory service (Novell NetWare's NDS, for example) can be represented in the Active Directory by means of *knowledge information*. This knowledge information is inserted in the AD at the point where the foreign directory should appear. The information represents the DNS name of the server holding the directory and a starting point for foreign directory search operations.

Windows 2000 Active Directory Overview

Windows 2000 Active Directory delivers a solution to all of your directory needs. As some of its benefits, this robust directory delivers scalability, extensibility, a hierarchical nature allowing top-down views of your directory objects, security, and replication abilities far improved on Windows NT.

Centralized Management

Centralized administration and management are provided by the AD for all objects within the directory including user, printers, volumes, databases, and any other objects existing in the AD.

DNS is used as the locator service for all objects in the AD and is a required system component for a Windows 2000 Active Directory.

The Active Directory tree is made up of one or more domains linked together; these domains in turn are organized hierarchically into organizational units (OUs). This structure allows a choice of centralized or distributed management, and this choice is configurable at any time.

Single Unified Directory

The AD can integrate with other directory services on non-Windows 2000 systems. Management of objects within these directories can be achieved through the AD, thus providing a single unified directory structure for your enterprise. Centralized management can still be a benefit even if your organization has been built up on many separate platforms. The use of the Lightweight Directory Access Protocol (LDAP) as the main protocol aids this cross-platform integration capability.

Scalability

The Active Directory engine is based on the Microsoft Exchange storage engine. Speed and efficiency are provided when retrieving directory information with this engine.

The Active Directory can scale from a single domain with a few hundred users to a huge installation with tens of millions of objects. When a directory structure starts to get this large, the speed and efficiency of the storage and retrieval engine is important. The administrative overheads do not rise in parallel to the scaling of object content because of the centralized administrative functionality.

Domain trees hold the key to the scalability of the Active Directory. Instead of one stored directory getting larger and larger as it is scaled upward in size, the Active Directory actually exists as domain trees grouped together under the same namespace. Each domain forms part of the larger AD. Therefore users who regularly use objects that exist in a particular part of the AD are created in that part of the tree. They can use objects in any other part of the AD if they have the correct permissions.

Domain Structure

With the Windows NT versions of the operating system, domain controller status is defined at installation time. Windows 2000 server installations do not include this choice. Instead, the installed server is promoted to domain controller status by the Dcpromo.exe program, which is a GUI-based wizard that guides the installer through the various choices for domain controllers.

Organizational Units (OU)

Domains are divided into organizational units, which are logical administrative boundaries that organize directory objects into areas that resemble an enterprise structure. For example, a domain created for the London office may have OUs created called Sales, Research, and Manufacturing, to mirror the business functions carried out by the organization. This way, all of the associated users and peripheral devices can be grouped together for administrative purposes. Figure 13.1 depicts a basic domain structure.

Active Directory Structure

The Active Directory is formed on the first Windows 2000 server to be promoted to domain controller status. This forms the first partition of the Active Directory. The first domain in the Active Directory is the root domain. All other domains are formed as child nodes from the root domain. This can be seen in Figure 13.2.

During installation of future domain controllers, certain choices are made that affect the structure and layout of the AD:

■ First, whether to join a preexisting domain or to form a new domain

■ If forming a new domain, then whether to include this domain in the existing AD or to form a separate AD

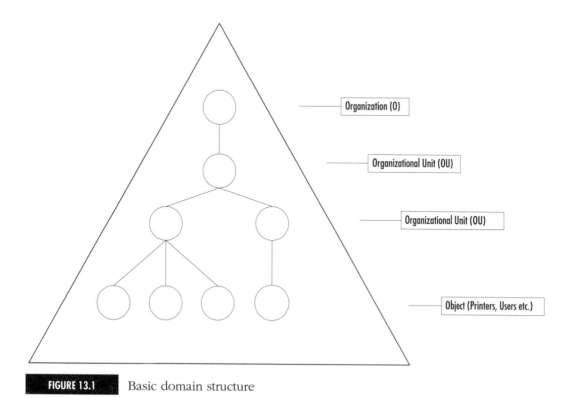

Organization (0)

Organizational Unit (OU)

Organizational Unit (OU)

Object (Printers, Users etc.)

FIGURE 13.1   Basic domain structure

- If creating a new directory, then the domain is formed as the root domain
- If joining an existing directory, then the domain can be joined at any point below the existing root domain. There can only be one root domain per Active Directory

You should carefully plan the placement of the new domain in an existing directory, bearing in mind the required security and administrative structures you wish to implement. The placement will be influenced by the manner in which you wish to use the *inheritance* and *transitive trust* features of the AD. These features are discussed later in the *Domains and Trust Relationships* section.

A domain joined into the AD below another domain is known as a child domain. The domain above the child is known as a parent domain. All domains can be both a child and a parent domain in that they can all have domains above and below them in the directory structure. The only exception to this is the root domain, which can be a parent but never a child. In the domain setup procedures, you choose the placement of a domain in the AD by choosing which domain is to be the parent of the new (child) domain.

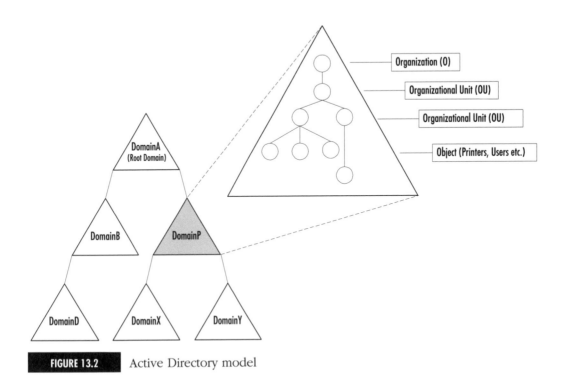

FIGURE 13.2 Active Directory model

Naming Support

The Active Directory is a namespace, that is, an area within which a name can be resolved by some available method. DNS is used as the locating and name resolution service for the Active Directory. The root domain is used as the beginning of the DNS naming system. All domains created after this point are named with the root domain name plus their individual name.

All objects in the Active Directory are named in this fashion. For example, the user object at the bottom of DomainP shown in Figure 13.2 might be called o=ibs.ou=london.ou=sales.cn=user1. The Active Directory supports many other naming conventions for objects within the Active Directory. Applications often need to request an object and have a built-in format for naming the object. The AD can support many naming formats and so provide added functionality that many directory services do not offer. The user object mentioned earlier is shown below in different, supported naming conventions.

- LDAP—LDAP://IBS01/ibs.com/cn=user1,ou=sales,ou=london, o=ibs,c=uk
- UNC—\\Ibs.com\London.sales.user1
- HTTP—HTTP://IBS01.ibs.com/london/sales/user1
- RFC822—(Internet) User1@ibs.com

Partitions

Each domain makes up one distinct partition of the Active Directory. All domains added together form the whole of the AD. Copies of the partitions are held on each domain controller DC within the domain.

MultiMaster Replication

The idea of primary and backup domain controllers is not supported in Windows 2000. The Windows 2000 domain recognizes all domain controllers as peers. In Windows NT, any changes to objects in the domain (e.g., user additions or amendments) could only be made on the PDC. The replica information stored on BDCs was read-only. This led to severe restrictions to the scalability of the server systems.

Each DC in a Windows 2000 domain contains a full read-write copy of the AD partition. Replication is performed automatically among the DCs at timed intervals. Update sequence numbers (USN) are used instead of time-stamps to control system changes that may clash. If a user password is changed on two separate copies of the partition, then the changes are replicated to partners and the USNs decide which conflicting change to apply. In a tie-break situation where USN number match, then timestamps break the deadlock and only the last change is applied. This ability to have more than one read-write partition copy makes scaling upwards much easier because workloads can be shared evenly. It also means that no one server is any more important than another for Active Directory reasons.

Active Directory Security

Administration

Administrative functionality can be fine-tuned to the design of the Active Directory. It would be good practice in a large organization to divide administrative responsibility within the AD. Security boundaries do not have to stop at the domain edge, but it may make sense in your own structure to have them stop there.

The most important thing to remember about administration of an AD is that it can be delegated in any way that you feel is right for your own network design. Delegation of the Control wizard is discussed later in the chapter.

Secondary Logon

Secondary logon allows an administrator (or anyone with access to an administrative account) to run programs or tasks in an administrative context while logging on as a normally privileged user. The benefit of this approach is that a system administrator can be logged on as a normal user and still perform administrative functions without having to log off. This feature addresses the security issues concerned with overuse of the Administrator account.

For secondary logon to work, system administrators are required to hold two accounts: a normally privileged account and an Administrator-equivalent account. The process involves setting up *trusted administrative applications*. The system administrator logs on as a normal user, so the security context for performing any tasks is set as being equivalent to that user. When a system task needs to be completed, the system administrator invokes the trusted administrative application and supplies the administrative credentials. The security context of this one task is then set to be Administrator-equivalent. If the system administrator were to visit a Web site at the same time and download malicious code, the code would only be able to operate in the security context of a normal user because of the separation of contexts maintained by the secondary logon service.

Trusted Administrative Applications

Trusted administrative applications are simply any applications that you wish to set up to use the secondary logon process to achieve an administrative security context to run in. The applications are the same as when they are run directly under the Administrator account. The only difference is the way they are invoked. The steps necessary to set up the secondary logon feature in Windows 2000 and to configure a sample application are outlined below.

ACTIVATING THE SECONDARY LOGON SERVICE

Before a secondary logon can take place, the secondary logon service needs to be started.

1. Select **Programs > Administrative Tools > Computer Management** from the **Start** menu.

2. Expand the **System Tools** menu, and select **Services** to display a list of the available services and their status. By default, the Secondary Logon Service startup mode is Manual. Figure 13.3 shows the Services node of the Computer Management tool.

3. Double-click the **Secondary Logon Service** to display the properties dialog box. Figure 13.4 shows the Secondary Logon Service properties dialog box.

4. If the status is Stopped, select the **Start** button. A message informs you of the attempt to start the service.

5. Change the startup type to **Automatic** if you want the service to start after every boot.

6. Select **OK**.

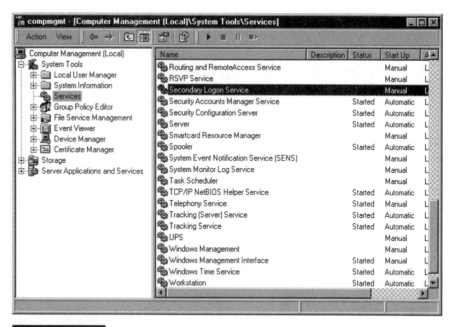

FIGURE 13.3 Services pane in the Computer Management tool

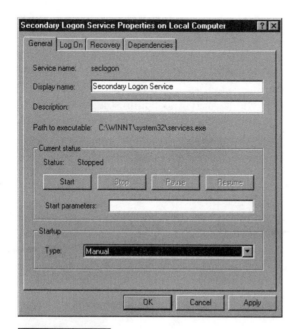

FIGURE 13.4 Secondary Logon Service properties dialog box

CREATING A TRUSTED ADMINISTRATIVE APPLICATION

Trusted administrative applications can be run from a command line by the runas command or as a Windows program run from a shortcut. Figure 13.5 shows the runas command line and available parameters.

The following instructions show you how to set up the MMC program to run under an administrative context.

1. Log on as a nonadministrative user.

2. Right-click the desktop and choose **New > Shortcut**.

3. In the command line, type the following command. **Runas /user:<Domain name>\administrator "MMC %windir%\ system32\svcmgmt.msc"**

4. Select **OK**. A new shortcut should appear on the desktop.

5. When this command is run, a command-line box asks for the password to the administrator account. Enter the password and press <Enter>. The MMC application should start and load the Services Management tool, shown in Figure 13.6.

As you can see, the ability to perform administrative tasks from a non-administrative account is simple and can reduce the amount of time that the Administrator account is used on a day-to-day basis.

Delegation of Administrative Rights and Processes

An important feature of the Active Directory is the ability to granulate security control within the namespace. The structure of the domain in Windows 2000 not only allows for the creation of a logical organizational structure that can closely match the actual structure of your enterprise but also allows for almost any part of the security and administration of the individual OUs to be entrusted to nonadministrative users.

The benefit of this granularity control is that you can tune your administration as you want it to be. If you would like the IT administrator in a branch office to be able to create and delete users in the container used to house the objects relating to that branch office, then you can localize the settings to meet your needs exactly.

The following examples show some of the uses of this Windows 2000 feature. To perform these functions you must be logged on as a user with administrative rights in the area of the domain on which you wish to work. Note that by the very nature of the delegation feature, the logged on user does not necessarily mean the Administrator account if delegation functions have already been used.

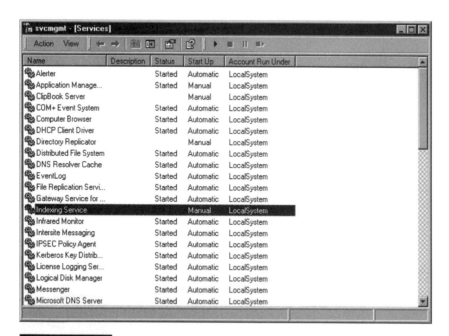

FIGURE 13.5   runas command line

FIGURE 13.6   Service Management application run in administrative
context

DELEGATION OF CONTROL—USER SETUP

This step-through example shows you how to delegate the control of user creation function within an OU in the Active Directory. The first step is to create a user entity to which you wish to delegate control. If you already have a user or group created for this purpose, then skip to the next section.

1. Start the **Active Directory Manager**. Select **Start > Programs > Administrative Tools > Directory Management**.

2. Expand your Active Directory in the scope pane and right-click the container in which you wish to create the user account.

3. Select **New > User**. Enter the **First Name** and a **User logon name** (TestUser is the account used in the following example). Select **Next**.

4. Enter valid password information. Select **Next**.

5. Select **Finish** to confirm the creation.

User TestUser is now created and will be the target of the delegation of Control wizard functions.

DELEGATING USER SETUP CONTROL

We can now run the delegation of Control wizard and pass on administrative rights to the new user. Remember that the target of the delegation of Control wizard could just as easily be another user or a group.

1. Start the **Active Directory Manager** as in step 1

2. Navigate to the target container in the scope pane.

3. Right-click the container and choose **Delegate control** to start the wizard and see an overview of the functionality.

4. Select **Next**. The name of the container within which you wish to delegate control is specified by default. Select **Next**.

5. If this is the first delegation function on the specified container the User and Group Selection list is empty. Select **Add**.

6. Select your target user or group from the supplied list. You may have to navigate the directory to find the container that holds the user.

7. Select **Add** to add the user to the list and **OK** to confirm.

8. Select **Next** to move to the Directory Object Type Selection screen.

9. Select the **Delegate control on this container** radio button.

10. Select **Next**. In the Access to Delegate screen, the filter is set to **Show General Rights** by default.

11. Select the **Show creation/deletion of subobjects rights** radio button to see the extra options needed to delegate user creation.

12. In the Access to Delegate box, select **Create User objects** and **Delete User objects**.

13. Select **Next**.

14. The final screen, shown in Figure 13.7, shows the user or group that you have chosen, the container where the rights are applied, and the rights delegated.

15. Select **Finish**.

The preceding example shows you how easy it is to set up and maintain a distributed administration model within the enterprise. Centralized administration can be used for certain functionality while distributing the ability to perform localized tasks.

Windows 2000 Authentication Process

Users can be authenticated in the Active Directory from many different client platforms by the Kerberos authentication protocol. From a Windows 2000 client, the logon process is as follows.

- The Secure Attention Sequence (Ctrl-Alt-Del) is initiated.
- The user credentials (without password) are passed by the local Kerberos SSP to the Key Distribution Center (KDC) for the domain. Note that only a representation of the password in the form of a hash value is sent to the KDC.

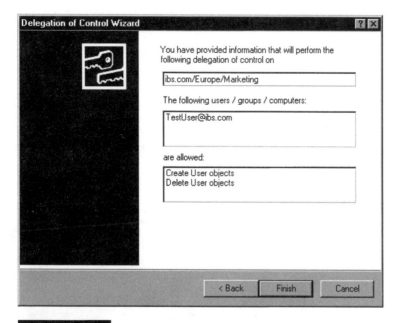

FIGURE 3–7 Delegation of Control Wizard selections

- The hash value of the password is compared to the stored hash value, and an initial Kerberos Ticket Granting Ticket (TGT) is created, based on the hash value. The TGT is used by the client to get further session tickets for other services that may be needed.

- The TGT is returned to the client and is stored on the client in the user's context by the LSA. The TGT is stored in an encrypted format protected by a shared key encryption system. The TGT contains the system identifiers relative to the user and any group associations.

Session tickets are required for network service use. When a client attempts to use a network service, the ticket cache is searched for a valid session ticket. If a valid ticket is not found, then the TGT is sent along with a request for a session ticket. The resulting session ticket is stored and can be used until its expiration regardless of whether sessions are disconnected from services in the meantime (unlike NTLM, which requires another credential check if a session is disconnected). Session ticket requests are handled in the same way, regardless of which services are requested on the network. The two scenarios below request session tickets for local machine access and network server access.

Local Machine Authentication

- The client sends its TGT along with a request to access the local machine resource to the KDC running as a service on a domain controller.
- The KDC checks the access rights and creates a relevant session ticket, which is encrypted and sent back to the client.
- The session ticket is received and the authorization data is used to grant access to the local resource.

Application Server Authentication

- The client sends its TGT along with a request to access the application server resource to the KDC running as a service on a domain controller.
- The KDC checks the access rights and creates a relevant session ticket, which is encrypted and sent back to the client.
- The session ticket is received and sent along with connection setup information to the application server.
- The application server verifies the authorization data in the session ticket and grants access.

As you can see, the KDC acts as the central interface to the security database and is used to fulfill requests for session tickets. The process for requesting and receiving these tickets is similar, regardless of the target of the client access request.

Domains and Trust Relationships

The implementation and management of trust relationships in Windows 2000 have been simplified to fit in with the design goal of making a large enterprise network easier to control. Some of the key features of the new domain structure are discussed below.

Inheritance

Inheritance within the domain structure means that security can be set at a high level in the OU structure and can be allowed to filter down to the lower levels. Security should be applied whenever possible at the highest point in the domain and only blocked or amended at lower points where absolutely necessary.

Transitive Trusts

Trust relationships between domains in the Active Directory are automatically created as domains are added to the tree. These Kerberos trusts are transitive by nature, and no further work need be done on trust relationships. The two-way trust allows interdomain communications without compromising the security structure. Security boundaries still exist by default at the edge of every domain.

Advantages of the Directory System

Object Organization

User accounts, printers, servers, and all other objects within the AD are organized and stored within OUs in the Active Directory. If the directory is planned and implemented to reflect your enterprise structure, then these objects can be placed and administered in a logical representation of your business. When changes occur within your business, they are easily reflected in the structure of your AD. When a user moves within the business, the associated objects (user accounts, etc.) can be moved to the corresponding location in the directory. Inheritance ensures that attributes assigned to the new location (OU) are applied to the user moved into that location.

Scalability

The Active Directory can scale to much larger sizes than can individual Windows NT domains. With the scaling of the AD, performance is not degraded in the same way that it is when a Windows NT registry is scaled beyond certain limits.

Replication

MultiMaster replication supports multiple copies of the account security information and allows real-time updates to any of these copies. This feature improves performance and makes administration easier than using the single master copy of account information on a primary domain controller.

Groups

Many good Windows NT administrators have had difficulty at some time understanding the need for local and global groups and the correct way to use them within the domain. The group structure has been simplified so that only one type of group object exists. Backward compatibility with programs requiring local and global groups exists, but the overall structure of grouping users is simplified, adding to the ease of management.

Granularity of Access Controls

The nature of the Active Directory means that all user accounts and information are stored as objects with the directory. Finer-grained access controls can be used to delegate the ability to control objects within the directory. Now, the head of a group of people can be given control over the accounts for that group alone without the need to make him an account operator. Control can be further granulated so that the head of a department only has access to certain attributes of the user account, such as Full Names or Location, and cannot affect other attributes such as passwords.

Management Interfaces

New, intuitive management interfaces have been introduced to Windows 2000, providing features such as drag-and-drop administration so that the management of ever-growing enterprise IT structures remains as easy as possible. The management interfaces are configurable and can be accessed from one central console.

Summary

The Active Directory in Windows 2000 can be developed to be a scalable, logical representation of your enterprise and so allows changes to be made easily as your enterprise changes. It holds all of the information relevant to the IT structure within your enterprise, including users, printers, servers, and volumes in an easily accessible form. Security and administration are implemented in either a centralized or distributed fashion, depending on the requirements of the organization, and management is simplified by the use of graphical tools gathered together to run on one host platform.

Security Configuration Tool Set

Security management can be one of the most important and time consuming tasks performed by the network administrator today. Windows 2000 can scale enormously within the enterprise, possibly leading to an extra workload in this area as well as others. The Microsoft Management Console enables an administrator to bring together all necessary system tools under one common platform and helps keep down any overheads that might have arisen otherwise.

This chapter discusses the Microsoft Security Configuration Tool Set. This set of administrative tools form the backbone of the security implementation and analysis functions in Windows 2000. The tool set and the implementation of the individual tools and services are discussed in detail in this chapter.

Follow the step-through guides to configuring system security in this chapter in the order in which they are provided to derive the greatest benefit from them.

Introduction

The Security Configuration Tool Set is a group of system services and MMC snap-in tools that act together to help build and maintain the system security model. The set includes tools to set up security from the time of installation, tools to change the security configuration, tools to benchmark and measure security implementations, and analysis tools to query the installed security base.

The Security Configuration Tool Set is made up of the following distinct modules.

- **The Security Configuration Server service.** This system service runs on all Windows 2000 machines and acts as the interface between all of the security-related system tools and the NT security subsystem.

- **Initial security setup.** On a new installation of Windows 2000 (as opposed to an upgrade of a previous version), this portion of the NT setup program is responsible for the initialization of a Local Computer Policy database. On an upgrade installation, this portion of the NT setup program is responsible for importing the existing security settings into the newly initialized Local Computer Policy database.

- **Security Configuration Editor.** This standalone MMC snap-in tool is used to define security templates, which can be saved as .INF files and used later on this machine or transmitted to any other machine.

- **Security Configuration Manager.** This standalone MMC snap-in tool implements the saved templates created by the Security Configuration Editor. These templates can be imported into a system and implemented as live settings or used as a baseline against which to measure existing settings. Analytical features of the SCM are much improved over downlevel OS capabilities. Windows NT 4.0 and below have basic auditing capabilities and use the event viewer to gather the results of the audit policies in place. Nobody will deny that the event viewer is very basic and leaves a lot to be desired. The analysis capabilities provided by the SCM provide you with an in-depth look at the security setup for your Windows NT network as a whole or as separate entities. Now, Windows NT can deliver real audit and analysis ability—all within the same security tool structure used for implementation.

- **Group Policy Editor, Security settings extension.** The Group Policy Editor is a standalone snap-in in its own right. A set of extension snap-ins is available for the Group Policy Editor, one of which is the security settings extension. This extension allows security settings to be configured on a *group policy object*. The GPE applies policies created by the other tools to a larger selection of targets.

Some of the tools and services mentioned above are discussed in more detail throughout this chapter.

Building Your Security Management Console

Although the tool set comprises many distinct modules, one of the design goals of Windows 2000 is to enable flexible management in either a centralized or distributed management model.

One of the first tasks that you should complete when starting the security model implementation is to gather the tools necessary to complete all of the functions that will be needed. You can create a Microsoft Management Console containing only the tools related to security setup. When this console is saved, either you can then use it for centralized management control or you can send the console file to others for use in a distributed management model.

Benefits of Saved Console

Windows NT 4.0 has many built-in features that help administrators implement a secure network architecture. Tools exist for setting account policies and managing user accounts. Tools exist for setting permissions for users. Tools exist for auditing system events. All of the basic aspects of a secure system are present in this version of the Windows operating system and the tools necessary to implement and maintain that system are provided as well.

But don't you wish that you didn't have to go to three or four different places to complete these tasks? Don't you wish that your time wasn't wasted moving around the system trying to complete what should basically be one system task, securing your network? Now add the extra complications of the vast scalability of the Windows 2000 active directory and other new features such as the Encrypting File System. This is where a saved console containing all of the elements of the Security Management Tool Set becomes useful.

One of the design goals for the tool set was to lower the cost of managing the security of your network. To work toward this goal, Microsoft developed the MMC interface so that all of the necessary tools could be brought together in one place. The correct console design means that you no longer have to start three different applications to complete one task. To utilize the system tools efficiently, a worthwhile exercise is to build your own console containing all of the tools necessary to control the security settings on your network. The following sections describe the tools and services mentioned above in more detail and provide step-by-step instructions on how to build your security management console as you go along.

New Console Creation

The first step toward building your Security Management console is to create a new blank console screen. Follow the steps outlined below to do this.

1. Select **Run** from the Start Menu.
2. Enter **MMC** and select **OK**.

3. Select **Save As** from the Console menu.

4. Enter a name for your console. For the remainder of the book, assume a name of **Security Management**.

5. Select **Save**. Figure 14.1 shows the saved Security Management console.

You are now ready to populate the new console with the security management tools described above.

Security Configuration Server service

The Security Configuration Server service runs on all Windows NT machines as a system service. By default, the service is installed and set to start automatically at system startup.

ADD SERVICE MANAGEMENT
TO THE SECURITY MANAGEMENT CONSOLE

The steps outlined below add the system service management snap-in to your Security Management console so that the status of the Security Configuration Server service (and any other services) can be monitored.

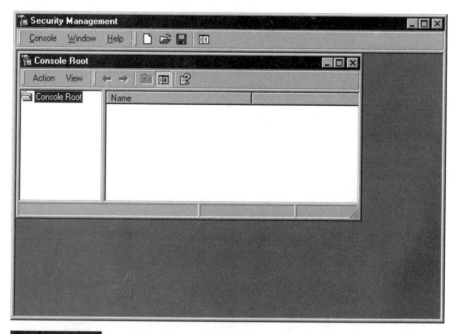

FIGURE 14.1   Newly created Security Management console

1. If it is not already running, start the **MMC** as described above in *New Console Creation*.

2. Select **Open** from the **Console** menu. Highlight the **Security Management** console, and select **Open**.

3. Select **Add/Remove snap-in** from the **Console** menu. The snap-in list should be blank at this point.

4. Select **Add** to display a list of available standalone snap-ins.

5. Scroll down the list and select **System Service Management**.

6. Select **Add** to open a computer selection dialog box. Ensure the **Local Computer** radio button is selected (default).

7. Select **Finish**.

8. Select **Close**.

The snap-in has been added as **Services on Local Computer**. This is the first entry made to the list of existing standalone add-ins (which was blank). This add-in has three extension add-ins available. To ensure that all three are selected (default option), follow these steps.

1. Select the **Extensions** tab in the **Add/Remove Snap-in** dialog box.

2. The **Add all extensions** radio button should be selected. Figure 14.2 shows the System Service Management available extension snap-ins.

3. Select **OK**.

The **Services on Local Computer** selection has been added to the console. To commit these changes, choose **Save** from the **Console** menu.

CHECK STATUS OF THE SECURITY CONFIGURATION SERVER SERVICE

1. If it is not already running start the **MMC** as described in *New Console Creation*.

2. Select **Open** from the **Console** menu. Highlight the Security Management console, and select **Open**.

3. Select **Services on Local Computer**.

4. Scroll down the list of system services in the results pane (right side) until you find **Security Configuration Server**. By default, this service is started and the startup option is set to **Automatic**.

5. If the service is in a **Stopped** state or the startup option is not **Automatic,** double-click the service. Figure 14.3 shows Security Configuration Management service startup options.

6. Select the **Start** button to immediately run the service.

7. Set the Startup option to **Automatic** to have the service start on boot-up.

8. Select **OK** to confirm the changes, or select **Cancel** to quit without saving.

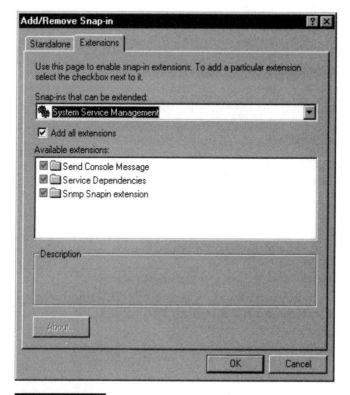

FIGURE 14.2   System Service Management available extensions

Security Configuration Editor (SCE)

The Security Configuration Editor (SCE) is an MMC snap-in tool that configures text-based templates containing security-related settings for the systems and users. These files can then be imported into the security setup at a later date or used as a baseline model to measure security settings against.

This section contains the step-by-step instructions for adding the SCE to the Security Management console.

1. If it is not already running start the **MMC,** as described in *New Console Creation.*

2. Select **Open** from the **Console** menu. Highlight the Security Management console, and select **Open.**

3. Select **Add/Remove snap-in** from the **Console** menu.

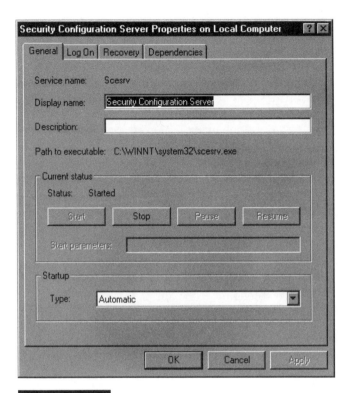

FIGURE 14.3 Security Configuration Management service startup options

4. Select **Add** to display a list of available standalone snap-ins.

5. Scroll down the list and select **Security Configuration Editor**.

6. Select **Add** > **Close** > **OK**.

The Security Configuration Editor snap-in does not have any available extensions to enable or disable.

Figure 14.4 shows the updated Security Management console. Remember to save the console after any deliberate change. If you make accidental changes to the console or layout and format changes, you will be prompted to save when you exit; then, you can decide whether to confirm or not.

Security Configuration Manager (SCM)

You add the Security Configuration Manager (SCM) snap-in to your saved console in the same way as the previous snap-ins.

1. Run the **MMC** and open the **Security Management** console.
2. Select **Add/Remove snap-in** from the Console menu.
3. Select **Add** to display a list of available standalone snap-ins.
4. Scroll down the list and select **Security Configuration Manager**.
5. Select **Add > Close > OK**.

The Security Configuration Manager snap-in does not have any available extensions to enable or disable.

The console now contains all of the tools necessary to apply security policies to a Windows 2000 computer.

Group Policy Editor

The Group Policy Editor snap-in is added to the Security Management console in a similar manner as the previous examples. There are however some differences in the choices offered after you select the snap-in. Group policies can be applied to different levels of the domain tree structure. The GPE applies policies through the domain or AD. The GPE is discussed in Chapter Fifteen, *Group Policies*.

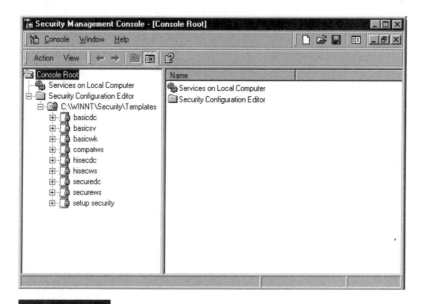

FIGURE 14.4   Updated Security Management console

Introduction to Security Policies

The definition and implementation of security policies form the backbone of the security model in Windows 2000. A security policy is a set of parameters governing one aspect of the security setup on a machine. The Security Configuration Tool Set (SCTS) described above can be loosely split into two parts. The first part includes all of the tools except the Group Policy Editor (GPE). The second part contains the GPE.

The first part of the SCTS allows security policies to be defined, measured, analyzed against benchmark settings, and implemented for the *local* machine.

The addition of the second part of the SCTS containing the GPE enables the administrator to use the defined policies across the enterprise throughout the Active Directory. The following discussions include instructions for setting up a security model, using the local machine as the target for the implementation. Once the model is defined, we introduce the Group Policy Editor and show how Group Policy objects can be used to control security settings on the local machine, the domain tree, and the active directory.

System security policies are stored on each machine in the Local Computer Policy database mentioned earlier. When a new installation of Windows 2000 is made (i.e., not an upgrade) the policy database only contains the predefined policy settings shipped with the product. If an upgrade takes place, the policy database contains settings brought forward from the previous installation.

Security policy configuration template files are discussed in more detail in the next section.

Security Configuration Editor (SCE)

The SCE is accessed through the Microsoft Management Console GUI interface, as described above. The GUI interface gives you full access to the different security configurations templates for your local machine or enterprise. From here, you can configure policy templates to control user access permissions, default system policies, specific policies for different groups of users, and directory tree object security. You can create and manage policy templates that make it easier to apply the policies to one or more systems. The security policy files created or amended with this snap-in tool are used by the Security Configuration Manager to implement new security policies or to analyze existing policies against these templates.

Preinstalled Security Policy Templates

You can use the Security Management console created earlier to view the preinstalled security policy templates for the local machine. To do this, follow the instructions below.

1. Start the **MMC** and open the **Security Management** console. See *New Console Creation* for details.

2. Expand **Security Configuration Editor** > **%SystemRoot%\Security \Templates**.

Figure 14.5 shows the nine preinstalled security policy templates found in each installation of Windows 2000. The nine security policy file names are shown in the scope pane (left-hand side).

The security setup on all Windows 2000 machines is split into eight separate *security areas*. Each of the nine configuration files shown in Figure 14.5 contains settings for those security areas. Table 14.1 lists the security areas and gives a brief description of the contents of each.

The nine preinstalled security configuration templates shown in Figure 14.5 and any other templates you decide to create are stored in the `%SystemRoot%\Security\Templates` directory as plaintext files with the extension of `.inf`.

The preinstalled files can be grouped into the sections listed after Table 14.1. The security settings become more restrictive as you work down the list, and the ability to run and benefit from the full functionality

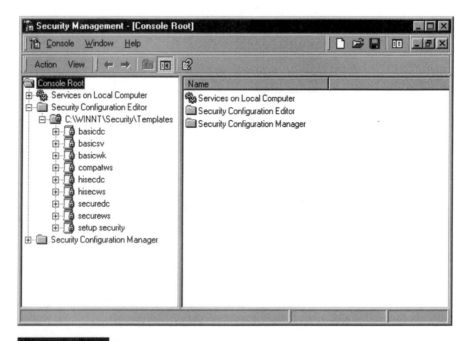

| **FIGURE 14.5** | Default security policy configuration files

TABLE 14.1 Security areas

Area Name	Area Contents
Account Policies	Password policy
	Account lockout policy
	Kerberos policy (in NT domains)
Local Policies	Audit policy
	User rights assignment
	Security options for the local machine. Many of these options are specific registry entries on the local machine.
Event Log	Settings for event logs
Restricted Group	This area is used to set policies for membership to groups the administrator deems to be sensitive. This could include the domain Admins group and the Account Operators group as well as any other groups necessary. This area also allows group nesting on domain controllers (one group residing within another) for policy application.
System Services	Settings for service startup mode and security
	Access control for network file shares
	Settings controlling networked services such as printing and network connectivity and startup/configuration options for system services
Registry	Registry access control
File System	This area is used to grant rights and permissions for users in the domain or from trusted domains to files and directories.
Active Directory Objects	Assigned on domain controllers only to apply access control to objects within the Active Directory

of applications becomes more limited. As the security becomes more restrictive, you can be sure that if an application works under the most restrictive (high security) setting, then it will work under any of the others.

- **Basic templates.** This category includes `Basicws`, `Basicsv`, and `Basicdc`. These three files configure the security of a new Windows 2000 installation for workstation, standalone server, and domain controller, respectively. When you newly, install Windows 2000, the security settings will match one of these three templates. You can use these templates to return security settings to the default if you make a mistake while configuring your systems.

■ **Compatible templates.** The Compatws template has slightly improved security features over the basic template. It also contains Microsoft Office 97 specific file and folder settings. Note that any template containing settings specific to applications should be applied *after* the application is installed. In the trade-off between application functionality and security, this template favors the application.

■ **Secure templates.** This category includes Securdc and Securws. Securdc improves the security on a domain controller from the basic template, and Securws improves security on either a workstation or a standalone server. This security implementation favors tighter security over applications. More restrictions are placed on Microsoft Office 97, but some sites (those for limited Office 97 users or task-based workstation users) could benefit from the introduction of this policy.

■ **High security templates.** This category includes Hisecdc and Hisecws. These templates apply a high degree of security to domain controllers or workstation/standalone server machines, respectively. The restrictions placed on application functionality make these templates very unrealistic to implement. Microsoft hopes to guide applications developers toward producing security-conscious applications that could run on this type of restricted system.

The security templates can be amended to suit the needs of your enterprise for security restrictions, or brand-new templates can be created for the same purpose, as described in *Sample Security Implementation: Local Machine* later in this chapter.

Security Configuration Manager (SCM)

You can analyze your live system using any of the predefined security policy templates as a baseline measurement to see how secure your system really is. In this section, we compare the default Windows 2000 domain controller installation to the Hisecdc.inf template, which contains settings for a highly secure domain controller. This comparison should be made on a newly installed (not upgraded) Windows 2000 domain controller. If this is not possible on your system, then results will vary, depending on the way in which your previous (upgraded) NT domain controller was configured for security.

LOADING A COMPARISON TEMPLATE

1. Start the **MMC** and open the **Security Management** console.
2. Select the **Security Configuration Manager**. Figure 14.6 shows the Security Configuration Manager and the default settings for the password policy on a clean Windows 2000 domain controller installation.

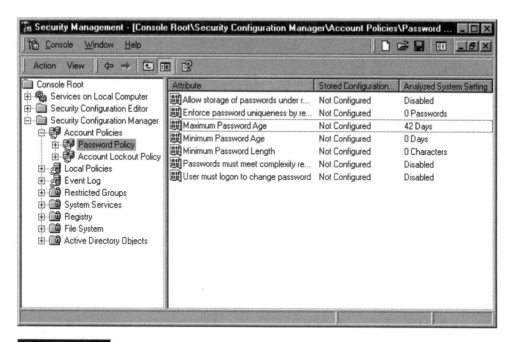

FIGURE 14.6 Default password policy on a Windows 2000 domain controller

3. Right-click the **Security Configuration Manager** in the scope pane (left-hand side).

4. Select **Set Database > Personal database**. The Local Computer Policy database is the live database containing your current security settings. By using a personal database, you can load the settings stored in any of the template files and compare them to the current settings.

5. Enter **Securdom** as the file name for your new database.

6. Select **Open**. The database file `securdom.sdb` will be created in the folder `%SystemRoot%\security\database` at the end of this process.

7. Navigate the **Look in** drop-down menu and select the file **hisecdc.inf** from the default template folder `%SystemRoot%\security\templates`.

8. Select **Open**.

This process creates the database file mentioned above and populates it with the settings from the `hisecdc.inf` template file. You are now ready to compare the settings stored in your Local Computer Policy database with the settings stored in your new personal database. Remember that at this point the new settings are only stored in your personal database and do not affect the live settings in any way. If you wish to run the analysis function later, you must save the console when closing the MMC. If the console is not saved, follow the instructions above to load the `hisecdc.inf` template into a personal database before running the analysis.

RUNNING AN ANALYSIS

Now that both the live security settings and the comparison template settings are available in a database, we can run the analysis function of the SCM and look at the results.

1. Ensure the **hisecdc.inf** template file is loaded into the current personal database as described above.
2. Right-click the **Security Configuration Manager**, and select **Analyze System Now**. The analysis can take a few minutes. Figure 14.7 shows the analysis screen and the different stages being processed.

VIEWING ANALYSIS RESULTS

When the analysis has completed, a screen shows the results of the comparison.

Expand the Security Configuration Manager in the scope pane to show the security areas valid for the type of system analyzed (i.e., if the system is not installed into an active directory, then this area will be missing from the list).

To see the results for individual objects, expand the area name in the scope pane and select a subtopic. Figure 14.8 shows the Password Policy screen after the analysis described above has been run.

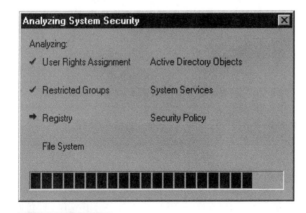

FIGURE 14.7   Security analysis with the Security Configuration Manager

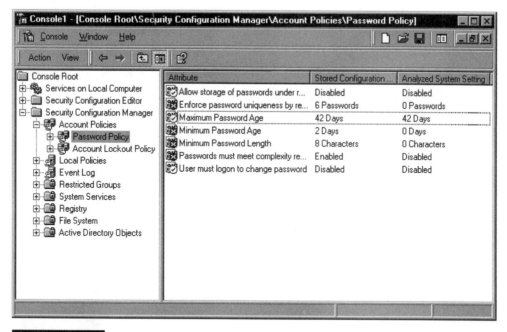

FIGURE 14.8 Security analysis results screen

The results pane shown in the figure above is divided into the following three columns.

- **Attribute.** This is the object that has been analyzed within the security area.
- **Stored Configuration Settings.** This is the value for the object found in the template file loaded for comparison (`hisecdc.inf` in this case).
- **Analyzed System Settings.** This is the value for the object currently in use on the system.

The Attribute column contains an indicator at the leftmost edge. There are three possible values for this indicator.

- **Red and white cross.** This signifies that the proposed security setting is stronger than the one already in place. This gives the best indication of possible areas for upgrading security.
- **Blue and white tick.** This signifies that the setting on the live system is at least as strong as the proposed configuration.
- **Neither sign.** This signifies that the setting is not present in the proposed configuration template.

The other two columns simply show the setting for the object being configured. The values contained in these two columns vary with the type of setting. There is one setting common to all objects configured in the security areas. The setting governs whether the item is included in security configurations and analysis in the future. To view this setting, follow the instructions below after completing an analysis, as described previously.

1. Expand the **Security Configuration Manager** in the scope pane.
2. Expand **Local Policies** and select **Security Options**.
3. Right-click **Extend user rights auditing completely** in the results pane.
4. Select **Security**.
5. The resulting dialog box has the radio button for **Exclude from future configurations and analysis** selected.
6. Select **Cancel**.
7. Now, right-click **Crash system if unable to audit**. The exclusion radio button exists here but is not selected. This exclusion radio button is used when building a template to show that an object is to be included in or excluded from the configuration, now and in any future analysis using this configuration.

Now that you are familiar with a simple security analysis and have seen how the SCE and the SCM fit into the bigger picture of security design and analysis, it is time to move on to a security implementation.

Sample Security Implementation: Local Machine

The instructions that follow take you through the required steps for a security configuration template build, a security analysis run comparing the template to the base install default settings, and the implementation of the new configuration template into the live system.

This sample security installation is based on a local security policy for a Windows 2000 workstation. The same methods can be employed to configure or amend a security policy for a standalone server or domain controller.

Build a New Template

The first thing to do after you have decided to create your own security templates is to understand where you should start from. The basic idea behind your template creation will be to start from one of the provided templates and either add or remove security features to suit your needs. You need to be familiar with the settings stored in each of the templates before basing your network security on that model. Take some time to familiarize yourself with the settings of the templates before choosing one from which to build your live system security.

The equivalent of starting completely from scratch would be to select one of the basic templates discussed earlier. The instructions that follow lead you through a sample template build to add security features to a workstation. The security features being added or enhanced include password policies, account lockout policies, and a restricted group setting.

1. Start the **MMC** and open the **Security Management** console.
2. Expand the **SCE** in the scope pane.
3. Expand the templates directory in the scope pane and select **basicws.inf**.
4. Select **Account Policies** in the scope pane.
5. Double-click **Password Policy**. Figure 14.9 shows the password policy default settings for a Windows NT workstation.

Users have been known to try very hard to keep a favorite password. To do this, users often change passwords when forced to do so and then change back to the original favorite one. Password history goes some way to defeating this practice but still some people would rather change the password six times in succession to defeat the history and keep a well-known (and often easy-to-guess) password. The following password policy uses a combination of restrictions to enforce password security.

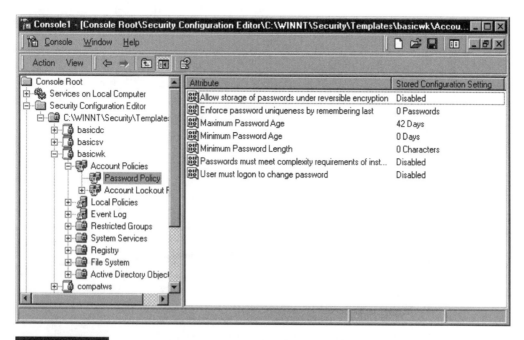

FIGURE 14.9   Default password settings for Windows NT workstation

1. Double-click **Enforce password uniqueness by remembering last** in the results pane.

2. Set this value to **8** and choose **OK**.

3. Double-click **Maximum Password Age**. Set this value to **40** and choose **OK**.

4. Double-click **Minimum Password Age**. Set this value to **5** and choose **OK**.

5. Double-click **Minimum Password Length**. Set this value to **8** and choose **OK**.

The combined object policies above mean that a password must be at least 8 characters in length and must be changed every 40 days. Because a password cannot be changed by the user for another 5 days and the history holds the last 8 passwords, the user could only get back to a favorite password after a minimum of 40 days, changing the password every 5 days. No password is so good that a user will go through the process just to hold it for 40 more days.

Now for account policies.

1. Double-click **Account Policies** in the scope pane.

2. Double-click **Account lockout count**. Set this value to **3**.

3. Double-click **Lockout account for**. Click on the **Exclude this setting from configuration** radio button to remove the tick mark. This will ensure that the object is included in the configuration.

4. Set the value for this object to **Forever**.

5. Double-click **Rest account lockout count after**. Click on the **Exclude this setting from configuration** radio button to remove the tick mark. This will ensure that the object is included in the configuration.

6. Set the value for this object to **1440** minutes (1 day).

With the account policy setting above, users (and intruders) will have three attempts at passwords before being locked out of the system until reset by an administrator. Any bad attempt at passwords will be discounted after one day. These types of settings help prevent unauthorized system access from brute-force or dictionary attacks on passwords.

Restricted group access is used to limit the users that can belong to certain high-risk groups on your system. The Administrators group is a typical example of this. How often do system administrators give extra access to users "temporarily" to accomplish a task and forget to remove it? Follow the steps below to configure the restricted group access.

1. Select **Restricted Groups** in the scope pane. Note that the results pane is empty.

2. Right-click **Restricted Groups** and select **Add Group**.

3. Select the **Administrators** group and then **Add > OK**. The Administrators group now appears in the results pane.

4. Right-click **Administrators** in the results pane and select **Security**.

5. Select **Add** and choose the **Administrator** user.

6. Choose **Add > OK**. This user is now the only one allowed to be a member of the Administrators group.

7. Select **OK**. The results pane shows the Administrators group and users allowed to be a member (Administrator in this case).

Note that this does not make Administrator a member of the group (although it already would be). This setting simply means that when an analysis is run, anybody who is a member of Administrators group except this one user will show up as a problem to be investigated. After all of these changes, save the new template.

1. Right-click **basicws** in the scope pane under the SCE.

2. Select **Save As**. Call the new template **SECPASS.inf**.

3. Select **Save**. The new file should now be listed in the scope pane.

Implement the New Template

The security settings contained in the new template (`secpass.inf`) are now ready to be implemented. Follow the steps outlined below to import these settings to the live system.

Ensure that the current database is the Local Computer Policy database.

1. Right-click **Security Configuration Manager**.

2. Select **Set Database > "Local Computer Policy" database**.

3. Select **Set Database > Import Configuration**. A security configuration dialog box warns you that you will be changing your current system settings. This change should not be made to a live system unless you are sure of the results.

4. Select **OK** to confirm (or Cancel to quit).

5. Select the **SECPASS.inf** template file.

6. Select the **Overwrite existing configuration** radio button.

7. Select **Open**. The Local Computer Policy database is now populated with the settings contained in the `secpass.inf` template file. This may take a few minutes.

The new template is now stored in the Local Computer Policy database. The new settings stored in this database will take effect automatically at next reboot. To force the changes into effect sooner, follow these steps.

1. Right-click **Security Configuration Manager**, and select **Set Database** > "**Local Computer Policy**" database.

2. Right-click **Security Configuration Manager**, and select **Configure System Now**.

3. Accept the default location for the log file or enter another location.

4. Select **OK** to put the settings stored in the Local Computer Policy database into the live system. This process may take a few minutes. Figure 14.10 shows the computer system security progress indicator.

Security Policy Violation and Analysis

Now we are going to purposely violate the security policy that has just been implemented and look at the results.

First, we need to violate the policy. We will add an unauthorized user to the Administrators group.

1. Right-click **My Computer** on the desktop, and select **Manage** to start the Computer Management console (compmgmt).

2. Expand **System Tools** > **Local User Manager** > **Users**.

3. Right-click the **Guest** user in the results pane and select **Properties**.

4. Select the **Membership** tab.

5. Select **Add**.

6. Select **Administrators** > **Add** > **OK**.

7. Select **OK** to confirm. Guest is now a member of the Administrators group.

Now that the policy has been violated, we can run an analysis to see the results.

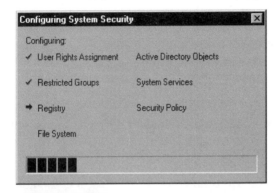

FIGURE 14.10 Configuring system security progress indicator

1. Right-click **Security Configuration Manager**, and select **Set Database > Personal database**.

2. Enter the database name **Secpass**, and select **Open** to open a new database file.

3. Select the **Secpass.inf** template and choose **Open**. This action populates the new personal database (`secpass.sbd`) with the security settings from the `secpass.inf` templates. This step may take a few minutes.

4. Right-click the **Security Configuration Manager**, and select **Analyze System Now**.

5. Select **OK** to choose the default log file setting and continue with the analysis. This may take a few minutes. When the analysis ends the Security Configuration Manager contains all of the analysis results.

6. Expand the **Security Configuration Manager**.

7. Double-click **Restricted Groups**. Note that the Administrators group in the results pane has an indicator in the **Attribute** column to show that this situation needs investigating.

8. Double-click the **Administrators** group in the results pane.

Figure 14.11 shows the Administrators group. Guest is shown to be an invalid member of the Administrators group: the expected result.

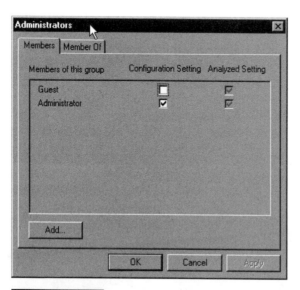

FIGURE 14.11   Screen showing Guest account violating Restricted Groups policy

The examples given above for template setup, configuration importing, security changes, and analysis have been a very simple introduction to the way that tools in the Security Configuration Tool Set work together to manage the security model. The examples are based on a single workstation security setup. When you need to extend this setup to many workstations or servers, even this simple method of applying security would become cumbersome without an extra tool to help distribute the security settings. Having to go to every machine and run these procedures would not work in a 10,000-users environment.

Group Policy Editor

The Group Policy Editor (GPE) is the only member of the tool set that has not been covered yet. The GPE is not a focused security tool in the same manner as the SCE and the SCM. The GPE is a component of the Windows 2000 Change and Configuration Management initiative. The GPE manages group policies in a Windows 2000 environment.

A Group Policy specifies settings for groups of users or objects on a single machine, at various levels of a domain or across the Active Directory. Group policies can contain settings for security, software distribution, startup or shutdown scripts, and files or folders.

The Group Policy Editor is the tool that allows security settings to be distributed throughout an enterprise in a controllable fashion. The GPE is covered in more detail later in the context of *Group Policies* (Chapter Fifteen).

Security Configuration Manager: Command Line

The functionality of the Security Configuration Manager is available in a command-line program. SECEDIT.exe provides all of the functionality of the GUI interface snap-in except for analysis viewing. Figure 14.12 shows the SECEDIT command line and some of the available parameters.

One of the great benefits of this command line is to initiate a system update after system security settings are changed either by the local policy editor (SCE and SCM) or by the Group Policy Editor, as discussed in the next chapter.

Use the instructions below to replace those described in *Implement the New Template*.

1. Select **Run** from the **Start** menu.

2. Enter **CMD** and select **OK**.

3. At the command line, type **CD \winnt\security\templates** and press **<Enter>**.

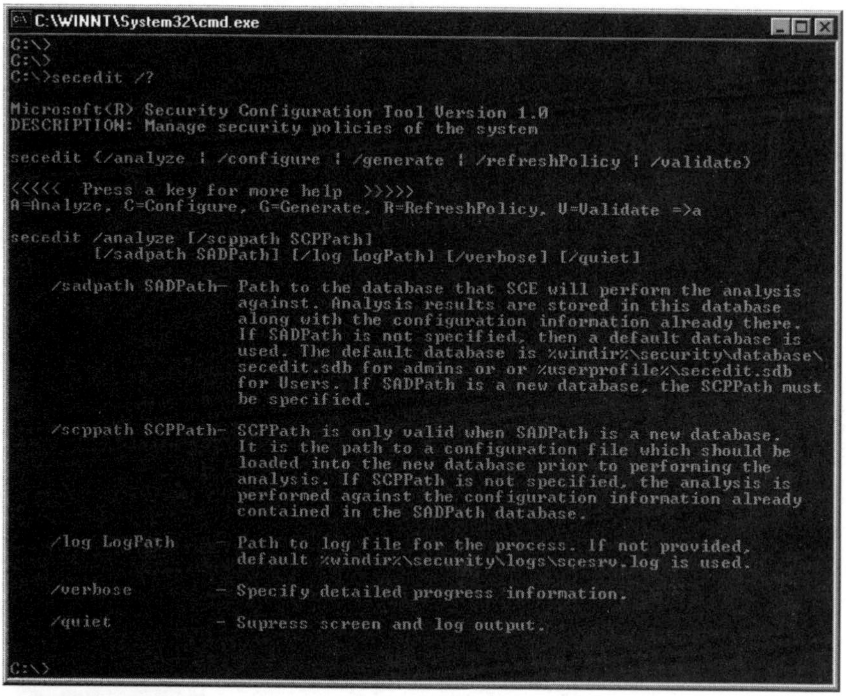

FIGURE 14.12   Secedit command-line utility

4. Type the command **Secedit /configure /scppath secpass.inf/overwrite /log secpass.log /verbose** and press **<Enter>**. A warning tells you that you will be overwriting current settings with the new ones.

5. Answer **Y <Enter>**. A percentage indicator displays the progress. When the command line returns, the configuration has been applied.

This command configures the security on the system with the template file secpass.inf. The overwrite command allows the Local Computer Policy database to be cleared and repopulated with the settings from this template file. The /verbose parameter adds full details to the log file.

Group Policies

This chapter discusses group policies in Windows 2000 and how they help to apply not only security settings but all other computer and user-related settings throughout the Active Directory.

Group policy design, implementation, and storage are covered in this chapter. Also covered is group policy application in a mixed environment containing Windows NT and Windows 2000 machines.

Introduction

In Windows 2000, security policies such as those discussed in the previous chapter can be configured, implemented, and managed on an enterprise level. This is accomplished by means of the group policy infrastructure provided by Microsoft as part of its Zero Administration for Windows (ZAW) initiative and the Change and Configuration Management initiative for Windows 2000.

Group Policies

Group policies are used in Windows 2000 to specify desktop and computer settings such as logon policies, software deployment, security settings, script usage, and startup and shutdown options. Group policies can be set for groups of users or on a per-machine basis. The Group Policy Editor (GPE) is run as a snap-in for the Microsoft Management Console and includes security-related snap-in extensions. The group policies are tied into the Active Directory, and Active Directory management tools such as *Active Directory Sites and Services Manager* can be used to set the scope for the GPE.

Group policies can be used to effectively change settings for large groups of users or computers with a minimum of effort and so lower the total cost of ownership. Administration can be centralized or decentralized with this tool.

The GPE is used by an administrator to control the policy categories described above. The entries made by the GPE are stored as a group policy object (GPO) in the Active Directory and are replicated to all DCs within the domain.

Group policies do not cross domain boundaries during replication; however, GPOs can be used by members of another domain if needed. This use can add time to system calls or to the function to which the GPO is attached, so it is not recommended. Group policies should be defined within each domain as necessary.

Readers who are familiar with the Windows NT 4.0 System Policy Editor (Poledit) can look at the Group Policy Editor as an extension to that tool.

Benefits of Group Policies

The group policy settings are fully integrated into the Active Directory. This means that settings stored as GPOs can be tied to other objects in the tree known as *containers*. Examples of containers are *sites*, *domains*, and *organizational units* (OU). Containers add an extra layer of granularity to the group policy control.

Some of the capabilities described below for the GPE have already been available for some time (with NT 4.0). The System Policy Editor in NT 4.0 was used to create desktop policies. The Group Policy Editor is an extension of the System Policy Editor and brings with it much more finely grained control over groups and computers.

One of the questions that should be asked by all developers of new systems is, What benefit does this product bring to the user? Another question to ask is, Why would the user want to change to this way of performing the task? The answers to these questions are set out below.

TOTAL COST OF OWNERSHIP (TCO)

Studies show that a major proportion of the TCO of a networked computer system with a large number of users is spent on time wasted at the desktop. The most popular reasons given for the amount of time spent there are:

- Users making changes to customize their desktop (damaging the system in the process)
- Complicated user desktops confusing the user and generally not being very user friendly
- Required changes to the desktop having to be made on a per-machine basis

With the introduction of the GPE, the total cost of ownership is reduced by bringing these desktop tasks under the control of a central administrative interface. All of the policies that can affect the use and appearance of a computer desktop are controlled by applying group policies centrally.

Policies can be tailored completely to the job responsibilities of a user or group of users. It is no longer necessary to have the same desktop look, full of all possible applications, on all machines. With less confusion on the part of the user, the management task becomes easier.

Desktops can be implemented in such a way as to deny the facility to change them. Powerful tools such as registry editors can be protected. The policies are totally configurable centrally so that the needs of your particular enterprise can be accommodated.

ACTIVE DIRECTORY INTEGRATION

Group policies are tied in with the Active Directory. As the Active Directory scales, group policies can scale with it. Because of the close integration, group policies can be defined at all of the granular levels of the Active Directory (domain level, OU level, or computer level).

The Active Directory integration also allows a choice between centralized or distributed management of policy options.

COMMON INTERFACE

The Group Policy Editor has been developed as an MMC snap-in. This means that as with all of the other security features in Windows 2000, group policies are defined and implemented through the same common interface that is used for all of the other system-related tasks. This common interface not only centralizes administration to one computer on the network but also moves the administration to one simple-to-use interface on that one computer. No more searching for the different tools required just for one job.

On the subject of centralized management, be advised that the integration of group policies into the Active Directory allows for either centralized or decentralized management of policies and settings. Management choice is accomplished by means of the delegation abilities of the directory structure and is in line with Microsoft's future plans for management. The choice of centralized or decentralized management is yours to make, depending on your circumstances.

The Group Policy Editor also allows certain extensions to be used. Extensions are extra facilities attached to a snap-in module. The extensions require that the parent snap-in be available. An example of an extension is the Application Deployment Editor used for deploying applications to the desktop. It is called from within the Group Policy Editor parent snap-in.

Group Policy Categories

Windows 2000 group policies are divided into the six main categories listed in Table 15.1.

Uses of Group Policies

Group policies can manage the desktop settings for both users and computers. The following sections describe some of the different type of policies available for use. Although only one of these policy types is specifically referred to as security policies, all of the others have security ramifications also. For example, access to the registry editor can be controlled with the software policy settings, but obviously this is a security issue as well.

TABLE 15.1 Windows 2000 group policies

Policy Name	Policy Description
Software policies	Registry entries written to the HKEY_LOCAL_MACHINE and HKEY_LOCAL_USER registry hives. These control desktop looks, application settings, and any system services related to installed software.
Software installation	Controls the *advertisement* and *publishing* of software packages.
Security settings	Controls the security settings at both computer and domain level and also for network-related security values.
File deployment	Controls the files to be placed on the desktop in any of the special folders (e.g., Start menu or Favorites).
Folder redirection	Controls the ability to redirect special desktop folders such as Favorites or My Documents to network drives for protection and speed of logon/logoff.
Script running	Controls the use of scripts at startup and shutdown or user logon and logoff.

User and Computer Settings

The Group Policy Editor namespace contains two items known as nodes. The two node names are Computer Settings and User Settings.

Computer settings controlled by group policies take effect at system initialization before a user interacts with the machine. These settings can include scripts to run at startup. Settings include desktop settings, operating system settings, application deployment settings, and, of course, security settings.

User settings are implemented at logon and can include application access, desktop settings, application deployment settings, and any scripts to be run at logon time.

As you can see, there is a certain amount of overlap in the available settings for each node type. This duplication gives administrators the choice of setting desktop configurations so that they move with a user from machine to machine or so that they appear on a certain machine regardless of the user.

Security Groups

Security groups apply one further layer of granularity to the process of applying group policies. Security groups can filter policy settings applied to Active Directory containers. Membership in a security group can shield the user or computer from the effects of a group policy.

Software Policies

Software policies control the same policy information that the Windows NT 4.0 Policy Editor controlled. Operating system components and installed applications are controlled under this policy. Software policies are applied to either users or computers. All information regarding the software policies for a given user logged on to a machine is stored in the registry hive HKEY_CURRENT_USER. All software policy information for a given computer is stored in the registry hive HKEY_LOCAL_MACHINE.

Software Management

Software management takes advantage of the snap-in extension called the Application Deployment Editor. This extension tool enables you to define which applications can be used on a computer or by a specified user or group. This tool also allows applications to be installed directly onto the computer when the user chooses to use them. There are two ways to deploy the application in question.

The first method is to assign the application to a user or group. This assignment gives the correct permissions to install the application and run it. The application does not need to be preinstalled on the desktop, thus reducing the management overhead for distributed applications. This assignment is called an *application advertisement*. When the user next logs on to a machine, the application shortcut is placed in the Start menu and the necessary registry entries for installation are made. When the application shortcut is activated for the first time the installation takes place. From then on, the application is available for normal use. This obviously saves time from a desktop management point of view and works well for those applications that lend themselves to a simple installation.

The second method involves making no changes at all to the computer's Start menu or registry. With this method, the application is *published*, that is, users are told that the application is available to them if they wish to install it. Users can see a list of available applications in the *Add/Remove software* section of Control Panel.

Software can also be updated or removed with this snap-in extension.

Scripting

Scripting is used to run scripts at user logon/logoff time or at system startup/shutdown. The contents of the script are completely configurable. The Windows Script Host (WSH) is included in Windows 2000 as a language-independent host mechanism for these scripts. VBScript and JScript engines are included with Windows 2000, and Microsoft expects other vendors to supply further scripting engines for languages such as PERL and REXX.

User File and Folders

Group policy settings can control the location and settings of any of the users' *special folders*. The special folders include the My Documents folder, Favorites folder, the desktop, and the Start menu. These folders are located by default under the %SystemRoot%\Profiles\%Username% folder.

Under the rules for roaming profiles in Windows NT 4.0, these files were copied down from the server at logon time and copied back up to the server at logoff time. This process added extra time to the logon and logoff processes.

Windows 2000 allows you to store these folders permanently on the server by redirecting the shortcuts. This approach has the advantage of ensuring that the folders are available wherever a user logs on and off, speeding up the logon and logoff time (fewer folders are copied up and down to the workstation).

The most likely candidate for relocation would be the My Documents folder. This tends to be the largest folder and adds most time to the logon/logoff process. This folder also holds documents that you may want to protect with server backups.

Depending on the policy method used (computer or user), the folders are made available at either system initialization (after network initialization) or user logon. Files relocated under the computer settings policy will be available to that one computer regardless of who the user is. Files relocated under the user settings policy will be available to that user regardless of the network machine used for logon.

User files and folder settings redirect these folders and also add any shortcuts or files to these folders.

Group Policies vs. Local Policies

When looking at the Security Management Tool Set and especially at the GPE and the SCE, you would be forgiven for thinking that they perform very similar functions. The easiest way to distinguish between the two roles played by these tools is to think about a standalone workstation and a computer joined to a domain.

The SCE in conjunction with the SCM applies security policies to the local machine. On a standalone workstation or a machine that needs different security settings to all others, these tools can be used to define and apply the policy.

The GPE adds to the basic functionality of the SCE and SCM the ability to apply the security to anywhere in the Active Directory or from anywhere in the Active Directory. For an enterprise with a large Windows 2000 installed base, this is an invaluable extension to the base security policy product.

Now we are faced with policy being applied in different places, and we need to understand the flow of these policies.

Security policies are applied in a cumulative fashion. That is, the first policy is applied and then the next relevant policy is applied on top (and can overwrite anything applied already), then the next policy is applied, and so on. Figure 15.1 shows an example domain; the security policy flow is described below.

In the Windows 2000 domain scenario shown in Figure 15.1 the application of policies is such that the local policy on computer PC1 is applied first. If a site policy exists, it is applied next. Then, the domain policy is applied; it overwrites any conflicting settings already established. Then, any OU policies are applied, working from the highest OU in a direct line above the computer in the domain tree (Asia) down to the OU that contains the computer (Sales). Not all OUs will necessarily have a group policy object to be applied to this computer, but if they do, the strict order of precedence is followed.

All of the settings combined from working through the list of policies are stored on the machine in the System Security Policy database. This database is first populated with the local settings and then with domain and OU policy settings. Group policies can also be applied to Active Directory *sites* (usually defined by IP subnet). This task of applying the security policies is carried out at the following times:

- On every reboot
- When a group policy is propagated
- When the SCM option *Configure System Now* is chosen
- When the period group policy processing time arrives (every 8 hours by default, but configurable from 7 seconds to 45 days)
- When the `Secedit` command-line option `RefreshPolicy` is chosen

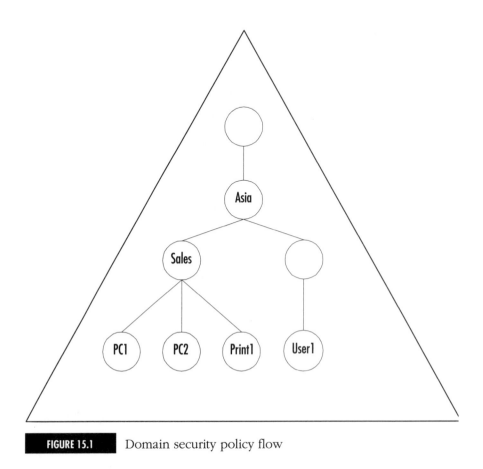

Domain security policy flow

A number of group policies can be applied to one container within the AD. The Administrator can use the GPE to rank the multiple GPOs in order of precedence.

The inheritance of GPOs is set to be the default nature of the policy structure. This behavior can be overcome, and any setting that is configured to be enforced cannot be overwritten by inheritance or cumulative applications of multiple GPOs. Therefore, settings that must be guaranteed not to be overwritten should be set in the group policy closest to the object in question; that is, settings for a particular computer should be set as a local policy and enforced.

Group Policy Storage

Group policy objects created with the GPE are stored in different places, depending on their configuration.

LOCAL GROUP POLICY OBJECTS

Local GPOs are stored on each individual computer. By default, they are held in the `%SystemRoot%\system32\GroupPolicy` folder. By default, Administrators and System have Full Control permission and all users have Read access.

Local group policies can be disabled. A file called `GPT.ini` is in the `\%SystemRoot%\system32\GroupPolicy` folder. This file holds a flag that can be set to disable the policy.

ALL OTHER GROUP POLICY OBJECTS

All group policy objects that are not defined as local are associated with a container in the Active Directory. This container may be a site, an OU, or a domain. Some information pertaining to the GPOs associated with these containers is stored in the Active Directory in a group policy container. Information such as version numbers and status are stored here. As the Active Directory exists only on domain controllers, the reality is that this information physically resides on a DC. The remaining information is stored in a template file in the Sysvol volume under the `\Policies` folder. This is the information modified when a GPO associated with a particular container is changed.

A computer can be made exempt from these group policies in the same way as the local policy can be disabled. To exempt a computer, edit the registry key DiasableGPO in the `HKEY_LOCAL_MACHINE\Software\Policies\Microsoft\Windows\System` hive. Values are 1 = disabled, 0 = enabled.

As always with registry changes, be careful not to make a mistake because the changes are committed instantly. View the registry in read-only mode first to make sure you are in the correct hive.

Backward Compatibility

Previous versions of the Windows operating system (NT 4.0 and below) and also Windows 95/98 are not accommodated in the group policy model for Windows 2000. Use the system policy editor tool (`Poledit.exe`) to configure policy for NT 4.0 and Windows 95/98.

Group Policy Administration Requirements

There are a few requirements that must be fulfilled before you can set group policies within the Active Directory.

- At least one Windows 2000 domain controller must be installed in the AD.
- The user must have Read/Write permissions for the system volume (\Sysvol folder) on the DC.
- The user must have Modify permission for the directory object that is set as the current scope for the group policy object (i.e., the object to which you wish to apply the policy).

With the minimum requirements in place, you are ready to start looking at group policies in more detail.

Group Policy Migration Pattern

Windows NT 4.0 has a well-established user base and is deployed in many large organizations today. The migration path from NT 4.0 to Windows 2000 is likely to be a gradual one (as Microsoft has made it easy to stop and start almost at will), so the chances of there being a mixed network are quite good.

As mentioned earlier, Windows NT 4.0 cannot take advantage of the group policies that may exist in a Windows 2000 environment. Group policies are tied into the Active Directory, and NT 4.0 nodes never become an active member of the AD.

It is important to understand throughout the migration where your policies are coming from. Table 15.2 shows the possible combinations of NT 4.0 and Windows 2000 in workstation and server formats and links these scenarios with the source of the policy that will be applied to each type of machine.

Group Policy Implementation

Certain fundamental principles and design implications surround the implementation of group policies. It is easy to focus on one aspect of this powerful tool set and forget about the other activities and settings affected by GPOs. I have listed some guidelines below to help you design your group policy. This list is not exhaustive, but it will help to prevent you from falling into the most common traps when you implement your design.

- Group policies are associated with sites, domains and OUs. This means that your Active Directory design will affect your ability to implement a workable and sustainable group policy design. Understand what can be achieved with group policies (which is much more than security policy implementation) and at least consider your group policy design when designing your AD.

	NT 4.0 Client	Windows 2000 Client
TABLE 15.2 Group policy migration matrix		
Domain Type	**Runs This Policy**	**Runs This Policy**
NT 4.0	NT 4.0	Local group policy + NT 4.0 policy
Windows 2000 AD native mode	NT 4.0	Local group policy, site, domain, OU policies
Windows 2000 AD mixed mode (default install)	NT 4.0	Local group policy, site, domain, OU policies, NT 4.0
Windows 2000 AD mixed mode, all Windows 2000 DCs are down, NT 4.0 BDCs are up	NT 4.0	Local group policy, site, domain, OU policies (all from cached credentials) + NT 4.0. Reverts to local group policy + NT 4.0 policy after timeout
Workgroup (no domain)	One of: No policy Manual NT 4.0 policy Remains of domain NT 4.0 policy if machine was removed from a domain	One of: Local group policy Manual NT 4.0 policy Remains of Windows 2000 domain policy if machine was removed from a domain

- Group policies are inherited and cumulative in the AD by default. Some existing mechanisms use ACL editors to either enforce policies or deny policy application. Be very wary about using these techniques. Group policies can be complicated things, and putting blocking mechanisms in place will make them more complicated. Learn the natural flow of group policies and design them so that their inheritance and cumulative nature work in your favor.

- Keep the number of different group policies affecting an object to a minimum. You can apply numerous group policies to a specific container, but this should be a rare occurrence. If you are tempted to add a second GPO to a container, then look at the order in which you intend to rank them and then combine the two GPOs into one. This is a manual task and not as easy as it may sound, but in the long run the benefits of a simplified system will be the reward.

- User logon time will be affected by the number of group policy objects associated with the containers in the Active Directory path above them. Minimize the number of GPOs applied to a user object to speed up the logon process.

- Although it is possible for a GPO associated with a container anywhere in the Active Directory to be applied to a user, try not to cross domain or site boundaries. This is especially important if one of the domains is located across a WAN link.

- Remember that your security design and implementation will only be as good as your group policy design, which in turn will only be as good as your Active Directory design. Everything needs to be built up from a solid foundation. Understand Active Directories and the full functionality of group policies before commencing.

This is by no means an exhaustive list, but the scope of this security book will not allow for an in-depth look at group policies.

Summary

Group policies control many aspects of the Windows 2000 computing environment, including software, application availability, desktop look and feel, and security settings.

Group policies add scalability to the security settings that can be applied to a single machine or user and allows those settings to be applied throughout the domain to many users, groups, computers, sites, or containers.

File Systems

This chapter introduces the file system security features of Windows 2000. The first part of the chapter discusses the new features that enhance the scalability of the Windows operating system, such as the Distributed File System and the security issues surrounding their implementation. The second part of the chapter covers the new Windows 2000 Encrypting File System in some detail.

Distributed File System

The Distributed File System (DFS) provides the simple means for an administrator to build in to a single namespace a hierarchical view of the file systems and shares on multiple computers. Files and shares are no longer tied to a particular server as far as the user is concerned. Users can now see *logical shares* that point to their critical files. These logical shares can be placed in the most convenient position in the tree for the user. Users no longer need concern themselves with the physical location of these files and directories. Transparency of the physical location is provided to the user by the DFS.

As enterprises grow and file systems become larger, we find ourselves faced with the ever-growing need to access data in many locations and on different platforms. The original way of accessing files on a server was to map a direct drive letter (e.g., X = \\server1\driectory1). Then, we navigated the drive letter to find files and directories. This was not scalable beyond the allowable drive letters. Then UNC came along and relieved the problem of no more drive letters. However, having to make a separate connection to all of the different locations in which we store files today means the UNC approach is cumbersome and time consuming. DFS brings the many file systems together in one namespace, regardless of the physical location.

DFS is administered through a GUI interface and can connect disparate file systems through NT redirectors or gateway services.

Securing Your Data in a DFS

Load Balancing

Load balancing with DFS increases the availability of files by providing alternate locations, transparently to the user. DFS does not perform data synchronization tests; the administrator must ensure the integrity of the data on the *alternate volumes*. This situation raises the issue of data integrity and trusted sources. It is important to ensure that the security applied to any file system is replicated on alternate volumes.

Disparate File Systems

DFS works on disparate file systems. This means that the file format and the security model for the foreign system may not be the same all over. When connecting disparate systems in DFS, remember that you may be lowering the security level of your network by this connection. If you have an NTFS partition with file security applied, it is not a good idea to synchronize this partition onto a FAT partition on another system as an alternate volume. The FAT partition will not have the same security structure available, and file security will be lost for anybody using the alternate volume.

ACLs

No security configuration is done through the DFS, for the following reasons.

- Many different file systems can be connected together as a logical volume, and no reasonable way of passing on ACL protection to non-NTFS volumes is possible.

- There would be an extra security overhead. DFS security could not replace the physical NTFS security. While taking part in the DFS, the NTFS volumes can still be addressed physically. Because the DFS can be bypassed like this, there would still be a need for NTFS security.

- The engine for monitoring storage quotas would have to traverse the logical volumes to check the storage amounts utilized.

Encrypting File System (EFS) Architecture

The EFS is based on shared (symmetric) key security (see Chapter Six, *Cryptography*, for more details). The encryption algorithm shipped in the first release is a DES variant (DESX) and so will allow 128-bit North American encryption and only 40-bit international encryption. This first algorithm will make way in future releases for a wider choice of encryption schemes because the EFS architecture enables almost any public-key encryption scheme to be used.

NTFS Integration

The encryption system is interwoven with the NTFS system. If an application such as MS Word opens an encrypted document, the ensuing temporary work file is encrypted as well. This technique addresses one of the problems inherent in application encryption systems. The EFS also works in kernel mode, using the nonpaged memory pool, instead of in user mode (where an encryption application would work), so the use of the page file is avoided. Memory and page leaks are therefore not an issue with EFS.

Low Administrative Overhead

File encryption is very easy to implement. The EFS is a system service and does not need installing or configuring. Users can control whether or not their files are encrypted. The operation to encrypt or decrypt is a function attached to the context-sensitive toolbars in the same way as the *Delete* command or the *Rename* command. Files can be encrypted individually or by directory. The public key pair required for encryption and decryption is generated automatically, if the user does not already have one, when the first encryption command is given.

The file encryption attribute is transitive. If you copy an encrypted file from an encrypted directory to a non-encrypted directory, the file will still be encrypted (as long as the target partition is NTFS). If you copy a non-encrypted file into an encrypted directory, the file will be encrypted automatically.

Files can be encrypted both on local workstations and also on network servers. One point worth noting on network server disk encryption is that only the storage of the file/directory is encrypted. Files are decrypted on a block-by-block basis as the byte stream leaves the disk. This means that when an encrypted file is read, it is transmitted over the network in its decrypted form. You can use protocols such as SSL and PCT to provide secure channel services to protect the transmission of data.

File Encryption, Decryption, and Recovery Mechanisms

File Encryption

File encryption on an EFS volume takes place transparently to the user. The EFS runs as a system service and is tightly integrated into the NTFS and operating system.

When a file (or folder) is set for encryption for the first time, a randomly generated file encryption key (FEK) is created for that file or folder. If the encryption target is a folder containing more files, then each individual file has a randomly generated FEK of its own. This facilitates file movement because a file can be moved from an encrypted directory to another NTFS location and keeps its encryption status, regardless of what happens to the original directory.

The FEK, which is a fixed-length key, is used by the DESX algorithm to encrypt the file. The FEK is then encrypted itself for decryption purposes, using the user's own public key. The RSA algorithm is used for this public key encryption. The FEK is encrypted for a second time by the encryption recovery agent, using its public key.

Accessing Encrypted Files

Access to encrypted files is still governed by the access permissions for the particular user. The ACL is checked on the file to see if the user has the correct permissions needed to carry out the request. The complete transparency of the EFS system ensures that if a user has the correct permissions (and the correct private key), then the access is granted with no extra steps necessary for decryption. The only real way for a user to tell if a file or directory is encrypted is to check the properties for the object and look for the encrypted attribute.

File Decryption

The file decryption mechanism is almost the reverse of the encryption mechanism. Files are decrypted by user request (a read request, turning off the encryption attribute, etc.). The request takes the user's private key to decrypt the stored FEK (encrypted by the users public key). Once the FEK is decrypted then it can be used to decrypt the file that was encrypted by a shared key algorithm. The same key is used to both encrypt and decrypt with a shared key algorithm.

File Recovery

As a safety precaution, the key used for file encryption (the FEK) is stored twice: once in a form encrypted with the user's public key and once using the recovery agent's public key. If the user were to lose the certificate containing the public/private key pair or if the certificate was damaged, the private key could not be used to decrypt the FEK and so the FEK could not be used to decrypt the file. The recovery agent is used in this case (usually by a security officer or administrator) to decrypt the copy of the FEK with its private key. This is a safety mechanism to guard against file and data loss.

In the first release of Windows 2000, encrypted file sharing is not supported. Therefore, the FEK is only encrypted by one user's private key. However, multiple recovery agents are supported, so a copy of the FEK can be encrypted by the private keys of several agents.

File Sharing

It is worth mentioning again that file sharing is not supported in the initial release of Windows 2000 Encrypting File System.

As you can see from the section above, encryption takes place by means of a shared key protocol, but the key itself (the FEK) must then be stored securely. This security is accomplished with the individual user's public key; so, the only key that can unlock the FEK is the user's private key (apart from the recovery agent). This means that only the one user can open an encrypted file.

This drawback in the EFS will be addressed in future releases by removing the FEK encryption responsibility from one individual using his own public key.

Encryption and Decryption Processes

Implementing File and Folder Encryption

File and directory encryption is implemented by use of the context-sensitive menus in Windows NT Explorer.

1. Select **Programs** from the **Start** menu.
2. Select **Windows NT Explorer**.
3. Navigate the Explorer window until you can select the files or directory you wish to encrypt.
4. Right-click the selection to show the context menu.
5. Select **Properties**. Figure 16.1 shows the Properties dialog box.
6. Click the **Advanced** button.

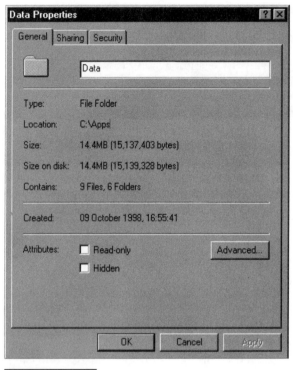

FIGURE 16.1 Folder Properties dialog box

7. Select **Encrypt contents to secure data**. Figure 16.2 shows the Advanced attributes dialog box for folder encryption.

8. Select **OK**.

9. Select **OK** again in the **Properties** dialog box.

If you are encrypting a file or a selected file range, then this is the end of the process. The files are now encrypted. Remember that these files cannot be shared from now on because file and folder encryption does not allow for shared access in its first release in Windows 2000.

If you are encrypting a folder, there is one more step. You are asked to choose from the two options provided at this point.

1. Apply changes to this folder only encrypts the current folder only. No files or subfolders are included.

2. Apply changes to this folder, subfolders and files encrypts everything in the directory tree at this level and below. Note that the procedure may fail if any files in the directory structure are in use at the time of encryption.

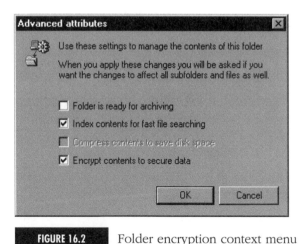

FIGURE 16.2 Folder encryption context menu

Remember that this is not a manual task that needs to be completed continuously to secure or access a file. You run the encryption once for a file or directory. From then on, any file access is granted through your private key; the file is decrypted as it is read from disk. Similarly, as you close a document and write to disk, the file is encrypted. You only need to use this procedure to change the attribute on a file or folder.

If you encrypt a directory, then all future file or subdirectories created there are encrypted as well. To create a secure repository for sensitive information, you can create the top-level directory and encrypt it. From then on, all files copied into this location are automatically encrypted. Even when a directory is encrypted, a user with the appropriate rights (RX)( ) can list the files within the directory.

Folder encryption is favored over file encryption. When individual files are chosen for encryption, the management task becomes more difficult.

Note that the \%SystemRoot% folder (usually C:\Winnt) and its contents cannot be encrypted. EFS runs as a system service and so is not available for encrypting and decrypting until after the system has started. If system files were encrypted, then they could not be read at startup and the system start would fail. Normally, this would not be a problem, but remember that nonsystem files are stored in this path, too. Profile folders containing the My Documents folder are in this path. Files stored in this default My Documents folder location cannot be secured with EFS.

Implementing File and Folder Decryption

File and directory decryption uses the same context menu as the encryption process. This action is not necessary to access the file because data decryption is done automatically for the user who encrypted the file. If you need to share an encrypted file, then it must be decrypted first because file sharing is not supported in the first release version of EFS. The steps necessary to decrypt an encrypted file or directory are outlined below.

1. Select **Programs** from the **Start** menu.
2. Select **Windows NT Explorer**.
3. Navigate the Explorer window until you can select the files or directory you wish to encrypt.
4. Right-click the selection to show the context menu.
5. Select **Properties**.
6. Click the **Advanced** button.
7. Deselect **Encrypt contents to secure data**.
8. Select **OK**.
9. Select **OK** again in the **Properties** dialog box.

As with file encryption, if you are decrypting a file or a selected file range, then this is the end of the process. The files are now decrypted. These files and folders can now be shared.

If you are decrypting a folder, there is one more step. You are asked to choose from the two options provided at this point.

1. **Apply changes to this folder only** decrypts the current folder only. No files or subfolders are included.

2. **Apply changes to this folder, subfolders, and files** decrypts everything in the directory tree at this level and below. Note that the procedure may fail if any files in the directory structure are in use at the time of decryption.

As well as the GUI interface for file encryption and decryption, you can use a command-line utility when you need more administrative control over the operation. Figure 16.3 shows the `Cipher` command-line utility.

To use the `Cipher` command-line utility to encrypt the `D:\data` folder and all of its subfolders and files, enter this command: **Cipher /E /S:d:\data /I <Enter>**. The `/I` switch allows the command to carry on processing if it encounters an error such as a file in use. Remember, though, that any files in use will not have their encryption attribute changed.

Copying Encrypted Files and Folders

A cautionary note on copying files. Windows 2000 introduces the concept of Distributed File Systems, as described earlier in this chapter. These file systems can be physically located on many disparate platforms, and so they may not share the same security functionality as Windows 2000.

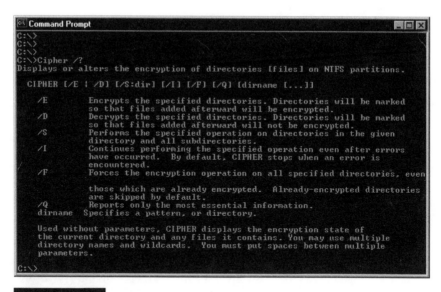

FIGURE 16.3 Cipher command-line utility

A simple copy command run on an encrypted file by the user will produce different results depending on the target file system. Table 16.1 shows the way in which a copy command or file drag and drop in Windows Explorer will treat the encryption attribute of a file.

TABLE 16.1 File copying and the encryption attribute

Original Folder Attribute	File Attribute	Destination Partition Type	Destination Folder Attribute	Resulting File Attribute
Encrypted	Encrypted	NTFS v5.0	Encrypted	Encrypted
Encrypted	Encrypted	NTFS v5.0	Normal	Encrypted
Encrypted	Encrypted	Non-NTFS v5.0	Normal	Normal
Encrypted	Normal	NTFS v5.0	Encrypted	Encrypted
Encrypted	Normal	NTFS v5.0	Normal	Normal
Encrypted	Normal	Non-NTFS v5.0	Normal	Normal
Normal	Encrypted	NTFS v5.0	Encrypted	Encrypted
Normal	Encrypted	NTFS v5.0	Normal	Encrypted
Normal	Encrypted	Non-NTFS v5.0	Normal	Normal
Normal	Normal	NTFS v5.0	Encrypted	Encrypted
Normal	Normal	NTFS v5.0	Normal	Normal
Normal	Normal	Non-NTFS v5.0	Normal	Normal

Certain rules become apparent from Table 16.1.

- The destination must always be an NTFS v5.0 partition if a file is to retain or receive the encryption attribute.
- If a file has the encryption attribute set (whether from inheritance or directly applied), then it will keep the attribute regardless of the folder settings of the destination.
- If a file does not have the encryption attribute, it can still inherit it from the destination folder.

If you use the encryption feature of Windows 2000, then you must take care when copying files around your network. No warnings are given when circumstances mean that the encryption attribute is going to be removed from a file. If you copy an encrypted file from an NTFS v5.0 partition to a volume in your Active Directory that physically resides on an NT 4.0 server, then the encryption is removed automatically and without warning.

The rules mentioned above are only broken when the `\%SystemRoot%` folder is used. Files and folders in this directory path are mainly for system use and cannot be encrypted, so even if this folder is on an NTFS v5.0 partition, copying or moving files into this folder will remove any encryption without warning.

Backing Up Encrypted Files and Folders

Encrypted files and folders can be backed up with the NTbackup utility. The difficulties faced when copying files is overcome by the backup utility never having to decrypt the files to back them up. They are moved to tape or to a backup set on disk by the system in encrypted form and remain encrypted until they are restored and the user's private key is used for decryption.

Encrypted files and folders are backed up in the same way as any other files or folders. The fact that some files are stored on the disk in an encrypted fashion is completely transparent to the NTbackup utility. Remember that this is the backup utility shipped with Windows 2000. A third-party product may not be able to backup encrypted files, depending on the method of access.

For more help on using the NTbackup utility, see the online help.

Restoring Encrypted Files and Folders

The NTbackup utility restores the files in the same way as any other backed-up files are restored. Again, as with the backup tool, the restore tool does not need to decrypt the files and so does not need access to the user's private key.

Complications can arise from restoring encrypted files to a destination other than the original. You must always remember that for the files to be of use, the user's private key must be available to decrypt them after the restore. If encrypted files are backed up on one machine, and then restored to another machine the user must have access to that machine and the user must also have access to his private key store at the same time. This could be a problem when two physically distinct locations are involved.

This case means that either the certificate store must be available, which would be the case if the restore was made onto another machine in the same domain, or the certificate containing the private key must be exported to a file and copied to the destination. It can then be imported into the local certificate manager and used to decrypt the file. Follow the instructions below to set up an MMC console, using the Certificate Manager snap-in.

1. Log on as Administrator.
2. Start the **MMC**.
3. Select **Add/Remove snap-ins**.
4. Select **Add**.
5. Select **Certificate Manager** from the list of available snap-ins.
6. Select **Add**. Figure 16.4 shows the Certificate Manager snap-in dialog box.
7. Select **My User Account**.
8. Select **Finish > Close > OK**.

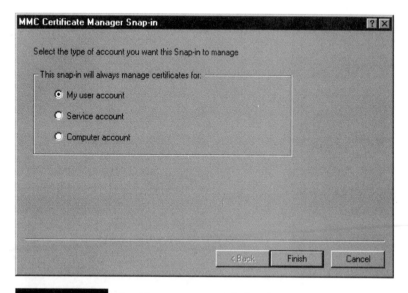

FIGURE 16.4   Certificate Manager dialog box

The Certificate Manager snap-in is now installed in the console, and the focus is set to the user account currently logged on. The next step is to find the correct certificate and export it to a file so it can be moved to the new location.

1. Expand the **Certificate Manager** node in the scope pane.

2. Expand **Personal** and select **Certificates**. Figure 16.5 shows the results pane containing the personal certificates configured for the logged-on user (Administrator, in this case). If no other certificate activity has taken place with this user, the list should only contain an EFS certificate because Administrator is the default recovery agent.

3. Right-click the certificate intended for EFS use, and select **Task > Export** to initiate the Certificate Manager Export Wizard.

4. Select **Next** to continue. You are now asked if you want to export your private key, and you are warned about password protection. The private key is the one requirement for decrypting files on another system, so you must export it.

5. Ensure that **Yes, export the private key** is selected.

6. Select **Next**.

7. Accept the default PFX file format and options. Select **Next**.

8. Enter a private key protection password and confirm it.

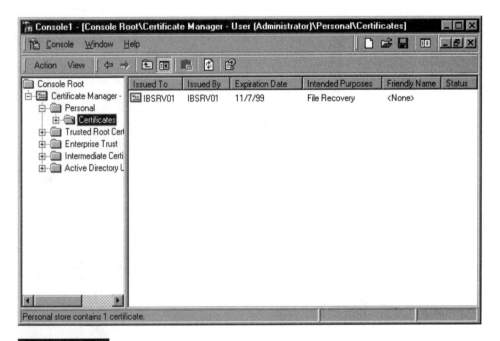

FIGURE 16.5   Personal certificates stored on the local machine

9. Select **Next**.

10. Choose the path and file name for the export file.

11. Your certificate options are displayed, and you are asked to complete the operation.

12. Select **Finish**. The export file is created, and you are notified on successful completion.

The export file can now be moved to the system on which the restore has taken place. The next step is to import the certificate into a certificate store valid for the current user (on the destination machine).

1. Start the import process. You can follow the same instructions outlined in steps 1 through 3 for exporting a certificate, substituting **Import** for **Export**. This will start the Certificate Manager Import Wizard. A much easier way is to double-click the certificate file in Windows Explorer. All .pfx files are associated with the Certificate Manager Import Wizard by default in Windows 2000.

2. Select **Next**.

3. Enter the certificate file name and path and select **Next**.

4. Enter the password you selected for private key protection. Forgetting this password means that the certificate file is no good and you have to start the export over again.

5. Select **Place all certificates in the following store**.

6. Use the Browser to select the **Personal** store. Select **OK > Next**.

7. Select **Finish** to complete the import. The successful import in confirmed.

The user on the destination node who has imported the certificate containing the original private key can now transparently decrypt the restored files.

Always bear in mind when backing up encrypted data that you must have the correct private key or recovery key available to you if you need to restore. If these backups are for disaster recovery purposes, then consider exporting recovery keys, password protecting them, and backing them up as well.

Encrypted File Recovery Process

Public keys used to encrypt the file encryption key can be lost or damaged, so there is a need for a recovery system to be in place to safeguard against the possibility of lost data. EFS will not work unless the data recovery policy is set in the domain (or on a standalone computer). Recovery agents (people defined within the enterprise responsible for this job function) should be identified for your enterprise. The default recovery agent is the local or domain administrator, but if your company has a compliance or data security officer, then company policy may dictate that this person be the recovery agent. If data is inaccessible because the user certificate is lost or has been removed because a user left the company, then the data can be recovered by the recovery agent.

Defining Recovery Agents

When you look at your EFS recovery policy, you must decide who will become a recovery agent. By default, the local Administrator (standalone machine) or domain administrator is defined as a recovery agent.

A recovery agent is defined by access to a recovery key. Recovery keys are held in certificates in the certificate store by default and are used only when a file cannot be decrypted by the original user for some reason.

APPLY USER RIGHTS

To give the recovery agent status to a user, the user must first be given the right to request a recovery key from a Certificate Authority (CA). Before you can grant this right you must ensure that the Certificate Services is installed and that an Enterprise CA exists in your domain. For details on Certificate Services, see the online help.

REQUESTING A RECOVERY CERTIFICATE

Once a user has been given the rights to request a recovery certificate, the process can be completed by the user. This allows the process to be removed from the control of administrators as the removal of overall control from administrators is a requirement in some enterprises. Follow the instructions below to request a recovery certificate. These instructions need to be carried out by the user who requires the recovery certificate.

1. Start the **MMC** and add the **Certificate Manager** snap-in.
2. Expand the **Certificate Manager** node in the scope pane.
3. Right-click the **Personal** store, and select **Task > Request New Certificate** to start the Certificate Request Wizard.
4. Select **Next**. You are asked to choose a Certificate Authority to send the request to.
5. Choose the appropriate CA.
6. Select **Next**. You are asked to choose the type of certificate that you wish to receive.
7. Select **EFS Recovery Agent**.

8. Select **Next**.

9. Give your certificate a distinguishable name and an optional description.

10. Select **Next**. The certificate summary page appears.

11. Check the information on the summary page, and select **Finish**. The certificate request is confirmed.

EXPORTING THE RECOVERY CERTIFICATE

The certificate now exists in your personal certificate store. You must export the certificate in two formats. The first is without your private key attached. To perform the export, follow the instructions below.

1. Expand the **Certificate Manager** node in the scope pane.

2. Expand **Personal** and select **Certificates**.

3. Right-click the certificate intended for EFS use, and select **Task > Export** to initiate the Certificate Manager Export Wizard.

4. Select **Next** to continue. You are now asked if you want to export your private key and are warned about password protection.

5. Ensure that **No, do not export the private key** is selected.

6. Select **Next**.

7. Select the **DER encoded binary X.509 (CER)** file format. Select **Next**.

8. Choose the path and file name for the export file.

9. Your certificate options are displayed, and you are asked to complete the operation.

10. Select **Finish**. The export file is created, and you are notified on successful completion.

This export file can now be used by the Administrator to add to the EFS Recovery Policy created earlier. The `.cer` file does not contain the user's private key and so is secure. The public key contained in the certificate will be used to encrypt a copy of the FEK for each encrypted file from now.

The second export is performed with the private key attached and in a `.pfx` format.

1. Follow steps 1 through 4 above.

2. Ensure that **Yes, export the private key** is selected.

3. Select **Next**.

4. Select the **.pfx** file format. Select **Next**.

5. Choose the path and file name for the export file.

6. Select **Next**.

7. Accept the default .pfx file format and options. Select **Next**.

8. Enter a private key protection password and confirm the password.

9. Select **Next**.

10. Choose the path and file name for the export file.

11. Your certificate options are displayed, and you are asked to complete the operation.

This certificate file is created for security reasons. The use of recovery agents should not be a frequent occurrence. In the day-to-day running of the systems, file encryption should be transparent and certificate services should be stable. If you leave the EFS recovery agent certificate on the system, it could be exported and used without your knowledge. Now that you have a secure copy of the certificate, keep it in a safe place (and don't forget the password) and delete the copy of the certificate on the system. To delete the certificate, right-click on the certificate in your **Personal** store and select **Delete**. Confirm the deletion.

Adding Recovery Agents

Once a recovery agent is defined and the certificate is exported and secure add the recovery agent to the list of recovery agents on the local machine or domain.

The Future of EFS

Later versions of EFS will allow file sharing with protection still afforded by public key technology. EFS uses the DESX encryption algorithm. Because of U.S. government export laws, only software intended for the North American market can contain an encryption system stronger than 40-bit. Therefore, the DESX encryption algorithm exported from the United States to its international market is only 40-bit. The encryption algorithm distributed in the United States is 128-bit. Files can be exported from a 40-bit system and imported into a 128-bit system. Files cannot travel in encrypted form from a 128-bit system to a 40-bit system. This may cause problems for international companies with offices in the United States. Microsoft is working for permission to allow stronger encryption systems to be exported and hopes to standardize on them.

System Policy File Listings

Common.adm

```
CLASS MACHINE

CATEGORY !!Network
   CATEGORY !!Update
      POLICY !!RemoteUpdate
      KEYNAME System\CurrentControlSet\Control\Update
      ACTIONLISTOFF
         VALUENAME "UpdateMode"      VALUE NUMERIC 0
      END ACTIONLISTOFF
         PART !!UpdateMode           DROPDOWNLIST REQUIRED
         VALUENAME "UpdateMode"
         ITEMLIST
            NAME !!UM_Automatic      VALUE NUMERIC 1
            NAME !!UM_Manual         VALUE NUMERIC 2
         END ITEMLIST
         END PART

         PART !!UM_Manual_Path       EDITTEXT
         VALUENAME "NetworkPath"
         END PART

         PART !!DisplayErrors        CHECKBOX
         VALUENAME "Verbose"
         END PART
```

```
            PART !!LoadBalance                              CHECKBOX
            VALUENAME "LoadBalance"
            END PART
        END POLICY
    END CATEGORY; Update

END CATEGORY  ; Network

CATEGORY !!System
    CATEGORY !!SNMP
        POLICY !!Communities
        KEYNAME System\CurrentControlSet\Services\SNMP\Parameters\ValidCommunities
            PART !!CommunitiesListbox               LISTBOX
                VALUEPREFIX ""
            END PART
        END POLICY

        POLICY !!PermittedManagers
        KEYNAME System\CurrentControlSet\Services\SNMP\Parameters\PermittedManagers
            PART !!PermittedManagersListbox         LISTBOX
                VALUEPREFIX ""
            END PART
        END POLICY

        POLICY !!Traps_Public
        KEYNAME System\CurrentControlSet\Services\SNMP\Parameters\TrapConfiguration\Public
            PART !!Traps_PublicListbox              LISTBOX
                VALUEPREFIX ""
            END PART
        END POLICY
    END CATEGORY ; SNMP

    CATEGORY !!Run
        POLICY !!Run
        KEYNAME Software\Microsoft\Windows\CurrentVersion\Run
            PART !!RunListbox                       LISTBOX EXPLICITVALUE
            END PART
        END POLICY
    END CATEGORY
END CATEGORY  ; System


CLASS USER

CATEGORY !!ControlPanel
    CATEGORY !!CPL_Display
        POLICY !!CPL_Display_Restrict
        KEYNAME Software\Microsoft\Windows\CurrentVersion\Policies\System

            PART !!CPL_Display_Disable              CHECKBOX
            VALUENAME NoDispCPL
            END PART
```

```
        PART !!CPL_Display_HideBkgnd              CHECKBOX
        VALUENAME NoDispBackgroundPage
        END PART

        PART !!CPL_Display_HideScrsav             CHECKBOX
        VALUENAME NoDispScrSavPage
        END PART

        PART !!CPL_Display_HideAppearance         CHECKBOX
        VALUENAME NoDispAppearancePage
        END PART

        PART !!CPL_Display_HideSettings           CHECKBOX
        VALUENAME NoDispSettingsPage
        END PART
      END POLICY
    END CATEGORY                    ; Display

END CATEGORY  ; Control Panel

CATEGORY !!Desktop
    KEYNAME "Control Panel\Desktop"
    POLICY !!Wallpaper
PART !!WallpaperName                              DITTEXT
VALUENAME "Wallpaper"
END PART
PART !!WALLPAPER_TIP1                             TEXT    END PART
PART !!WALLPAPER_TIP2                             TEXT    END PART

        PART !!TileWallpaper                      CHECKBOX DEFCHECKED
        VALUENAME "TileWallpaper"
        VALUEON "1" VALUEOFF "0"
        END PART
    END POLICY

    POLICY !!ColorScheme
        PART !!SchemeName                         DROPDOWNLIST
        KEYNAME "Control Panel\Appearance"
        VALUENAME Current                         REQUIRED
        ITEMLIST
          NAME !!Lavender VALUE !!Lavender
          ACTIONLIST
            KEYNAME "Control Panel\Colors"
            VALUENAME ActiveBorder                VALUE "174 168 217"
            VALUENAME ActiveTitle                 VALUE "128 128 128"
            VALUENAME AppWorkspace                VALUE "90 78 177"
            VALUENAME Background                  VALUE "128 128 192"
            VALUENAME ButtonDkShadow              VALUE "0 0 0"
            VALUENAME ButtonFace                  VALUE "174 168 217"
            VALUENAME ButtonHilight               VALUE "216 213 236"
            VALUENAME ButtonLight                 VALUE "174 168 217"
            VALUENAME ButtonShadow                VALUE "90 78 177"
            VALUENAME ButtonText                  VALUE "0 0 0"
            VALUENAME GrayText                    VALUE "90 78 177"
            VALUENAME Hilight                     VALUE "128 128 128"
```

```
    VALUENAME HilightText                    VALUE "255 255 255"
    VALUENAME InactiveBorder                 VALUE "174 168 217"
    VALUENAME InactiveTitle                  VALUE "90 78 177"
    VALUENAME InactiveTitleText              VALUE "0 0 0"
    VALUENAME Menu                           VALUE "174 168 217"
    VALUENAME MenuText                       VALUE "0 0 0"
    VALUENAME InfoText                       VALUE "174 168 217"
    VALUENAME InfoWindow                     VALUE "0 0 0"
    VALUENAME Scrollbar                      VALUE "174 168 217"
    VALUENAME TitleText                      VALUE "255 255 255"
    VALUENAME Window                         VALUE "255 255 255"
    VALUENAME WindowFrame                    VALUE "0 0 0"
    VALUENAME WindowText                     VALUE "0 0 0"
  END ACTIONLIST

NAME !!Tan256 VALUE !!Tan256
ACTIONLIST
    KEYNAME "Control Panel\Colors"
    VALUENAME ActiveBorder                   VALUE "202 184 149"
    VALUENAME ActiveTitle                    VALUE "0 0 0"
    VALUENAME AppWorkspace                   VALUE "156 129 78"
    VALUENAME Background                     VALUE "128 64 64"
    VALUENAME ButtonDkShadow                 VALUE "0 0 0"
    VALUENAME ButtonFace                     VALUE "202 184 149"
    VALUENAME ButtonHilight                  VALUE "228 220 203"
    VALUENAME ButtonLight                    VALUE "202 184 149"
    VALUENAME ButtonShadow                   VALUE "156 129 78"
    VALUENAME ButtonText                     VALUE "0 0 0"
    VALUENAME GrayText                       VALUE "156 129 78"
    VALUENAME Hilight                        VALUE "0 0 0"
    VALUENAME HilightText                    VALUE "255 255 255"
    VALUENAME InactiveBorder                 VALUE "202 184 149"
    VALUENAME InactiveTitle                  VALUE "156 129 78"
    VALUENAME InactiveTitleText              VALUE "0 0 0"
    VALUENAME Menu                           VALUE "202 184 149"
    VALUENAME MenuText                       VALUE "0 0 0"
    VALUENAME InfoText                       VALUE "202 184 149"
    VALUENAME InfoWindow                     VALUE "0 0 0"
    VALUENAME Scrollbar                      VALUE "202 184 149"
    VALUENAME TitleText                      VALUE "255 255 255"
    VALUENAME Window                         VALUE "255 255 255"
    VALUENAME WindowFrame                    VALUE "0 0 0"
    VALUENAME WindowText                     VALUE "0 0 0"
  END ACTIONLIST

NAME !!Wheat256 VALUE !!Wheat256
ACTIONLIST
    KEYNAME "Control Panel\Colors"
    VALUENAME ActiveBorder                   VALUE "215 213 170"
    VALUENAME ActiveTitle                    VALUE "0 0 0"
    VALUENAME AppWorkspace                   VALUE "173 169 82"
    VALUENAME Background                     VALUE "0 64 64"
    VALUENAME ButtonDkShadow                 VALUE "0 0 0"
    VALUENAME ButtonFace                     VALUE "215 213 170"
    VALUENAME ButtonHilight                  VALUE "235 234 214"
```

```
    VALUENAME ButtonLight                       VALUE "215 213 170"
    VALUENAME ButtonShadow                      VALUE "173 169 82"
    VALUENAME ButtonText                        VALUE "0 0 0"
    VALUENAME GrayText                          VALUE "173 169 82"
    VALUENAME Hilight                           VALUE "0 0 0"
    VALUENAME HilightText                       VALUE "255 255 255"
    VALUENAME InactiveBorder                    VALUE "215 213 170"
    VALUENAME InactiveTitle                     VALUE "173 169 82"
    VALUENAME InactiveTitleText                 VALUE "0 0 0"
    VALUENAME Menu                              VALUE "215 213 170"
    VALUENAME MenuText                          VALUE "0 0 0"
    VALUENAME InfoText                          VALUE "215 213 170"
    VALUENAME InfoWindow                        VALUE "0 0 0"
    VALUENAME Scrollbar                         VALUE "215 213 170"
    VALUENAME TitleText                         VALUE "255 255 255"
    VALUENAME Window                            VALUE "255 255 255"
    VALUENAME WindowFrame                       VALUE "0 0 0"
    VALUENAME WindowText                        VALUE "0 0 0"
END ACTIONLIST

NAME !!Celery VALUE !!Celery
ACTIONLIST
    KEYNAME "Control Panel\Colors"
    VALUENAME ActiveBorder                      VALUE "168 215 170"
    VALUENAME ActiveTitle                       VALUE "0 0 0"
    VALUENAME AppWorkspace                      VALUE "80 175 85"
    VALUENAME Background                        VALUE "32 18 46"
    VALUENAME ButtonDkShadow                    VALUE "0 0 0"
    VALUENAME ButtonFace                        VALUE "168 215 170"
    VALUENAME ButtonHilight                     VALUE "211 235 213"
    VALUENAME ButtonLight                       VALUE "168 215 170"
    VALUENAME ButtonShadow                      VALUE "85 175 85"
    VALUENAME ButtonText                        VALUE "0 0 0"
    VALUENAME GrayText                          VALUE "80 175 85"
    VALUENAME Hilight                           VALUE "0 0 0"
    VALUENAME HilightText                       VALUE "255 255 255"
    VALUENAME InactiveBorder                    VALUE "168 215 170"
    VALUENAME InactiveTitle                     VALUE "80 175 75"
    VALUENAME InactiveTitleText                 VALUE "0 0 0"
    VALUENAME Menu                              VALUE "168 215 170"
    VALUENAME MenuText                          VALUE "0 0 0"
    VALUENAME InfoText                          VALUE "168 215 170"
    VALUENAME InfoWindow                        VALUE "0 0 0"
    VALUENAME Scrollbar                         VALUE "168 215 170"
    VALUENAME TitleText                         VALUE "255 255 255"
    VALUENAME Window                            VALUE "255 255 255"
    VALUENAME WindowFrame                       VALUE "0 0 0"
    VALUENAME WindowText                        VALUE "0 0 0"
END ACTIONLIST

NAME !!Rose VALUE !!Rose
ACTIONLIST
    KEYNAME "Control Panel\Colors"
    VALUENAME ActiveBorder                      VALUE "207 175 183"
    VALUENAME ActiveTitle                       VALUE "128 128 128"
```

```
      VALUENAME AppWorkspace                      VALUE "159 96 112"
      VALUENAME Background                        VALUE "128 64 64"
      VALUENAME ButtonDkShadow                    VALUE "0 0 0"
      VALUENAME ButtonFace                        VALUE "207 175 183"
      VALUENAME ButtonHilight                     VALUE "231 216 220"
      VALUENAME ButtonLight                       VALUE "207 175 183"
      VALUENAME ButtonShadow                      VALUE "159 96 112"
      VALUENAME ButtonText                        VALUE "0 0 0"
      VALUENAME GrayText                          VALUE "159 96 112"
      VALUENAME Hilight                           VALUE "128 128 128"
      VALUENAME HilightText                       VALUE "255 255 255"
      VALUENAME InactiveBorder                    VALUE "207 175 183"
      VALUENAME InactiveTitle                     VALUE "159 96 112"
      VALUENAME InactiveTitleText                 VALUE "0 0 0"
      VALUENAME Menu                              VALUE "207 175 183"
      VALUENAME MenuText                          VALUE "0 0 0"
      VALUENAME InfoText                          VALUE "207 175 183"
      VALUENAME InfoWindow                        VALUE "0 0 0"
      VALUENAME Scrollbar                         VALUE "207 175 183"
      VALUENAME TitleText                         VALUE "255 255 255"
      VALUENAME Window                            VALUE "255 255 255"
      VALUENAME WindowFrame                       VALUE "0 0 0"
      VALUENAME WindowText                        VALUE "0 0 0"
   END ACTIONLIST

   NAME !!Evergreen VALUE !!Evergreen
   ACTIONLIST
      KEYNAME "Control Panel\Colors"
      VALUENAME ActiveBorder                      VALUE "47 151 109"
      VALUENAME ActiveTitle                       VALUE "0 0 0"
      VALUENAME AppWorkspace                      VALUE "31 101 73"
      VALUENAME Background                        VALUE "48 63 48"
      VALUENAME ButtonDkShadow                    VALUE "0 0 0"
      VALUENAME ButtonFace                        VALUE "47 151 109"
      VALUENAME ButtonHilight                     VALUE "137 218 186"
      VALUENAME ButtonLight                       VALUE "47 151 109"
      VALUENAME ButtonShadow                      VALUE "31 101 73"
      VALUENAME ButtonText                        VALUE "0 0 0"
      VALUENAME GrayText                          VALUE "31 101 73"
      VALUENAME Hilight                           VALUE "0 0 0"
      VALUENAME HilightText                       VALUE "255 255 255"
      VALUENAME InactiveBorder                    VALUE "47 151 109"
      VALUENAME InactiveTitle                     VALUE "31 101 73"
      VALUENAME InactiveTitleText                 VALUE "0 0 0"
      VALUENAME Menu                              VALUE "47 151 109"
      VALUENAME MenuText                          VALUE "0 0 0"
      VALUENAME InfoText                          VALUE "47 151 109"
      VALUENAME InfoWindow                        VALUE "0 0 0"
      VALUENAME Scrollbar                         VALUE "47 151 109"
      VALUENAME TitleText                         VALUE "255 255 255"
      VALUENAME Window                            VALUE "255 255 255"
      VALUENAME WindowFrame                       VALUE "0 0 0"
      VALUENAME WindowText                        VALUE "0 0 0"
   END ACTIONLIST
```

```
NAME !!Blues VALUE !!Blues
ACTIONLIST
    KEYNAME "Control Panel\Colors"
    VALUENAME ActiveBorder                      VALUE "161 198 221"
    VALUENAME ActiveTitle                       VALUE "0 0 0"
    VALUENAME AppWorkspace                      VALUE "69 139 186"
    VALUENAME Background                        VALUE "0 0 64"
    VALUENAME ButtonDkShadow                    VALUE "0 0 0"
    VALUENAME ButtonFace                        VALUE "164 198 221"
    VALUENAME ButtonHilight                     VALUE "210 227 238"
    VALUENAME ButtonLight                       VALUE "164 198 221"
    VALUENAME ButtonShadow                      VALUE "69 139 186"
    VALUENAME ButtonText                        VALUE "0 0 0"
    VALUENAME GrayText                          VALUE "69 139 186"
    VALUENAME Hilight                           VALUE "0 0 0"
    VALUENAME HilightText                       VALUE "255 255 255"
    VALUENAME InactiveBorder                    VALUE "164 198 221"
    VALUENAME InactiveTitle                     VALUE "69 139 186"
    VALUENAME InactiveTitleText                 VALUE "0 0 0"
    VALUENAME Menu                              VALUE "164 198 221"
    VALUENAME MenuText                          VALUE "0 0 0"
    VALUENAME InfoText                          VALUE "164 198 221"
    VALUENAME InfoWindow                        VALUE "0 0 0"
    VALUENAME Scrollbar                         VALUE "164 198 221"
    VALUENAME TitleText                         VALUE "255 255 255"
    VALUENAME Window                            VALUE "255 255 255"
    VALUENAME WindowFrame                       VALUE "0 0 0"
    VALUENAME WindowText                        VALUE "0 0 0"
END ACTIONLIST

NAME !!Teal VALUE !!Teal
ACTIONLIST
    KEYNAME "Control Panel\Colors"
    VALUENAME ActiveBorder                      VALUE "192 192 192"
    VALUENAME ActiveTitle                       VALUE "0 128 128"
    VALUENAME AppWorkspace                      VALUE "128 128 128"
    VALUENAME Background                        VALUE "0 64 64"
    VALUENAME ButtonDkShadow                    VALUE "0 0 0"
    VALUENAME ButtonFace                        VALUE "192 192 192"
    VALUENAME ButtonHilight                     VALUE "255 255 255"
    VALUENAME ButtonLight                       VALUE "192 192 192"
    VALUENAME ButtonShadow                      VALUE "128 128 128"
    VALUENAME ButtonText                        VALUE "0 0 0"
    VALUENAME GrayText                          VALUE "128 128 128"
    VALUENAME Hilight                           VALUE "0 128 128"
    VALUENAME HilightText                       VALUE "255 255 255"
    VALUENAME InactiveBorder                    VALUE "192 192 192"
    VALUENAME InactiveTitle                     VALUE "192 192 192"
    VALUENAME InactiveTitleText                 VALUE "0 0 0"
    VALUENAME Menu                              VALUE "192 192 192"
    VALUENAME MenuText                          VALUE "0 0 0"
    VALUENAME InfoText                          VALUE "192 192 192"
    VALUENAME InfoWindow                        VALUE "0 0 0"
    VALUENAME Scrollbar                         VALUE "192 192 192"
    VALUENAME TitleText                         VALUE "0 0 0"
```

```
      VALUENAME Window                          VALUE "255 255 255"
      VALUENAME WindowFrame                     VALUE "0 0 0"
      VALUENAME WindowText                      VALUE "0 0 0"
   END ACTIONLIST

   NAME !!TheReds VALUE !!TheReds
   ACTIONLIST
      KEYNAME "Control Panel\Colors"
      VALUENAME ActiveBorder                    VALUE "192 192 192"
      VALUENAME ActiveTitle                     VALUE "128 0 0"
      VALUENAME AppWorkspace                    VALUE "128 128 128"
      VALUENAME Background                      VALUE "64 0 0"
      VALUENAME ButtonDkShadow                  VALUE "0 0 0"
      VALUENAME ButtonFace                      VALUE "192 192 192"
      VALUENAME ButtonHilight                   VALUE "255 255 255"
      VALUENAME ButtonLight                     VALUE "192 192 192"
      VALUENAME ButtonShadow                    VALUE "128 128 128"
      VALUENAME ButtonText                      VALUE "0 0 0"
      VALUENAME GrayText                        VALUE "128 128 128"
      VALUENAME Hilight                         VALUE "128 0 0"
      VALUENAME HilightText                     VALUE "255 255 255"
      VALUENAME InactiveBorder                  VALUE "192 192 192"
      VALUENAME InactiveTitle                   VALUE "192 192 192"
      VALUENAME InactiveTitleText               VALUE "0 0 0"
      VALUENAME Menu                            VALUE "192 192 192"
      VALUENAME MenuText                        VALUE "0 0 0"
      VALUENAME InfoText                        VALUE "192 192 192"
      VALUENAME InfoWindow                      VALUE "0 0 0"
      VALUENAME Scrollbar                       VALUE "192 192 192"
      VALUENAME TitleText                       VALUE "255 255 255"
      VALUENAME Window                          VALUE "255 255 255"
      VALUENAME WindowFrame                     VALUE "0 0 0"
      VALUENAME WindowText                      VALUE "0 0 0"
   END ACTIONLIST

   NAME !!WindowsDefault VALUE !!WindowsDefault
   ACTIONLIST
      KEYNAME "Control Panel\Colors"
      VALUENAME ActiveBorder                    VALUE "192 192 192"
      VALUENAME ActiveTitle                     VALUE "0 0 128"
      VALUENAME AppWorkspace                    VALUE "128 128 128"
      VALUENAME Background                      VALUE "0 128 128"
      VALUENAME ButtonDkShadow                  VALUE "0 0 0"
      VALUENAME ButtonFace                      VALUE "192 192 192"
      VALUENAME ButtonHilight                   VALUE "255 255 255"
      VALUENAME ButtonLight                     VALUE "192 192 192"
      VALUENAME ButtonShadow                    VALUE "128 128 128"
      VALUENAME ButtonText                      VALUE "0 0 0"
      VALUENAME GrayText                        VALUE "128 128 128"
      VALUENAME Hilight                         VALUE "0 0 128"
      VALUENAME HilightText                     VALUE "255 255 255"
      VALUENAME InactiveBorder                  VALUE "192 192 192"
      VALUENAME InactiveTitle                   VALUE "192 192 192"
      VALUENAME InactiveTitleText               VALUE "0 0 0"
      VALUENAME Menu                            VALUE "192 192 192"
```

```
    VALUENAME MenuText                      VALUE "0 0 0"
    VALUENAME InfoText                      VALUE "192 192 192"
    VALUENAME InfoWindow                    VALUE "0 0 0"
    VALUENAME Scrollbar                     VALUE "192 192 192"
    VALUENAME TitleText                     VALUE "255 255 255"
    VALUENAME Window                        VALUE "255 255 255"
    VALUENAME WindowFrame                   VALUE "0 0 0"
    VALUENAME WindowText                    VALUE "0 0 0"
  END ACTIONLIST

NAME !!BlueAndBlack VALUE !!BlueAndBlack
ACTIONLIST
    KEYNAME "Control Panel\Colors"
    VALUENAME ActiveBorder                  VALUE "192 192 192"
    VALUENAME ActiveTitle                   VALUE "0 0 0"
    VALUENAME AppWorkspace                  VALUE "128 128 128"
    VALUENAME Background                    VALUE "0 0 128"
    VALUENAME ButtonDkShadow                VALUE "0 0 0"
    VALUENAME ButtonFace                    VALUE "192 192 192"
    VALUENAME ButtonHilight                 VALUE "255 255 255"
    VALUENAME ButtonLight                   VALUE "192 192 192"
    VALUENAME ButtonShadow                  VALUE "128 128 128"
    VALUENAME ButtonText                    VALUE "0 0 0"
    VALUENAME GrayText                      VALUE "128 128 128"
    VALUENAME Hilight                       VALUE "255 255 0"
    VALUENAME HilightText                   VALUE "0 0 0"
    VALUENAME InactiveBorder                VALUE "192 192 192"
    VALUENAME InactiveTitle                 VALUE "192 192 192"
    VALUENAME InactiveTitleText             VALUE "0 0 0"
    VALUENAME Menu                          VALUE "192 192 192"
    VALUENAME MenuText                      VALUE "0 0 0"
    VALUENAME InfoText                      VALUE "192 192 192"
    VALUENAME InfoWindow                    VALUE "0 0 0"
    VALUENAME Scrollbar                     VALUE "192 192 192"
    VALUENAME TitleText                     VALUE "255 255 255"
    VALUENAME Window                        VALUE "255 255 255"
    VALUENAME WindowFrame                   VALUE "0 0 0"
    VALUENAME WindowText                    VALUE "0 0 0"
  END ACTIONLIST

NAME !!Wheat VALUE !!Wheat
ACTIONLIST
    KEYNAME "Control Panel\Colors"
    VALUENAME ActiveBorder                  VALUE "192 192 192"
    VALUENAME ActiveTitle                   VALUE "128 128 0"
    VALUENAME AppWorkspace                  VALUE "128 128 128"
    VALUENAME Background                    VALUE "128 128 64"
    VALUENAME ButtonDkShadow                VALUE "0 0 0"
    VALUENAME ButtonFace                    VALUE "192 192 192"
    VALUENAME ButtonHilight                 VALUE "255 255 255"
    VALUENAME ButtonLight                   VALUE "192 192 192"
    VALUENAME ButtonShadow                  VALUE "128 128 128"
    VALUENAME ButtonText                    VALUE "0 0 0"
    VALUENAME GrayText                      VALUE "128 128 128"
    VALUENAME Hilight                       VALUE "128 128 0"
```

```
           VALUENAME HilightText               VALUE "0 0 0"
           VALUENAME InactiveBorder            VALUE "192 192 192"
           VALUENAME InactiveTitle             VALUE "192 192 192"
           VALUENAME InactiveTitleText         VALUE "0 0 0"
           VALUENAME Menu                      VALUE "192 192 192"
           VALUENAME MenuText                  VALUE "0 0 0"
           VALUENAME InfoText                  VALUE "192 192 192"
           VALUENAME InfoWindow                VALUE "0 0 0"
           VALUENAME Scrollbar                 VALUE "192 192 192"
           VALUENAME TitleText                 VALUE "0 0 0"
           VALUENAME Window                    VALUE "255 255 255"
           VALUENAME WindowFrame               VALUE "0 0 0"
           VALUENAME WindowText                VALUE "0 0 0"
        END ACTIONLIST
      END ITEMLIST
      END PART
    END POLICY
  END CATEGORY ; Desktop

CATEGORY !!Shell
   CATEGORY !!Restrictions
      KEYNAME Software\Microsoft\Windows\CurrentVersion\Policies\Explorer
        POLICY !!RemoveRun
        VALUENAME "NoRun"
        END POLICY

        POLICY !!RemoveFolders
        VALUENAME "NoSetFolders"
        END POLICY

        POLICY !!RemoveTaskbar
        VALUENAME "NoSetTaskbar"
        END POLICY

        POLICY !!RemoveFind
        VALUENAME "NoFind"
        END POLICY

        POLICY !!HideDrives
        VALUENAME "NoDrives"
        VALUEON NUMERIC 67108863     ; low 26 bits on (1 bit per drive)
        END POLICY

        POLICY !!HideNetHood
        VALUENAME "NoNetHood"
        END POLICY

        POLICY !!NoEntireNetwork
        KEYNAME Software\Microsoft\Windows\CurrentVersion\Policies\Network
        VALUENAME "NoEntireNetwork"
        END POLICY

        POLICY !!NoWorkgroupContents
        KEYNAME Software\Microsoft\Windows\CurrentVersion\Policies\Network
        VALUENAME "NoWorkgroupContents"
```

```
        END POLICY

        POLICY !!HideDesktop
        VALUENAME "NoDesktop"
        END POLICY

        POLICY !!DisableClose
        VALUENAME "NoClose"
        END POLICY

        POLICY !!NoSaveSettings
        VALUENAME "NoSaveSettings"
        END POLICY
    END CATEGORY
END CATEGORY  ; Shell

CATEGORY !!System
KEYNAME Software\Microsoft\Windows\CurrentVersion\Policies\System
    CATEGORY !!Restrictions
        POLICY !!DisableRegedit
        VALUENAME DisableRegistryTools
        END POLICY

        POLICY !!RestrictApps
        KEYNAME Software\Microsoft\Windows\CurrentVersion\Policies\Explorer
        VALUENAME RestrictRun
        PART !!RestrictAppsList LISTBOX
        KEYNAME Software\Microsoft\Windows\CurrentVersion\Policies\Explorer\RestrictRun
        VALUEPREFIX ""
        END PART
        PART !!RestrictApps_Tip1                    TEXT    END PART
        PART !!RestrictApps_Tip2                    TEXT    END PART
        PART !!RestrictApps_Tip3                    TEXT    END PART
        PART !!RestrictApps_Tip4                    TEXT    END PART
        END POLICY
    END CATEGORY
END CATEGORY  ; System


[strings]
Network="Network"
Update="System policies update"
RemoteUpdate="Remote update"
UpdateMode="Update mode"
UM_Automatic="Automatic (use default path)"
UM_Manual="Manual (use specific path)"
UM_Manual_Path="Path for manual update"
DisplayErrors="Display error messages"
LoadBalance="Load balancing"
System="System"
DisableFileSharing="Disable file sharing"
DisablePrintSharing="Disable print sharing"
ControlPanel="Control Panel"
CPL_Display="Display"
CPL_Display_Restrict="Restrict display"
```

```
CPL_Display_Disable="Deny access to display icon"
CPL_Display_HideBkgnd="Hide Background tab"
CPL_Display_HideScrsav="Hide Screen Saver tab"
CPL_Display_HideAppearance="Hide Appearance tab"
CPL_Display_HideSettings="Hide Settings tab"
Desktop="Desktop"
Wallpaper="Wallpaper"
WallpaperName="Wallpaper Name"
TileWallpaper="Tile Wallpaper"
Wallpaper_Tip1="Specifiy location and name (e.g. c:\winnt\winnt256.bmp)"
Wallpaper_Tip2="                         "
ColorScheme="Color scheme"
SchemeName="Scheme name"
Lavender="Lavender 256"
Celery="Celery 256"
Rose="Rose 256"
Evergreen="Evergreen 256"
Blues="Blues 256"
WindowsDefault="Windows Default"
BlueAndBlack="Blue and Black"
Teal="Teal"
TheReds="The Reds"
Wheat="Wheat"
Wheat256="Wheat 256"
Tan256="Tan 256"
Shell="Shell"
RemoveRun="Remove Run command from Start menu"
RemoveFolders="Remove folders from Settings on Start menu"
RemoveTaskbar="Remove Taskbar from Settings on Start menu"
RemoveFind="Remove Find command from Start menu"
HideDrives="Hide drives in My Computer"
HideNetHood="Hide Network Neighborhood"
NoEntireNetwork="No Entire Network in Network Neighborhood"
HideDesktop="Hide all items on desktop"
DisableClose="Disable Shut Down command"
NoSaveSettings="Don't save settings at exit"
SNMP="SNMP"
Communities="Communities"
CommunitiesListbox="Communities"
PermittedManagers="Permitted managers"
PermittedManagersListbox="Permitted managers"
Traps_Public="Traps for Public community"
Traps_PublicListbox="Trap configuration"
Restrictions="Restrictions"
DisableRegedit="Disable Registry editing tools"
Run="Run"
RunServices="Run services"
RunListbox="Items to run at startup"
RunServicesListbox="Services to run at startup"
NoWorkgroupContents="No workgroup contents in Network Neighborhood"
RestrictApps="Run only allowed Windows applications"
RestrictAppsList="List of allowed applications"
RestrictApps_Tip1="                         "
RestrictApps_Tip2="To create a list of allowed applications, click Show,"
RestrictApps_Tip3="then Add, and enter the application executable name"
```

```
RestrictApps_Tip4="(e.g., Winword.exe, Poledit.exe, Powerpnt.exe)."
DomainLogonConfirmation="Display domain logon confirmation"
NoDomainPwdCaching="Disable caching of domain password"
```

Winnt.adm

```
CLASS MACHINE

CATEGORY    !!Network
   CATEGORY !!Sharing
        KEYNAME System\CurrentControlSet\Services\LanManServer\Parameters

        POLICY !!WorkstationShareAutoCreate
           VALUENAME "AutoShareWks"
           VALUEON NUMERIC 1
           VALUEOFF NUMERIC 0
           PART !!ShareWks_Tip1                            TEXT     END PART
           PART !!ShareWks_Tip2                            TEXT     END PART
        END POLICY

        POLICY !!ServerShareAutoCreate
           VALUENAME "AutoShareServer"
           VALUEON NUMERIC 1
           VALUEOFF NUMERIC 0
           PART !!ShareServer_Tip1                         TEXT     END PART
           PART !!ShareServer_Tip2                         TEXT     END PART
        END POLICY

   END CATEGORY ; Sharing

END CATEGORY ; Network

CATEGORY    !!Printers
        KEYNAME System\CurrentControlSet\Control\Print
        POLICY !!PrintManager_Browser_Restrict
           VALUENAME DisableServerThread
           PART !!Disable_Server_Tip1                      TEXT
           END PART
           PART !!Disable_Server_Tip2                      TEXT
           END PART
        END POLICY

        POLICY !!Scheduler_Thread_Priority
        PART !!Scheduler_Priority                          DROPDOWNLIST
        VALUENAME SchedulerThreadPriority
           ITEMLIST
              NAME "Above Normal"    VALUE NUMERIC    1
              NAME "Normal"          VALUE NUMERIC    0
              NAME "Below Normal"    VALUE NUMERIC    -1
           END ITEMLIST
        END PART
        END POLICY
```

```
      POLICY !!Beep_Enabled
      VALUENAME BeepEnabled
        VALUEON NUMERIC 1
        VALUEOFF NUMERIC 0
      PART !!Beep_Tip1                                      TEXT    END PART
      PART !!Beep_Tip2                                      TEXT    END PART
      END POLICY
END CATEGORY

CATEGORY    !!RemoteAccess
KEYNAME System\CurrentControlSet\Services\RemoteAccess\Parameters
      POLICY !!MaximumRetries
        PART !!RAS_Length                           NUMERIC REQUIRED
        MIN 1 MAX 10 DEFAULT 2
        VALUENAME AuthenticateRetries
        END PART
      END POLICY
      POLICY !!MaximumTime
        PART !!RAS_Time                             NUMERIC REQUIRED
        MIN 20 MAX 600 DEFAULT 120
        VALUENAME AuthenticateTime
        END PART
      END POLICY
      POLICY !!CallBackTime
        PART !!INT_Time                             NUMERIC REQUIRED
        MIN 2 MAX 12 DEFAULT 2
        VALUENAME CallbackTime
        END PART
      END POLICY
      POLICY !!Auto_Disconnect
        PART !!Autodisconnect_Time                  NUMERIC REQUIRED
        MIN 0 DEFAULT 20
        VALUENAME AutoDisconnect
        END PART
      END POLICY
END CATEGORY

CATEGORY !!Shell

   CATEGORY !!CustomSharedFolders
      KEYNAME "Software\Microsoft\Windows\CurrentVersion\Explorer\User Shell Folders"

      POLICY !!CustomFolders_SharedPrograms
        PART !!CustomFolders_SharedProgramsPath       EDITTEXT REQUIRED   EXPANDABLETEXT
        DEFAULT !!CustomFolders_SharedProgramsDefault
        VALUENAME "Common Programs"
        END PART
        END POLICY

      POLICY !!CustomFolders_SharedDesktop
        PART !!CustomFolders_SharedDesktopPath        EDITTEXT REQUIRED   EXPANDABLETEXT
        DEFAULT !!CustomFolders_SharedDesktopDefault
        VALUENAME "Common Desktop"
        END PART
        END POLICY
```

```
        POLICY !!CustomFolders_SharedStartMenu
            PART !!CustomFolders_SharedStartMenuPath    EDITTEXT REQUIRED   EXPANDABLETEXT
            DEFAULT !!CustomFolders_SharedStartMenuDefault
            VALUENAME "Common Start Menu"
            END PART
        END POLICY

        POLICY !!CustomFolders_SharedStartup
            PART !!CustomFolders_SharedStartupPath    EDITTEXT REQUIRED   EXPANDABLETEXT
            DEFAULT !!CustomFolders_SharedStartupDefault
            VALUENAME "Common Startup"
            END PART
        END POLICY

    END CATEGORY
END CATEGORY  ; Shell


CATEGORY    !!System
    CATEGORY !!Login_Policies
        POLICY !!LogonBanner
        KEYNAME "Software\Microsoft\Windows NT\CurrentVersion\Winlogon"
        PART !!LogonBanner_Caption                    EDITTEXT
        VALUENAME "LegalNoticeCaption"
        MAXLEN 255
        DEFAULT !!LogonBanner_DefCaption
        END PART

        PART !!LogonBanner_Text                       EDITTEXT
        VALUENAME "LegalNoticeText"
        MAXLEN 255
        DEFAULT !!LogonBanner_DefText
        END PART
        END POLICY

        POLICY !!Shutdown_Restrict
        KEYNAME "Software\Microsoft\Windows NT\CurrentVersion\Winlogon"
        VALUENAME ShutdownWithoutLogon
        VALUEON "1"  VALUEOFF "0"
        PART !!Shutd_Tip1                              TEXT    END PART
        PART !!Shutd_Tip2                              TEXT    END PART
        PART !!Shutd_Tip3                              TEXT    END PART
        END POLICY

        POLICY !!LastUserName_Restrict
        KEYNAME "Software\Microsoft\Windows NT\CurrentVersion\Winlogon"
        VALUENAME DontDisplayLastUserName
        VALUEON "1"  VALUEOFF "0"
        PART !!Dont_Display_Tip1                       TEXT    END PART
        PART !!Dont_Display_Tip2                       TEXT    END PART
        PART !!Dont_Display_Tip3                       TEXT    END PART
        END POLICY

        POLICY !!Run_Logon_Script_Sync
```

```
        KEYNAME "Software\Microsoft\Windows NT\CurrentVersion\Winlogon"
        VALUENAME RunLogonScriptSync
        PART !!Script_Tip1                                      TEXT    END PART
        PART !!Script_Tip2                                      TEXT    END PART
        PART !!Script_Tip4                                      TEXT    END PART
        END POLICY


END CATEGORY  ; Login Policies

CATEGORY !!FileSystem
        KEYNAME System\CurrentControlSet\Control\FileSystem

        POLICY !!Disable8dot3Names
        VALUENAME "NtfsDisable8dot3NameCreation"
        END POLICY


        POLICY !!AllowExtCharsIn8dot3
        VALUENAME "NtfsAllowExtendedCharacterIn8dot3Name"
        PART !!ExtChars_Tip1                                    TEXT    END PART
        PART !!ExtChars_Tip2                                    TEXT    END PART
        END POLICY


        POLICY !!DisableLastUpdate
        VALUENAME "NtfsDisableLastAccessUpdate"
        PART !!LastAccess_Tip1                                  TEXT    END PART
        PART !!LastAccess_Tip2                                  TEXT    END PART
        END POLICY

    END CATEGORY ; File system

END CATEGORY ; System

CATEGORY    !!UserProfiles
KEYNAME "Software\Microsoft\Windows NT\CurrentVersion\winlogon"

        POLICY !!DeleteRoamingCachedProfiles
        VALUENAME "DeleteRoamingCache"
        PART !!DeleteCache_Tip1                                 TEXT    END PART
        PART !!DeleteCache_Tip2                                 TEXT    END PART
        END POLICY

        POLICY !!EnableSlowLinkDetect
        VALUENAME "SlowLinkDetectEnabled"
        END POLICY

        POLICY !!SlowLinkTimeOut
        PART !!SlowLinkWaitInterval                      NUMERIC REQUIRED
        MIN 1 MAX 20000 DEFAULT 2000
        VALUENAME SlowLinkTimeOut
        END PART
        END POLICY

        POLICY !!ProfileDlgTimeOut
        PART !!ProfileDlgWaitInterval                    NUMERIC REQUIRED
```

```
            MIN 0 MAX 600 DEFAULT 30
            VALUENAME ProfileDlgTimeOut
            END PART
            END POLICY

END CATEGORY


CLASS USER

CATEGORY !!Shell

    CATEGORY !!CustomShell
       KEYNAME "Software\Microsoft\Windows NT\CurrentVersion\Winlogon"

          POLICY !!ShellName
          PART !!ShellNameInst                    EDITTEXT REQUIRED
          VALUENAME "Shell"
          END PART
          END POLICY


    END CATEGORY


    CATEGORY !!CustomFolders
        KEYNAME "Software\Microsoft\Windows\CurrentVersion\Explorer\User Shell Folders"

        POLICY !!CustomFolders_Programs
        PART !!CustomFolders_ProgramsPath          EDITTEXT REQUIRED EXPANDABLETEXT
        DEFAULT !!CustomFolders_ProgramsDefault
        VALUENAME "Programs"
          END PART
          END POLICY

          POLICY !!CustomFolders_Desktop
          PART !!CustomFolders_DesktopPath          EDITTEXT REQUIRED  EXPANDABLETEXT
          DEFAULT !!CustomFolders_DesktopDefault
          VALUENAME "Desktop"
          END PART
          END POLICY

          POLICY !!HideStartMenuSubfolders
          KEYNAME Software\Microsoft\Windows\CurrentVersion\Policies\Explorer
          VALUENAME NoStartMenuSubFolders
          PART !!HideStartMenuSubfolders_Tip1        TEXT    END PART
          PART !!HideStartMenuSubfolders_Tip2        TEXT    END PART
          END POLICY

          POLICY !!CustomFolders_Startup
          PART !!CustomFolders_StartupPath          EDITTEXT REQUIRED  EXPANDABLETEXT
          DEFAULT !!CustomFolders_StartupDefault
          VALUENAME "Startup"
          END PART
          END POLICY
```

```
        POLICY !!CustomFolders_NetHood
        PART !!CustomFolders_NetHoodPath            EDITTEXT REQUIRED  EXPANDABLETEXT
        DEFAULT !!CustomFolders_NetHoodDefault
        VALUENAME "NetHood"
        END PART
        END POLICY

        POLICY !!CustomFolders_StartMenu
        PART !!CustomFolders_StartMenuPath          EDITTEXT REQUIRED  EXPANDABLETEXT
        DEFAULT !!CustomFolders_StartMenuDefault
        VALUENAME "Start Menu"
        END PART
        END POLICY

    END CATEGORY

    CATEGORY !!Restrictions
        KEYNAME Software\Microsoft\Windows\CurrentVersion\Policies\Explorer
        POLICY !!ApprovedShellExt
        VALUENAME "EnforceShellExtensionSecurity"
        END POLICY

        POLICY !!NoFileMenu
        VALUENAME "NoFileMenu"
        END POLICY

        POLICY !!NoCommonGroups
        VALUENAME "NoCommonGroups"
        END POLICY

        POLICY !!NoTrayContextMenu
        VALUENAME "NoTrayContextMenu"
        END POLICY

        POLICY !!NoViewContextMenu
        VALUENAME "NoViewContextMenu"
        END POLICY

        POLICY !!NoNetConnectDisconnect
        VALUENAME "NoNetConnectDisconnect"
        END POLICY

        POLICY !!DisableLinkTracking
        VALUENAME "LinkResolveIgnoreLinkInfo"
        END POLICY
    END CATEGORY

END CATEGORY ; Shell

CATEGORY    !!System
    POLICY !!Parse_Autoexec
    KEYNAME "Software\Microsoft\Windows NT\CurrentVersion\Winlogon"
    VALUENAME ParseAutoexec
    VALUEON "1" VALUEOFF "0"
```

```
    PART !!Parse_Tip1                                   TEXT    END PART
    PART !!Parse_Tip2                                   TEXT    END PART
    END POLICY


    POLICY !!Run_Logon_Script_Sync
    KEYNAME "Software\Microsoft\Windows NT\CurrentVersion\Winlogon"
    VALUENAME RunLogonScriptSync
    PART !!Script_Tip1                                  TEXT    END PART
    PART !!Script_Tip2                                  TEXT    END PART
    PART !!Script_Tip3                                  TEXT    END PART
    END POLICY

      POLICY !!DisableTaskMgr
      KEYNAME Software\Microsoft\Windows\CurrentVersion\Policies\System
      VALUENAME "DisableTaskMgr"
      END POLICY


      POLICY !!ShowWelcome
      KEYNAME "Software\Microsoft\Windows\CurrentVersion\Explorer\Tips"
      VALUENAME "Show"
      VALUEON NUMERIC 1
      VALUEOFF NUMERIC 0
      END POLICY


END CATEGORY

[strings]
Network="Windows NT Network"
Sharing="Sharing"
WorkstationShareAutoCreate="Create hidden drive shares (workstation)"
ServerShareAutoCreate="Create hidden drive shares (server)"
ShareWks_Tip1=Automatically create <drive letter>$ and Admin$ shares
ShareWks_Tip2=when Windows NT Workstation starts.
ShareServer_Tip1=Automatically create <drive letter>$ and Admin$ shares
ShareServer_Tip2=when Windows NT Server starts.
System="Windows NT System"
Login_Policies="Logon"
LogonBanner="Logon banner"
LogonBanner_Caption="Caption"
LogonBanner_Text="Text"
LogonBanner_DefCaption="Important Notice:"
LogonBanner_DefText="Do not attempt to log on unless you are an authorized user."
Shutdown_Restrict="Enable shutdown from Authentication dialog box"
Shutd_Tip1="When this box is checked, you can click Shut Down"
Shutd_Tip2="in the Authentication dialog box to select options."
Shutd_Tip3="Default: NT Server = Off, NT Workstation = On"
LastUserName_Restrict="Do not display last logged on user name"
Dont_Display_Tip1="When this box is checked, Windows NT does not"
Dont_Display_Tip2="automatically display the user name of the last person"
Dont_Display_Tip3="to log on in the Authentication dialog box."
Printers="Windows NT Printers"
PrintManager_Browser_Restrict="Disable browse thread on this computer"
Disable_Server_Tip1="When this box is checked, the print spooler does not"
Disable_Server_Tip2="send shared printer information to other print servers."
Scheduler_Thread_Priority="Scheduler priority"
```

```
Scheduler_Priority="Priority"
Thread_Priority_Above_Normal="Scheduler priority above normal"
Thread_Priority_Below_Normal="Scheduler priority below normal"
Thread_Priority_Normal="Scheduler priority normal"
Beep_Enabled="Beep for error enabled"
Beep_Tip1="A check in this box enables beeping (every 10 seconds) when a remote"
Beep_Tip2="job error occurs on a print server."
RemoteAccess="Windows NT Remote Access"
MaximumRetries="Max number of unsuccessful authentication retries"
RAS_Length="Number of retries"
MaximumTime="Max time limit for authentication"
RAS_Time="Length in seconds"
CallBackTime="Wait interval for callback"
INT_Time="Length in seconds"
Auto_Disconnect="Auto Disconnect"
Autodisconnect_Time="Disconnect after (minutes)"
UserProfiles="Windows NT User Profiles"
DeleteRoamingCachedProfiles="Delete cached copies of roaming profiles"
DeleteCache_Tip1="When users with roaming profiles log off,"
DeleteCache_Tip2="delete the locally cached profile (to save disk space)."
EnableSlowLinkDetect="Automatically detect slow network connections"
SlowLinkTimeOut="Slow network connection timeout"
SlowLinkWaitInterval="Time (milliseconds)"
ProfileDlgTimeOut="Timeout for dialog boxes"
ProfileDlgWaitInterval="Time (seconds)"
Parse_Autoexec="Parse Autoexec.bat"
Parse_Tip1="When this box is checked, environment variables declared"
Parse_Tip2="in autoexec.bat are included in the users environment."
Shell="Windows NT Shell"
CustomFolders="Custom folders"
CustomFolders_Programs="Custom Programs folder"
CustomFolders_ProgramsPath="Path to location of Programs items"
CustomFolders_ProgramsDefault="%USERPROFILE%\Start Menu\Programs"
CustomFolders_Desktop="Custom desktop icons"
CustomFolders_DesktopPath="Path to location of desktop icons"
CustomFolders_DesktopDefault="%USERPROFILE%\Desktop"
HideStartMenuSubfolders="Hide Start menu subfolders"
HideStartMenuSubfolders_Tip1="Check this if you use a custom Programs folder"
HideStartMenuSubfolders_Tip2="or custom desktop icons."
CustomFolders_Startup="Custom Startup folder"
CustomFolders_StartupPath="Path to location of Startup items"
CustomFolders_StartupDefault="%USERPROFILE%\Start Menu\Programs\Startup"
CustomFolders_NetHood="Custom Network Neighborhood"
CustomFolders_NetHoodPath="Path to location of Network Neighborhood items"
CustomFolders_NetHoodDefault="%USERPROFILE%\NetHood"
CustomFolders_StartMenu="Custom Start menu"
CustomFolders_StartMenuPath="Path to location of Start menu items"
CustomFolders_StartMenuDefault="%USERPROFILE%\Start Menu"
CustomSharedFolders="Custom shared folders"
CustomFolders_SharedPrograms="Custom shared Programs folder"
CustomFolders_SharedProgramsPath="Path to location of shared Programs items"
CustomFolders_SharedProgramsDefault="%SystemRoot%\Profiles\All Users\Start Menu\Programs"
CustomFolders_SharedDesktop="Custom shared desktop icons"
CustomFolders_SharedDesktopPath="Path to location of shared desktop icons"
CustomFolders_SharedDesktopDefault="%SystemRoot%\Profiles\All Users\Desktop"
```

```
CustomFolders_SharedStartMenu="Custom shared Start menu"
CustomFolders_SharedStartMenuPath="Path to location of shared Start menu items"
CustomFolders_SharedStartMenuDefault="%SystemRoot%\Profiles\All Users\Start Menu"
CustomFolders_SharedStartup="Custom shared Startup folder"
CustomFolders_SharedStartupPath="Path to location of shared Startup items"
CustomFolders_SharedStartupDefault="%SystemRoot%\Profiles\All Users\Start Menu\
   Programs\Startup"
Restrictions="Restrictions"
ApprovedShellExt="Only use approved shell extensions"
NoFileMenu="Remove File menu from Explorer"
NoCommonGroups="Remove common program groups from Start menu"
FileSystem="File system"
Disable8dot3Names="Do not create 8.3 file names for long file names"
AllowExtCharsIn8dot3="Allow extended characters in 8.3 file names"
ExtChars_Tip1="Short file names with extended characters may not be viewable"
ExtChars_Tip2="on computers that do not have same character code page."
DisableLastUpdate="Do not update last access time"
LastAccess_Tip1="For files that are only being read, do not update the last"
LastAccess_Tip2="access time. This will increase the file system's performance."
Run_Logon_Script_Sync="Run logon scripts synchronously."
Script_Tip1="Wait for the logon scripts to complete before starting"
Script_Tip2="the users's shell. If this value is also set in the"
Script_Tip3="Computer section, that value takes precedence."
Script_Tip4="User section, this value takes precedence."
NoTrayContextMenu="Disable context menus for the taskbar"
NoViewContextMenu="Disable Explorer's default context menu"
NoNetConnectDisconnect="Remove the "Map Network Drive" and "Disconnect Network Drive"
options"
DisableTaskMgr="Disable Task Manager"
DisableLinkTracking="Disable link file tracking"
ShowWelcome="Show welcome tips at logon"
CustomShell="Custom user interface"
ShellName="Custom shell"
ShellNameInst="Shell name (eg: explorer.exe)"
```

Proxy Server Logging Information

Services Logging Information

This section contains a list of fields available in the logging database for the Proxy Server services logging process. They are split into four separate types of fields as described below.

Server-Oriented Fields

- **Log Date.** The date the logged event occurred.
- **Log Time.** The time the logged event occurred.
- **Proxy Name.** The netbios name of the Windows NT 4.0 server computer that is running the Proxy Server software.
- **Referring Server Name.** The name of the downstream Proxy Server in a chained configuration that passed the request to the upstream server.
- **Service Name.** The name of the service to which the logged event belongs. The entry "CERNProxy" refers to the CERN-compliant Web Proxy service. The entry "WSProxy" refers to the Winsock Proxy service, and the name "Socks" refers to the Socks Proxy service.

Client-Oriented Fields

- **Authentication Status.** This field shows whether the request is using an authenticated client connection to the Proxy Server.
- **Client Agent.** This field can contain two different types of information. For the Winsock service, it gives the name of the client application generating the request. For the Web service, it contains header information from the client browser.
- **Client Platform.** This field is not used for the Web service. For the Winsock service this field contains an indicator denoting the client operating system.
  - **0:3.1** Windows 3.1
  - **0:3.11** Windows for Workgroups 3.11.
  - **0:3.95** Windows 95 (16 bit).
  - **1:3.11** Win32s.
  - **2:4.0** Windows 95 (32 bit).
  - **3:3.1** Windows NT 3.1.
  - **3:3.5** Windows NT 3.5.
  - **3:3.51** Windows NT 3.51.
  - **3:4.0** Windows NT 4.0.
- **Client User Name.** The Windows NT user name for the user logged on to the client machine when the request is issued.

Connection-Oriented Fields

- **Bytes Received.** This field is used by the Web Proxy service to indicate the number of bytes received from the remote system during this connection. This information may not be provided and so may be blank or contain a zero.
- **Bytes Sent.** This field is used by the Web Proxy service to show the number of bytes sent to the remote system for this connection. For the Winsock Proxy service, this field contains a number indicating the number of bytes sent at the end of a session.
- **Destination Address.** This field contains the IP address of the remote computer servicing a request. If this field is blank, the request may have been serviced from the Proxy Server cache.
- **Destination Name.** This field contains the domain name of the remote system servicing the request. A blank may mean that the request was serviced by the Proxy Server cache.

- **Destination Port.** This field contains the reserved port address on the remote computer.

- **Operation.** This field gives the current status of the connection. For Web Proxy service, it shows the current HTTP method used which may be GET, PUT, POST, or HEAD. For Winsock Proxy service, it shows the socket API call in use. This could be `Connect()`, `Accept()`, `SendTo()`, `RecvFrom()`, `GetHostByName()`, or `Listen()`.

- **Processing Time.** This field contains the total elapsed time that it took the server to facilitate the request (a measurement of how long the port was open). This may not be indicative of the speed of the network if items are retrieved from cache to fulfill a request.

- **Protocol Name.** This field holds the protocol name (HTTP, TCP, etc.) used for a Web Proxy service request or the well-known destination port number for a Winsock Proxy service request.

- **Transport.** For Web Proxy services, this field is always TCP/IP. For the Winsock Proxy service, the field can be TCP/IP, UDP, or IPX/SPX.

Object-Oriented Fields

- **Object MIME.** This field shows the MIME type for the current object when using Web proxy services.

- **Object Name.** This field contains the URL name requested through the Web Proxy service.

- **Object Source.** This fields gives the source of the current object for the Web Proxy service. The allowed values are:

  - **0**   No source information available
  - **Cache**   The cache of the Proxy Server
  - **Inet**   Sourced from the Internet and added to cache
  - **Member**   Sourced from another Proxy Server in the array
  - **NotModified** Sourced from cache with an "if-modified-since" request and object has not been modified
  - **NVCache**   Sourced from cache but the object cannot be verified to original source
  - **Upstream**   Sourced from an upstream Proxy Server cache
  - **Vcache**   Sourced from cache and verified to original source

- **Result Code.** This field holds a result code indicating the final status of the connection.

Packet Filter Logging Information

This section contains a list of fields available in the logging database for the logging process of the Proxy Server packet filter.

Service Information Fields

- **PFLogTime.** This field holds the time and date stamp showing when the packet was received.

Remote Information Fields

- **Protocol.** This field holds the transport-level protocol used for the connection. The protocol could be TCP, UDP, ICMP, etc.
- **SourceAddress.** This field holds the IP address of the remote computer that originated the packet.
- **SourcePort.** If the protocol is either TCP, UDP, or ICMP, this field indicates the service port number in use by the remote computer while the connection is live.

Local Information Fields

- **DestinationAddress.** This field holds the destination IP address of the local system (Proxy Server).
- **DestinationPort.** If the Protocol is either TCP, UDP, or ICMP, this field shows the service port number in use by the local system while the connection is live.

Filter Information Fields

- **FilterRule.** The only values allowed here are 0 for dropped packets and 1 for accepted packets. Only dropped packets are logged by default.
- **Interface.** This field denotes the interface that the packet was received on.

Packet Information Fields

- **IPHeader.** This field holds the IP header of the packet that initiated the alert event, stored in hex.
- **Payload.** This field contains a portion of the IP packet that initiated the alert event, starting from after the header information.
- **TcpFlags.** This field represents the TCP flag in the header of a TCP packet. Possible values are FIN, SYN, RST, PSH, ACK, and URG.

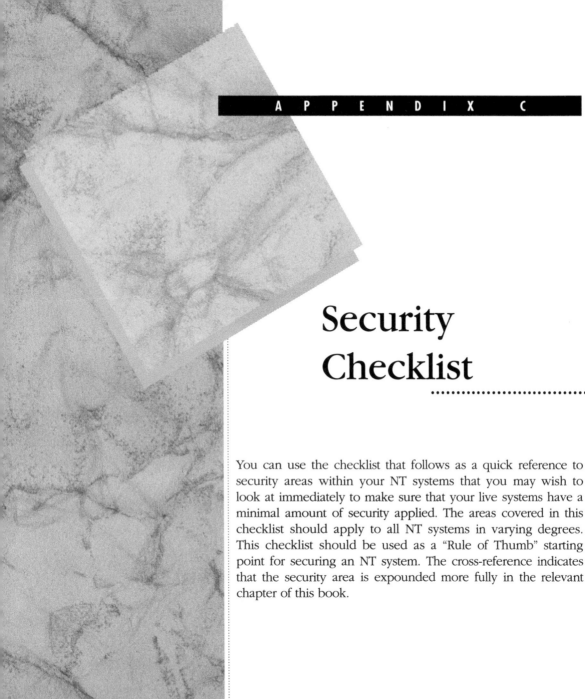

Security
Checklist

You can use the checklist that follows as a quick reference to security areas within your NT systems that you may wish to look at immediately to make sure that your live systems have a minimal amount of security applied. The areas covered in this checklist should apply to all NT systems in varying degrees. This checklist should be used as a "Rule of Thumb" starting point for securing an NT system. The cross-reference indicates that the security area is expounded more fully in the relevant chapter of this book.

Security Area	Description	Recommendation	See Chapter
File/Folder Permissions: Partitions	Partition types can be FAT or NTFS.	Use NTFS. NTFS allows ACLs to be used to secure files and folders.	3
File/Folder Permissions: \Winnt folder structure	The system files should be protected from unauthorized access.	Secure according to Tables 3.6 and 3.7. These tables contain the required settings for the \Winnt folder structure.	3
File/Folder Permissions: Everyone Group	All created users belong to the Everyone group, and you cannot change this.	Replace permissions for Everyone with Domain Users Group where possible. Control access to public folder areas with the Domain Users group. This gives you a certain amount of control because you can add or remove users from this group.	3
User Control: Mandatory Profiles	Mandatory, Roaming, or Local Profiles are available.	Mandatory Profile. User Profiles help to secure systems and lower the costs of maintenance by preventing inquisitive users from tampering with their system.	4
System Policy: Control Panel	Control access to the Control Panel; Display applet.	Hide the Settings tab. This prevents users from tampering with display settings that could render the system inoperable for a time	5
System Policy: System	Control access to system tools.	Disable the Registry Editors. This prevents users from running tools that could destroy the system.	5
System Policy: Shell	Control shell functionality.	Remove Taskbar from Settings on the Start Menu. This prevents access to the Taskbar which can open up access to the Profiles folder.	5
Audit Policy: Logon/Logoff	Track all user logons and logoffs.	Analyze failures. Tracking failed login attempts can help in the war against unauthorized system access.	9
Audit Policy: File and Object Access	Track access to files and printers.	Use discretion. Track access to sensitive files or folders as necessary or wise.	9
Audit Policy: Use of User Rights	Track event of a user exercising a User Right.	The use of this tracking tool is discretionary.	9

(continued)

Security Area	Description	Recommendation	See Chapter
Audit Policy: User and Group Management	Track changes to user accounts.	Track both successful *and* failed instances. This record can be used to track password changes or new user creations.	9
Audit Policy: Security Policy Changes	Track changes to security policies.	Track both successful *and* failed instances. This record can assure that your Audit Policy is not being tampered with.	9
Audit Policy: Restart, Shutdown, and System	Track system shutdown and restarts. Also, track events that affect system security or the security log.	Track both successful *and* failed instances. Use this record to track shutdowns on an NT Server or access to the security log.	9
Audit Policy: Process Tracking	Track events such as program activation and process exit.	The use of this tracking tool is discretionary.	9
Audit Review: Event Logs	Review the Event Logs.	Review the Security log weekly. An audit policy is virtually useless without a regular review of the audit logs.	9
Registry: Permission	Protect the registry structure from unauthorized access.	Match the entries in Table 8.1. Secure the Registry files and folder structure so that only authorized personnel can make changes.	8
Account Policy: Password Max Age	Force a password change at the end of a set period of time.	Set to 30 Days. The longer you keep the same password, the more likely it is to be discovered by third parties. Forcing a change too often can lead to confusion for users.	11
Account Policy: Password Min Age	Specify the period of time that must elapse after changing a password before you can change it again.	Set to 8 Days. Set this to a value that when multiplied by the Password Uniqueness value is greater than Max Age.	11
Account Policy: Password Length	Specify the minimum length of passwords.	Set to 8 characters. Fewer than 8 characters may lead to an easily guessed password.	11

(continued)

Security Area	Description	Recommendation	See Chapter
Account Policy: Password Uniqueness	Specify the number of previous passwords remembered.	Set to 4. Using this setting and the Min Age value, you can ensure that users cannot simply cycle passwords to arrive back at a well-loved (and possibly well-known) password.	11
Account Policy: Lockout	Enable or disable the Account Lockout feature for incorrect login attempts.	Enable lockout. Account lockout must be enabled to aid in preventing hacking attempts; once an account is locked, it should require Administrator intervention before it can be used again. This policy blocks repeated password hacking attempts.	11
Account Policy: Lockout After	Lock the account after the number of bad attempts is reached.	Allow 3 attempts. Nobody should require more than 3 tries at a password.	11
Account Policy: Reset After	Reset the bad attempt count after this amount of time.	Set for 1440 mins (24 hours). Reset the bad attempt count after this period.	11
Account Policy: Lockout Duration	Specify the period of time a locked-out account remains unusable.	Forever is the preferred setting. Lock the account until the circumstances of the lockout can be investigated.	11

INDEX